Law's Violence

The Amherst Series in Law, Jurisprudence, and Social Thought

Each work included in The Amherst Series in Law, Jurisprudence, and Social Thought explores a theme crucial to an understanding of law as it confronts the changing social and intellectual currents of the late twentieth century.

Law's Violence

Edited by

Austin Sarat and Thomas R. Kearns

Ann Arbor

THE UNIVERSITY OF MICHIGAN PRESS

First paperback edition 1995
Copyright © by the University of Michigan 1993
All rights reserved
Published in the United States of America by
The University of Michigan Press
Manufactured in the United States of America

1998   1997   1996   1995   4   3   2   1

Library of Congress Cataloging-in-Publication Data

Law's violence / edited by Austin Sarat and Thomas R. Kearns.
       p.   cm.—(Amherst series in law, jurisprudence, and social
thought)
    Includes bibliographical references and index.
    ISBN 0-472-10390-3 (alk. paper). — ISBN 0-472-08317-1 (pbk.:
alk. paper).
    1. Law—Philosophy. 2. Violence (Law) 3. Violence.   I. Sarat,
Austin. II. Kearns, Thomas R.   III. Series.
K235.L4   1992
340'.1—dc20   92-30306
                                                            CIP

A CIP catalogue record for this book is available from the British Library.

Acknowledgments

Writing and editing a book on *Law's Violence* has been part of an imagined conversation with Robert Cover, whose presence pervades our work and whose tragic absence is deeply felt. The subject of violence and its place in law and legal theory is at the center of the concerns of the Program in Law, Jurisprudence, and Social Thought at Amherst College. For their invaluable contributions to that program and their help in exploring the violence in and around law, we are grateful to our colleagues Lawrence Douglas and Victoria Saker. We have been greatly stimulated by the enthusiasm and interest of our students, and we acknowledge the help we have received in their many questions and provocations. Finally, we gratefully acknowledge the support of the Mellon Foundation and the sustaining interest of Amherst's President, Peter Pouncey.

Contents

Introduction

Austin Sarat and Thomas R. Kearns

In a previous book in this series, we noted the troubling lack of systematic thinking about the relationship of law and violence, and we argued that "...the general link between law and violence and the ways that law manages to work its lethal will, to impose pain and death while remaining aloof and unstained by the deeds themselves, is still an unexplored and hardly noticed mystery in the life of the law."[1] The essays collected in *Law's Violence* explore that mystery. Each recognizes that violence, as a fact and a metaphor, is integral to the constitution of modern law,[2] and that law is a creature of both literal violence, and of imaginings and threats of force, disorder, and pain. Each acknowledges that in the absence of such imaginings and threats there is no law, and that modern law is built on representations of aggression and disruption.[3] Law is, in this sense, an extended meditation on a metaphor.[4]

We are grateful for helpful suggestions made by Tom Dumm, Carol Greenhouse, and Victoria Saker.

1. Austin Sarat and Thomas R. Kearns, "A Journey Through Forgetting: Toward a Jurisprudence of Violence," in *The Fate of Law*, ed. Austin Sarat and Thomas R. Kearns (Ann Arbor: University of Michigan Press, 1991), 211.

2. See Thomas Hobbes, *Leviathan*, ed. C. B. MacPherson (New York: Penguin Books, 1986). See also Hans Kelsen, *General Theory of Law and the State*, trans. Anders Wedberg (New York: Russell and Russell, 1945); Noberto Bobbio, "Law and Force," *Monist* 48 (1965): 321; Walter Benjamin, "Critique of Violence," in *Reflections*, trans. Edmund Jepchott (New York: Harcourt Jovanovich, Brace 1978); Peter Fitzpatrick, "Violence and Legal Subjection," University of Kent, 1991, Photocopy).

3. Sarat and Kearns, "Journey," 222.

4. Drucilla Cornell suggests that the "foundation" of law is allegorical rather than metaphorical.

> [T]he Law of Law is only "present" in its absolute absence. The "never has been" of an unrecoverable past is understood as the lack of origin "presentable"

But law's possibility is built on more than metaphors. The violence that makes law possible is made all too real in the almost unlimited physical damage it is capable of doing. Were it possible adequately to respond to that damage with metaphors alone, law would be superfluous. Thus, were there to be no occasion or need for an all-too-literal violence, there would be no occasion or need for law.[5]

Law exists in the tangle of the literal and metaphorical.[6] Yet it constantly appears and presents itself as a means of disentangling the literal from the metaphorical, of legislating, in words, symbols, and metaphors, what counts as the real and what really counts. Law seeks to be, or define, the boundary between the real and the fictive, the possible and the unimaginable. Moreover, the existence of law stands as a monument to the hope that words can contain and control violence, that unspeakable pain can be made to speak, and that aggression and desire can be tamed. If law is to succeed in this role, it must always conquer, or appear to conquer, force and calm, or appear to calm, turmoil.[7] Violence stands as the limit of law, as a reminder of both law's continuing necessity and its ever-present failing. Without violence, law is unnecessary, yet, in its presence, law, like language and representation themselves, may be impossible.[8]

While each of the essays in *Law's Violence* speaks about that subject in its own way, each, at least implicitly, recognizes relations of necessity and possibility between law and violence. They all remind

only as allegory. The Law of Law, in other words, is the figure of an initial fragmentation, the loss of the Good. But this allegory is inescapable because the lack of origin is the fundamental truth.
See Drucilla Cornell, "From the Lighthouse: The Promise of Redemption and the Possibility of Legal Interpretation," *Cardozo Law Review* 11 (1990): 1689.

5. "If a law cannot exist apart from the exercise of force, then laws *must* desire transgressions. Since law *is* the resistance of transgression, law needs and yet cannot bear transgression. Transgressions, in turn, are not really lawless but are other laws that themselves desire transgressions." See Mark Taylor, "Desire of Law/Law of Desire," *Cardozo Law Review* 11 (1990): 1272. See also Jan Narveson, "Force, Violence, and Law," in *Justice, Law, and Violence*, ed. James Brady and Newton Garver (Philadelphia: Temple University Press, 1991), 150.

6. Carol Greenhouse suggests that the phrase "literal violence" is itself metaphorical. Literal violence is violence according to the letter, yet it is used to suggest force applied to bodies (letter to editors, August 20, 1991).

7. Carl Wellman, "Violence, Law, and Basic Rights," in *Justice, Law, and Violence*, ed. James Brady and Newton Garver (Philadelphia: Temple University Press, 1991), 177–80.

8. Elaine Scarry, *The Body in Pain* (New York: Oxford University Press, 1985), 3–6.

us that law's violent constitution does not end with the establishment of legal order. The law constituted, in part, in response to meta-phorical violence is a doer of literal violence; law as the peaceful alternative to the chaos and fury of a fictive state of nature inscribes itself on bodies.[9] It "deal[s] pain and death,"[10] and calls the pain and death that it deals "peace."[11] Once established, law is maintained through force; it is maintained as an apparatus of violence that disorders, disrupts, and repositions preexisting relations and practices all in the name of an allegedly superior order.[12] That order demon-strates its "superiority" in ferocious displays of force, and in sub-jugating, colonizing, "civilizing" acts of violence.[13] Violence thus

---

9. Michel Foucault, *Discipline and Punish*, trans. Alan Sheridan (New York: Vintage Books, 1979), chap. 1. See also Franz Kafka, "In the Penal Colony," in *The Penal Colony: Stories and Short Pieces*, trans. Willa Muir and Edwin Muir (New York: Schocken Books, 1976). As Virginia Held puts it, "The legal rules of almost any legal system permit the use of violence to preserve and enforce the laws, whether these laws are just or not, but forbid most other uses of violence." See Virginia Held, "Violence, Terrorism, and Moral Inquiry," in *Ethical Theory and Social Issues: His-torical Texts and Contemporary Readings* (New York: Holt, Rinehart and Winston, 1988), 475.

10. Robert Cover, "Violence and the Word," *Yale Law Journal* 95 (1986): 1609.

11. The tendency to use violence for the sake of "peace," to use violence and call it "peace," is not contained within national boundaries. It also marks the con-ditions that exist between and among states. What we do to those who violate domestic law is also what we do to "international outlaws." This was, of course, vividly displayed in the recent war in the Persian Gulf. As President Bush put it in his speech to the nation announcing the attack on Iraq, "We have before us the opportunity to forge for ourselves and for future generations a new world order, a world where the rule of law, not the law of the jungle, governs the conduct of nations." See *Vital Speeches of the Day* 57 (February 1, 1991): 227.

12. See Benjamin, "Critique of Violence," 287; also see Karl Olivecrona, *Law As Fact* (Copenhagen: Einar Munksgaard, 1939), chap. 4; Martha Minow, "Words and the Door to the Land of Change: Law, Language, and Family Violence" (Harvard Law School, 1990, Photocopy), 14. As Minow puts it, "Law is itself violent in its forms and methods. Official power effectuates itself in physical force...."

13. Edgar Friedenberg contends that,
   The police often slay; but they are seldom socially defined as murderers. Students who block the entrances to buildings or occupy a vacant lot and attempt to build a park in it are defined as not merely being disorderly but violent; the law enforcement officials who gas and club them into submission are perceived as restorers of order, as, indeed, they are of the *status quo ante* which was orderly by definition.
See Edgar Friedenberg, "The Side Effects of the Legal Process," in *The Rule of Law*, ed. Robert Paul Wolff (New York: Simon and Schuster, 1971), 43. As Fitzpatrick puts it,
   ... [T]his association of law with order, security and regularity rapidly became general and obvious, the violence associated with the establishment of law and

constitutes law in three senses: it provides the occasion and method for founding legal orders,[14] it gives law (as the regulator of force and coercion) a reason for being,[15] and it provides a means through which the law acts.[16]

Yet law denies the violence of its origins,[17] as well as the disorder engendered by its ordering, peacemaking efforts, by proclaiming the force it deploys to be "legitimate."[18] As Robert Paul Wolff argues, violence is, in the eyes of the law, "... *the illegitimate or unauthorized use of force to effect decisions against the will or desire of others. Thus murder is an act of violence, but capital punishment by a legitimate state* is not."[19] Law is that which monopolizes, or seeks to monopolize, the violence that is transformed into "legitimate" force.[20] In and through its claims to legitimacy, what law does is privileged and distinguished from "the violence that one always deems unjust."[21] Legitimacy is thus the minimal answer to skeptical questions about the ways law's violence differs from the turmoil and disorder law is

order assuming insignificance in the immeasurability of the violence and disorder of savagery.
See Fitzpatrick, "Violence and Legal Subjection," 15; see also Tzvetan Todorov, *The Conquest of America: The Question of the Other,* trans. Richard Howard (New York: Harper and Row, 1984).

14. See Jacques Derrida, "Force of Law: The 'Mystical Foundation of Authority,'" *Cardozo Law Review* 11 (1990): 981.

15. Hobbes, *Leviathan,* 185; also see Fitzpatrick, "Violence and Legal Subjection," 2–14.

16. Cover, "Violence and the Word."

17. Derrida, "Force of Law," 983–84.

18. See Robert Paul Wolff, "Violence and the Law," in *The Rule of Law,* ed. Robert Paul Wolff (New York: Simon and Schuster, 1971); see also Bernhard Waldenfels, "The Limits of Legitimation and the Question of Violence," in *Justice, Law, and Violence,* ed. James Brady and Newton Garver (Philadelphia: Temple University Press, 1991). For a classic discussion of legitimacy, see Max Weber, *Max Weber on Law in Economy and Society,* ed. Max Rheinstein (Cambridge, Mass.: Harvard University Press, 1954). An important study of the way legal legitimacy is produced is Douglas Hay, "Property, Authority and the Criminal Law," in *Albion's Fatal Tree: Crime and Society in Eighteenth-Century England,* ed. Douglas Hay, Peter Linebaugh, John G. Rule, E. P. Thompson, and Cal Winslow (New York: Pantheon Books, 1975).

19. Wolff, "Violence and the Law," 59.

20. Weber, *Law in Economy,* 5.

21. Derrida, "Force of Law," 927; see also Friedenberg, "Side Effects."
If by violence one means injurious attacks on persons or destruction of valuable inanimate objects ... then nearly all the violence done in the world is done by legitimate authority, or at least by the agents of legitimate authority engaged in official business. ... Yet their actions are not deemed to be violence. (43)

allegedly brought into being to conquer.[22] In this claim to legitimacy, in this minimal answer, is the further claim that law's violence is rational, controlled, and purposive, that law makes force the servant of the "word."

To say that law's violence is legitimate is, in the modern age, to juxtapose the alleged rationality of legal coercion and the irrationality of a violence that knows no law. It is to claim that law's violence is controlled through the legal articulation of values, norms, procedures, and purposes external to violence itself. It is to claim that the force of law serves common purposes and advances common aims in contrast to the anomic or sectarian savagery beyond law's boundaries.[23]

In the presence of these claims, one must ask whether rationality can really survive its encounter with violence,[24] whether violence can be made to obey law, and whether its destructive energies can be made constructive. The answers to such questions hardly seem obvious. Yet we know that the complexity of law's relationship to violence is deepened by the variability of that relationship.

Constitutional, democratic, humane legal orders are distinguishable from their lawless, authoritarian, and barbaric counterparts by the ways they authorize and use the coercive force at their disposal. We sense the difference in our almost universal preference for the former and aversion to the latter. We recognize the difference, in part, by mood and temper—by the circumspection and ambivalence associated with the use of authorized force in constitutional, democratic, humane legal orders, in contrast to the enthusiams and bloodthirstiness of other legal regimes. Yet constitutional violence is violence nonetheless; it crushes and kills with a steadfastness equal to a violence undisciplined by legitimacy.[25]

---

22. Wolff, "Violence and the Law."

23. See Susan Jacoby, *Wild Justice: The Evolution of Revenge* (New York: Harper and Row, 1983); see also Jonathan Rieder, "The Social Organization of Vengeance," in *Toward A General Theory of Social Control,* ed. Donald Black (New York: Academic Press, 1984). As Justice Stewart put it in his concurring opinion in Furman v. Georgia, 408 U.S. 238 (1972): "The instinct for retribution is part of the nature of man and channelling that instinct in the administration of criminal justice serves an important purpose in promoting the stability of a society governed by law" (309).

24. See Sarat and Kearns, "Journey," 269; see also Waldenfels, "Limits of Legitimation," 101.

25. Even in constitutional legal orders the imperatives of violence may be so

In all legal orders, the violence inside law threatens to undo
law.[26] It threatens to expose the facade of law's dispassionate reason
as just that—a facade[27]—and to destabilize law by forcing choices
between the normative aspirations of law and the need to maintain
social order through force.[28] It threatens to swallow up law and
leave nothing but a social world of forces arrayed in aggressive
opposition.[29] Where violence is present, can there be anything other
than violence?

But, unfortunately, except in the utopian imagination, there is
no symmetry in the relationship of law and violence. Law never
similarly endangers violence. Even when we realize the way law itself
exaggerates the threat of violence *outside* law, we can never ourselves
imagine that law could finally conquer and undo force, coercion, and
disorder; its best promise is a promise to substitute one kind of force—
legitimate force—for another.[30]

The association of law and violence is visible in the discrete acts
of law's agents—the gun fired by the police, the sentence pronounced
by the judge, the execution carried out behind prison walls. It is,
moreover, audible in the ease and comfort with which we speak about
enforcing the law. "'Applicability, enforceability' is not," as Derrida
puts it,

---

overwhelming as to distort and destroy prevailing normative commitments. Two
powerful examples are provided by Justice Powell in McCleskey v. Kemp, 107 S. Ct.
1756 (1987), holding that statistical evidence of racial discrimination may not be used
to establish a prima facie case of discrimination in death penalty cases, and by Justice
Rhenquist in Payne v. Tennessee, 90-5721 (1991), devising a new understanding of
the bindingness of precedent to overturn two decisions forbidding the use of victim
impact information in death penalty litigation.

26. Benjamin argues that "in the exercise of violence over life and death more
than in any other legal act, law reaffirms itself. But," he continues, "in this very
violence something rotten in law is revealed, above all to a finer sensibility, because
the latter knows itself to be infinitely remote from conditions in which fate might
imperiously have shown itself in such a sentence" (Benjamin, "Critique of Violence,"
286). See also Albert Camus, "Reflections on the Guillotine," in *Réflexions sur la
Peine Capitale,* by Albert Camus and Arthur Koestler (Paris: Calmann-Lévy, 1957).

27. Sarat and Kearns, "Journey," 269.

28. See *McCleskey v. Kemp* for a powerful example of this dilemma. See also
Robert Cover, *Justice Accused* (New Haven: Yale University Press, 1975).

29. For an examination of how violence may come to swallow up law in the
work of certain legal theorists, see Dominick LaCapra, "Violence, Justice, and the
Force of Law," *Cardozo Law Review* 11 (1990): 1065.

30. See Justice Stewart in *Furman.*

an exterior or secondary possibility that may or may not be added as a supplement to law. . . . The word *enforceability* reminds us that there is no such thing as law that doesn't imply in itself, a priori, . . . the possibility of being "enforced," applied by force. There are, to be sure, laws that are not enforced, but there is no law without enforceability, and no applicability or enforceability of the law without force, whether this force be direct or indirect, physical or symbolic.[31]

As pervasive as the relationship of law and violence is, as visible and audible as are its manifestations, it is, nonetheless, difficult to speak about that relationship or to know precisely what one is talking about when one speaks about law's violence. This difficulty results, in part, from three different trends within legal scholarship, each distinct in its emphasis but each of which displaces that subject. The first is perhaps the most well recognized in terms of its displacement of the subject of violence from the study of law.[32] It is associated with the law and humanities movement.

Humanists emphasize the meaning-making, community-building character of law, and deemphasize its coercive aspects. In law, they see a vehicle for binding persons together through its engagement of our imaginations and its demands on our interpretive energies. Humanists liken law to literature, as a resource in building humane societies.[33] Where they bow to, or acknowledge, violence in law, they do so only to give impetus to their own effort to identify the culture of argument and principle that allegedly gives law its defining character.[34]

---

31. Derrida, "Force of Law," 925.

32. See Cover, "Violence and the Word," 1601, n. 2.

33. See, for example, James Boyd White, *Justice As Translation* (Chicago: University of Chicago Press, 1990).

34. As Ronald Dworkin argues,

Day in and day out we send people to jail, or take money away from them, or make them do things they do not want to do, under coercion of force, and we justify all this by speaking of such persons as having broken the law or having failed to meet their legal obligations. . . . Even in clear cases . . . , when we are confident that someone had a legal obligation and broke it, we are not able to give a satisfactory account of what that means or why it entitles the state to punish or coerce him. We may feel confident that what we are doing is proper, but until we can identify the principles we are following we

The second displacement is part of the scientific study of legal institutions and practices. Here, violence becomes a subject of inquiry, but the nature of its connection to law, as well as the way it gives meaning to law, is nonetheless displaced. This is the result of specification, disaggregation, and reluctance to speak about law as something other than the discrete acts of its agents or the discrete performances of its institutions.[35] In scientific studies, force and coercion are disconnected from law by dismantling law so as to specify its practices. Thus, we have a rich and important body of research on punishment[36] and a proliferation of valuable empirical studies of police[37] and of sentencing.[38] This research and those studies make particular acts of coercive force visible, but disconnect them from what is essential to law itself. As a result, the relationship of law to violence is denied a theory, as theory itself is displaced in favor of observation.

The third trend within legal scholarship appears, on first glance, to respond to the defects of both humanistic and scientific scholarship by speaking about many different types of violence and theorizing about their connection to law. Under the forces of critical theory and deconstruction, the use of the word *violence* proliferates; we are reminded that law is violent in many ways—in the ways it uses language and in its representational practices,[39] in the silencing of perspectives and the denial of experience,[40] and in its objectifying

cannot be sure they are sufficient. . . . In less clear cases, . . . the pitch of these nagging questions rises, and our responsibility to find answers deepens. (Dworkin, *Taking Rights Seriously* [Cambridge, Mass.: Harvard University Press, 1977], 15)

35. This critique is suggested in David Trubek, "Where the Action Is: Critical Legal Studies and Empiricism," *Stanford Law Review* 36 (1984): 575.

36. See, for example, David Garland, *Punishment and Modern Society* (Chicago: University of Chicago Press, 1990).

37. A fine example is provided by Jerome Skolnick, *Justice Without Trial* (New York: Wiley, 1967).

38. See Stanton Wheeler, Ken Mann, and Austin Sarat, *Sitting in Judgment: The Sentencing of White Collar Criminals* (New Haven: Yale University Press, 1988).

39. See Catharine MacKinnon, *Feminism Unmodified* (Cambridge, Mass.: Harvard University Press, 1987). For an interesting treatment of representation as violence in a nonlegal context, see Nancy Armstrong and Leonard Tennenhouse, eds., *The Violence of Representation: Literature and the History of Violence* (London: Routledge, 1989).

40. See Martha Minow, *Making All the Difference* (Ithaca: Cornell University Press, 1989); also see Joan Scott, "The Evidence of Experience," *Critical Inquiry* 17

epistemology.[41] In addition, we find increasingly ingenious and surprising pathways to the subject of violence; thus, Samuel Weber says, "To render impure, literally; to 'touch with' (something foreign, alien), is also to violate. And to violate something is to do violence to it. Inversely, it is difficult to conceive of violence without violation, so much so that the latter might well be a criterion of the former: no violence without violation, hence, no violence without a certain contamination."[42]

Where once it seemed quite obvious that when one talked about law's violence one would be referring to the direct, unmediated infliction of physical force by officials invested with legal authority, today, critical theory and deconstruction have, as Peter Fitzpatrick recently wrote, ". . . left 'violence' with a confusion of meaning."[43] Fitzpatrick suggests that,

> in its narrow perhaps popular sense, violence is equated with unrestrained physical violence. . . . A standard history of the West would connect a decline in violence with an increase in civility. Others would see civility itself as a transformed violence, as a constraining even if not immediately coercive discipline. . . . The dissipation of simple meaning is heightened in recent sensibilities where violence is discerned in the denial of the uniqueness or even existence of the "other." . . . These expansions of the idea of violence import a transcendent ordering—an organizing, shaping force coming to bear on situations from outside of them and essentially unaffected by them.[44]

The expansions of the idea of violence about which Fitzpatrick

---

(1991): 773; Teresa de Lauretis, "The Violence of Rhetoric: Considerations on Representation and Gender," in *The Violence of Representation: Literature and the History of Violence,* ed. Nancy Armstrong and Leonard Tennenhouse (London: Routledge, 1989).

41. Robin West, "Disciplines, Subjectivity, and Law," in *The Fate of Law,* ed. Austin Sarat and Thomas R. Kearns (Ann Arbor: University of Michigan Press, 1991).

42. Samuel Weber, "Deconstruction Before the Name: Some [Very] Preliminary Remarks on Deconstruction and Violence" (University of California, Los Angeles, 1990, Photocopy), 2.

43. See Fitzpatrick, "Violence and Legal Subjection," 1; also see Wolff, "Violence and the Law," 55.

44. Fitzpatrick, "Violence and Legal Subjection," 1.

writes threatens to undo the subject itself. If everything is violent,
then the word and the idea lose their meaning and their normative
and critical bite. If the critique of violence must take on all cognitive,
linguistic, and cultural practices, then it is overwhelmed and undone.
Thus, the first act in the effort to understand law's forceful, coercive
character must be a "violent" act of repositioning our language; we
must insist on clarity and distinctiveness against our better understandings of the dangers of such insistence.

Our own efforts in that direction, as well as the efforts of several
of the authors who have contributed to this volume, find their point
of departure in the work of Robert Cover.[45] Cover argued that the
meaning-making, community-building, literary quality of law should
not distract us from the fact that, as he put it, "Legal interpretation
takes place in a field of pain and death."[46] In addition, he worked
hard to reconnect the seemingly discrete and isolated violent acts of
judges, police, wardens, and executioners to a theory of law. And,
he insisted, even at the price of doing linguistic violence, that ". . .
the violence . . . [of law] is utterly real—in need of no interpretation,
no critic to reveal it—a naive but immediate reality. Take a short
trip to your local prison and see."[47] The coercive character of law,
he contended (against humanist, positivist, and postmodern critics),
is central to law, systematic, and quite unlike the "psychoanalytic
violence of literature or the metaphorical characterization of literary
critics and philosophers."[48]

Cover invited us to imagine and construct a jurisprudence of
violence, and to theorize about law by attending to its pain-imposing,
death-dealing acts. This book—*Law's Violence*—is a response to that
invitation and a contribution to building that jurisprudence. While
it does not present a systematic overview of the nature, uses, and
meaning of force in law, it contributes to a jurisprudence of violence
by providing examples, glimpses perhaps, of answers to three different
questions.

First is the question of institutional design. Here we ask, does
it matter—in terms of the nature, uses, and meaning of legal force—

---

45. See Cover, "Violence and the Word."

46. Cover, "Violence and the Word," 1601.

47. See Robert Cover, "The Bonds of Constitutional Interpretation: Of the Word,
the Deed, and the Role," *Georgia Law Review* 20 (1986): 818.

48. Cover, "Constitutional Interpretation," 818–19.

what procedures authorize its use and who is authorized to deploy it? Second is the question of the meaning of law's violence in culture and history. How does it vary across cultures and over time? What is the significance of violence in different cultures, and when is law's reliance on coercion and physical force most frequent and intense? The final question is one of the impact of law's violence on law itself and on the culture in which it is embedded. Each of the essays in this collection take up one or more of these questions. Each pursues and develops its own perspective on the relationship of law and violence, yet each insists that that relationship be made central to our understanding of the history, nature, and purposes of law.

The contributions by Elaine Scarry and Patricia Wald take up the question of institutional design. Scarry, in "The Declaration of War: Constitutional and Unconstitutional Violence," begins our consideration of law's violence by focusing on the most dramatic and dangerous instance of violence—nuclear war.[49] For her, the subject of nuclear war demands a careful reexamination of the procedures through which wars are declared and given legal authorization.[50] In her view, it is doubtful that nuclear war could or would ever be a legally authorized act, that nuclear war could ever be a form of law's violence.

Scarry's essay explicates and defends the constitutional requirement of a congressional declaration of war against the doctrine of presidential first-use of nuclear weapons. Presidential first-use is or would be, in her account, profoundly incompatible with the Constitution, which allocates the power to declare war to Congress, not the president. What is at stake in the debate about presidential first-use is thus the very idea of the rule of law.[51] The power of Congress

---

49. For a related effort, see Antonio Cassese, *Violence and the Law in the Modern Age*, trans. S. J. K. Greenleaves (Princeton: Princeton University Press, 1988).

50. Similar concerns, concerns that go to the relationship between nuclear war and the rule of law, are expressed in George Kateb, "Nuclear Weapons and Individual Rights," *Dissent* 33 (1986): 161.

51. While the declaration of war provision of the Constitution is a restraint on violence imposed by a framework of laws, the only restraint in presidential first-use is the restraint of personal goodwill. As Scarry puts it,

The grant of power by the population to the executive government was never a grant of power to give or retract the lives of millions of people. . . . Not even the most benign and generous leader can make contractually tolerable a national arms policy that holds out to other populations this kind of threat—the threat

to declare war is the only way, in Scarry's view, for war to become a form of law's violence; otherwise war is always an extralegal, illegal violence no matter what its substantive justifications.

In addition, the processes of deliberation through which Congress goes about declaring war make a profound difference in the likelihood of war itself. Whereas presidential first-use eases the way toward nuclear war, the declaration of war provisions of the Constitution, Scarry believes, have the effect, when translated into congressional practice, of making that kind of world-ending violence less likely. Her explication and defense of the congressional declaration of war as the only legally appropriate means to authorize acts of war, the only way to make that violence into law's violence, is presented as an analysis of the way language and representation work when war is "declared" in the prescribed manner.[52]

Each of the linguistic and representational properties of the declaration of war that Scarry identifies is an occasion for deliberation and reflection, for thought and, more important, second thought.[53]

of annihilation to be restrained by purely personal (rather than transpersonal and legal) inhibitions on violence.

52. Scarry believes that, to sustain an argument for congressional control over acts of war, one must be committed to a particular view of representation and language that, she fears, is increasingly discredited.

Because so many descriptive sentences have failed to represent the world accurately and because so many performative sentences have been spoken by the wrong speaker, it sometimes seems that a general skepticism has arisen so that we no longer aspire to have descriptive sentences that are true and performative sentences constrained by the authorization to speak. But to lose this aspiration imperils our world. It takes away the ground from which we can criticize language that has ceased to be true and resist speakers who oblige us to live outside the rule of law.

53. Scarry identifies three linguistic properties of congressional declarations of war that she believes materially alter the prospects for war. The first, what she calls "exact repeatability," arises from the need to attain the consent of a majority of the 535 members of Congress. It means that many voices will be heard; many must make their assent or disagreement known. This "inlaying of voices" leads to the second linguistic property of the declaration of war, the tendency to "dismantle the object." Dismantling the object is a technique through which those who oppose war carry out their opposition; they verbally detach actions from the alleged enemy and show how those same actions are being, or have been, taken by the United States itself or an allied country. The third linguistic property—also a result of the "inlaying of voices" in the congressional declaration—is what Scarry calls "inlaying the material object." By this she means that, in the process of declaring war, Congress must and will consider the human and material consequences that flow from that declaration, the persons who must be enlisted to fight and die, the treasure that must be spent to sustain the war.

Each, Scarry contends, is missing in presidential first-use. In her view, presidential first-use would be a performative—Scarry relies on J. L. Austin's analysis of performative sentences[54]—that "misfires," but, unlike other misfiring performatives that have no material consequences, "In presidential first-use, the absence of a verbal declaration does not prevent injuries from taking place. The performative is disabled; it misfires; yet millions of persons die. The president has the technological power to bring war into being through instant materialization at the precise moment that any claim to authority for the verbal declaration has ceased."

While Scarry points to the importance of particular institutional arrangements as an alternative to a world in which ultimate violence is a matter of personal responsibility or irresponsibility, the author of the second essay—Patricia M. Wald—considers the ways in which institutional arrangements encourage or discourage personal responsibility in the use of legal force. Wald's essay, "Violence under the Law: A Judge's Perspective," moves the consideration of law's violence from the threat of nuclear war to the more ordinary, if not mundane, coercion and force that is authorized or condoned by the law everyday. Judge Wald asks us to consider the everyday world of criminal sentencing and family violence, of prison conditions and environmental danger. She speaks about the capacity of law to rule violence, in each of these areas, from the perspective of a sitting judge—someone who has the power to unleash or restrain the coercive power of law. Like Cover, she argues that violence gives law its distinctive character, a character that cannot be captured adequately in and by the texts of law. Like Scarry, she argues that institutional arrangements and legal doctrines matter. Such arrangements and doctrines either invite restraint or they ease the path to violence.

Judge Wald favors those institutional arrangements and doctrines that require legal decision makers, especially judges, to confront, in a concrete and immediate way, the pain their decisions authorize, condone, or ignore. Thus she worries, for example, about the recently created United States Sentencing Commission and the movement to impose rigid and mechanical sentencing guidelines. In such a system, Judge Wald contends, "The sentencing commissioners never see

54. See J. L. Austin, *How to Do Things with Words*, 2d ed. (Cambridge, Mass.: Harvard University Press, 1962).

individual defendants during trial; they only read about the unique facts of their cases or lives in cold print. And the judge who does see and hear the defendant is constrained as to what punishment to impose. The imposition of law's violence has been depersonalized." Depersonalization diminishes accountability and means that law's violence will be imposed in a more ruthless and less responsible manner.

Similarly, when she writes about the agonizing problems posed when judges are asked to decide whether to continue life-sustaining, extraordinary medical care for those unable to speak for themselves, Wald contends that institutional arrangements and legal doctrines matter. She criticizes the so-called substituted judgment rule that enjoins judges to act as they imagine incompetent patients would themselves act. This rule allows judges to avoid confronting their own judgment and responsibility "in approving the use of violence on an unconsenting individual."

In this area and the others she considers, Wald criticizes arrangements and doctrines that "distance the judge from responsibility for the violence he or she authorizes" through abstraction, depersonalization, and neglect. She urges her readers to look within the framework of the rule of law to consider alternative possibilities. She believes that, within that framework, judges and others should be held accountable for the painful impositions they authorize or condone, and that such personal accountability would insure that law's violence would be dealt with more reasonably and responsibly.

From questions of institutional design, the next two essays move to questions of culture and history. Those essays—by Carol J. Greenhouse and Douglas Hay—remind us that law's violence is dynamic and varied, constantly defining and redefining contexts of interaction, and that it cannot be understood apart from the particular cultural contexts that give it meaning.

Greenhouse begins her essay, "Reading Violence," by making explicit the problem to which both Scarry and Wald address themselves—namely, the relationship of language and violence. This is, of course, at the heart of any debate about law and force, about the rationality, control, and purposiveness of the violence that law does. Greenhouse connects the conventional distinction between language and violence to old evolutionary approaches in sociocultural anthropology, which stipulated that one sign of cultural "progress" was the move from

physical force to the symbolic force of words in the regulation of interpersonal conflict. She notes that Robert Cover's work, whose premise
is an axiomatic distinction between violence and ordinary language,
draws on this legacy.

In the course of her analysis of the cultural meaning and variability of law's violence, she examines two of Cover's claims, claims
that she believes pose fundamental epistemological and ethical challenges to those committed, as she is, to an interpretivist understanding
of culture and law. The first of these claims is that violence cannot
be adequately represented in texts and that interpretive approaches
in legal scholarship cannot grasp the power, pain, and problems
associated with law's use of coercive force. The second is that interpretive approaches necessarily assume the completeness and sharing
of meanings within communities and, as a result, are unable to grasp
the wrenching divisions and incompatibilities that are necessarily part
of the meaning of all legal texts.

Greenhouse tests and contests the first of these claims by drawing
on ethnographies of a community of headhunters in the Philippines—
the Ilongot—and of a horticultural community in Papua, New
Guinea—the Kaluli. She contends that these case studies demonstrate
that violence can be, and is, part of the narrative and textual life of
communities, that violence can give meaning to textual artifacts and
can be both symbolically and literally incorporated into them.[55] From
these two case studies, Greenhouse argues—contra Cover—that violence itself does not destroy the world of text, interpretation, and
meaning. On the contrary, "the violence in the texts extends, circulates, modifies, or contains—or fails to do these things—the violence in the world." In the cultures of the Ilongot and the Kaluli,
certain texts become legible through, and would be illegible without,

---

55. With regard to the Ilongot, Greenhouse claims, drawing on Rosaldo's original ethnography (Renato Rosaldo, *Ilongot Headhunting 1863–1974: A Study in History and Society* [Stanford: Stanford University Press, 1980]), that the remembrance
of headhunting gives shape to the historical narratives through which they make
sense of who they are as a people. "Violence," Greenhouse argues, "was at the core
of Ilongot textuality." Similarly, Greenhouse, borrowing from Schiefflin (Edward
Schiefflin, *The Sorrow of the Lonely and the Burning of the Dancers* [St. Lucia:
University of Queensland Press, 1976]), describes how, among the Kaluli, central
cultural rituals, the Gisaro dance, successfully recreate memories of violence and
destruction in their audience. The intention and effect is to provoke a literally violent
response. The violence of that response "does not disrupt the performance because
it is absorbed and contained within it."

their very embodiment of the physical force that is present in everyday life. For Greenhouse, the frightening thing about violence, including law's violence, "is not that it cannot be read or interpreted textually . . . but that it can be so easily."

But Greenhouse recognizes that any representation of force, whether inside or outside law, works against a background of something even more destructive than violence, something truly unspeakable. From the cultural perspectives she describes in her essay, it is not violence in itself that destroys meaning, but violence from this other realm. She argues that the task of interpretive work is not to demonstrate the unity of culture, but its essential contradiction, and that interpretivists can do so by "discovering the contours of the text against the unspeakable that it keeps at bay. Attending to the law's textuality offers one means of holding the law accountable to something beyond law—something like a connection between language and life." She illustrates this claim by discussing a U.S. case—*Perry v. Louisiana*—in which a man sentenced to die argued that it would be unconstitutional for the state forcibly to administer antipsychotic drugs in order to make him competent to be executed.

Interpreting the text of *Perry*, Greenhouse identifies meanings that she argues are, for the state seeking to execute him and for Perry, mutually exclusive and contradictory. Indeed, she argues that the text is interpretable only to the extent that those oppositions are recognized and acknowledged. From this she contends—again contra Cover—that interpretation does not require agreement, consensus, and solidarity. The job of the interpretivist is, in her view, first, to find those places in culture and law where oppositions and contradictions are denied as well as where the unspeakable is kept at bay and, then, to expose them. Here Greenhouse reminds us that there can be no general universal modus operandi; while texts, including legal texts, can and do contain violence, the ways in which they do so, as well as the meaning of the text and its violence, in her view, involve fundamental cultural contests and contingencies.

A similar interest in the contingency of law's violence animates the essay by Douglas Hay. Hay, like Greenhouse and Wald, begins with Cover. While he appreciates the value and significance of Cover's writing about law's violence, he argues that it is "teleological in its implication of a blueprint, formalist in its apparent assumption that the hierarchy of state violence has the same contours as the hierarchy of legal institutions. [And] above all, it is static, with perhaps unintended connotations of fixed stability." Hay's essay is devoted to the last of these concerns, to showing "how the violence of state law fluctuates over time."

In "Time, Inequality, and Law's Violence," Hay examines fluctuations in the incidence of capital punishment and incarceration—as indicators of law's violence—in England from the seventeenth to and into the twentieth century. He argues that law's reliance on physical force is responsive to changes in the social context and environment within which law operates. In particular, he notes that the incidence of coercive repression increases during periods of increasing social inequality and decreases during periods where inequality is ameliorated. This pattern is as visible in the twentieth century as it was in the seventeenth. Thus, ". . . the violence of the law, measured by prosecutions and punishments, was," Hay concludes, "determined by the need to contain the effects of substantial social inequality, and particularly changes in its incidence." While he acknowledges that the "causal connections are undoubtedly multiple" his argument suggests that law's violence is typically a repressive response to social injustice.

Hay also argues that the reliance of law on brute force is not a simple response to levels of violence outside the law. In fact, he suggests that "the violence of the state may be a powerful *determinant* of violence in society." The violence of law may, if Hay is right, actually inspire extralegal, illegal violence. This dynamic of law responding to injustice violently, and, in so doing, encouraging disorder and criminality, precipitates, in Hay's account, the ameliorative efforts of poor relief and welfare. But these efforts exist precariously as supplements to law's violence. They do not, and cannot, go very far toward displacing or limiting it given continuing (Hay might say deepening) commitments to market economies and their self-help ideologies.

Moreover, despite occasional, highly visible demonstrations of the evenhandedness of law and of its commitment to justice regardless of class, it is the imperatives of class, not justice, that give meaning to law's violence. Hay's comparison of England and the United States suggests a similar dynamic in this country, and cautions those (like Scarry and Wald) who would look to doctrinal developments or institutional rearrangements internal to law to govern or ameliorate its violence. As Hay puts it (here echoing Cover), "The coercive impact of law is the important element for those who, in fact, are the most direct victims of its violence, the poor; the legitimation of the word is most compelling to those predisposed to believe it, who share it, who articulate it."[56]

Hay's arguments about the latent consequences of law's violence, as well as his concern to understand the social dynamics attendant to it, provide a historical context within which to consider the last two essays in *Law's Violence*. Robert Weisberg and Sarat and Kearns address the question of the impact of law's violence, first on culture and society, and then on law itself.

Weisberg's project in "Private Violence as Moral Action: The Law as Inspiration and Example" is to blur the asserted distinction between law's legitimate violence and the allegedly irrational, uncontrolled, anomic conditions outside law. For him, as for Hay, law's use of force provides an example, if not an inspiration, that is imitated beyond law's boundaries. "[R]ather than view law as punishing or deterring criminals, while finessing the issue of whether we must use violence to achieve those goals, we might," Weisberg suggests, "view law as inspiring and emboldening these criminals." Moreover, Weisberg claims that extralegal violence is neither as irrational, uncontrolled, nor anomic as defenders of law would have us believe. Crime, Weisberg contends, often feels like law for the perpetrator; it represents an act of lawmaking or law enforcement without the sanction of law itself. "In fact," he says, "much crime, rather than offering a general moral counterclaim to society's vision of the good, is a directly parallel and purportedly supplementary form of moral claiming and, indeed, law enforcement."

---

56. As Cover put it,
   The perpetrator and victim of organized violence will undergo achingly different experiences. For the perpetrator, the pain and fear are remote, unreal, largely unheard.... On the other hand, for those who impose the violence, the justification is important, real and carefully cultivated. Conversely, for the victim, the justification for the violence recedes in reality and significance in proportion to the overwhelming reality of the pain and fear that is suffered. (Cover, "Violence and the Word," 1629)
Here, Cover draws on Scarry's *The Body in Pain*, though, as Scarry herself put it in a personal letter to the editors (August 26, 1991), "I am saying, when discrepancies between 'perpetrator and victim' exist of this severity, then it should be called torture and not law, whereas you are introducing the possibility that the same is true of law (I would answer, it is being miscalled law; it doesn't deserve the name law)."

Distinguishing law's violence from its extralegal counterpart is complicated, Weisberg argues, by the social psychology of crime—namely, most homicide victims are well known to their killers, who often see their acts as morally justified, and many property crimes are "aggressive forms of debt collection"—and by the long history of self-help as a legitimate means of law enforcement. Thus, even group violence against alleged transgressors—like that recently seen in Howard Beach and Bensonhurst[57]—may be inspired by some lawlike attachment to ideas of territorial or cultural defense. "Armed with the belief that it is acting in the name of the law, a group of rioters," Weisberg reminds us, "feels like a state itself, a body politic."[58]

According to Weisberg, efforts to take account of, and displace, self-help (for example, the Victorian reform movement and the defense of retribution as a basis for punishment) run up against a continuing and widespread ambivalence about such acts. That ambivalance is seen within law itself, in doctrines that excuse or justify crimes, and it insures that law's violence will often provide a model for, rather than a deterrent to, extralegal violence. If this is true, then Weisberg's work suggests that the violence of law may be as much an impediment as it is an aid to the articulation and realization of social forms in which the role of force is minimized.

Just as law's violence may be an impediment to the realization of certain social forms, the conditions necessary to sustain that violence may alter or limit the possibilities of law itself. This is the argument that Sarat and Kearns develop in the last essay in this volume, "Making Peace with Violence: Robert Cover on Law and Violence."

Sarat and Kearns suggest that Cover was both a critic of, and an apologist for, law's violence. In his critical mode, he saw the fury of state law as a barrier to the achievement of a normatively rich, legally plural community, and he urged judges to go far in tolerating and respecting the normative claims of communities whose visions of the good did not comport with the commands and requirements of state law. He argued that unless judges could articulate normative arguments more compelling than those presented by such

---

57. For an especially insightful discussion, see Patricia Williams, *The Alchemy of Race and Rights* (Cambridge, Mass.: Harvard University Press, 1991), chap. 4.

58. For a contrasting view, see Edward Banfield, *The Unheavenly City: The Nature and Future of Our Urban Crisis* (Boston: Little, Brown, 1970).

communities, a just legal order would respect and accommodate the latter rather than violently impose itself. It is never enough, in Cover's view, for a judge to retreat to the positivist assertion that deference and obedience is required merely because state law commands it.

Yet Sarat and Kearns contend that Cover recognized the need for law's occasional violent impositions, and that he attended carefully to the prerequisites for law's successful use of violence. For law to achieve such success, its social organization would have to find resources both to overcome and to regulate cultural and moral inhibitions against the use of physical force. To overcome those inhibitions, Cover suggested that strong justifications would have to be provided and that such justifications, when combined with a well-articulated structure of roles and offices, might then assure relatively automatic compliance with the violence-authorizing (or -restraining) orders of judges. Thus, for law's violent impositions to work in the world—for words to be translated into violent deeds—justifications, strong justifications, would have to be provided. Here Cover was more apologist than critic.

As Sarat and Kearns read the corpus of Cover's work, they find a twofold message; "Wherever possible, withhold violence and let new worlds flourish; but do not forget that, for the sake of life, law's violence will sometimes be necessary and the conditions of its effective deployment must be carefully provided for. . . . To do its job, then, law *must* be violent, but *sparingly.*" Cover, they contend, was too hopeful that this twofold admonition could be realized in fact. As they see it, the conditions necessary for the effective deployment of force—in particular, the generation of strong justifications—promote excess, not restraint, universalism, not toleration. Attention to Cover's work, Sarat and Kearns contend, demonstrates how the imperatives of violence radically limit the possibilities for law and dictate the terms of law's relationship to the world.

Somewhere between Cover's message of hope—which is reflected most acutely in Scarry and Wald's essays—and the despairing thought that law's violence, like an invisible toxin, corrupts all it touches, sits the everyday reality of law. Law traffics in violence out of claimed or imagined necessity; yet, in every legal order, violence—officially authorized and actually dispensed—tends to excess. Finding the resources of understanding that will allow effective opposition to excess while encouraging an accurate perception of the necessities of law's reliance on force is the remaining task for the jurisprudence of violence to which we hope the essays in this volume contribute.

The Declaration of War: Constitutional and Unconstitutional Violence

Elaine Scarry

> Mr. Bush took a photograph out of his pocket—a family group, people of various generations on some cliffs by the sea. He said, "Here's the guarantee that we will never use nuclear weapons first, this is my family, my wife, children and grandchildren. I don't want them to die. No one on earth wants that."
>
> —Andrei Sakharov

Shortly before he died, Andrei Sakharov urged the president of the United States to formally renounce the strategic policy of presidential first-use of nuclear weapons. Although the president—drawing a photograph from his wallet—gave his personal assurance, what Sakharov wanted was not this act, but an official announcement. "[I]f," said Sakharov to Bush, "you insist that you will not strike first, you must make an official announcement of that, put it into the law." Mr. Bush was silent.[1] This opposition—a restraint imposed by personal goodwill or instead one imposed by a framework of laws—is as old as the idea of a republic. The distance between the two can be measured by assessing how the act of "representation" works in each. In articulating his reluctance to use nuclear weapons offensively, the president

My thanks to the Institute for Advanced Study in Berlin, where much of the work on this essay took place.

1. Andrei Sakharov, "Sakharov on Gorbachev and Bush," *Washington Post,* December 3, 1989; "Presidents' Answers Don't Always Answer," *International Herald Tribune,* December 4, 1989.

introduced into the visual space a "representation," a photograph, a fragile slip of paper. Both aesthetic representation and political representation were entailed—as they must always be entailed in the question of how other persons come before the mind in the moment one considers inflicting great injury upon them.

As Sakharov may or may not have been aware, a formal legal prohibition of presidential first-use of nuclear weapons already exists. Article I, section 8, clause 11 of the U.S. Constitution requires a congressional declaration of war: it stipulates that the full House and Senate together (the full assembly of Representatives) are obligated to oversee the country's entry into war. The stark incompatibility of this constitutionally required declaration with the longstanding strategic policy of presidential first-use has, since 1984, been repeatedly observed in both foreign policy and law journals.[2] The observation has been made not only by scholars, academics, and dissident intellectuals, but also by those at the center of executive power. At least where formerly classified presidential and National Security Council Memoranda have been made available, the severity of the constitutional breach has been acknowledged. President Eisenhower, for example, was prepared to use nuclear weapons during both the 1954–55 Taiwan Straits Crisis and the 1959 Berlin Crisis, but he repeatedly acknowledged, that, without congressional authorization, his action would be unconstitutional. "If Congressional authorization were not obtained," a memorandum records him as saying, "there would be logical grounds for impeachment. Whatever we do must be done in a Constitutional manner."[3]

The specter of a constitutional violation so grave it warrants impeachment has not, over the last four decades, stopped the pro-

---

2. For the journal articles and law cases that address the discrepancy between Art. I, sect. 8, cl. 11 of the U.S. Constitution and the country's policy of presidential first-use, see Elaine Scarry, "War and the Social Contract: Nuclear Policy, Distribution, and the Right to Bear Arms," *University of Pennsylvania Law Review* 139 (1991): 1267, 1268 nn. 32, 33.

3. U.S. Department of State, "Memorandum of Discussion at the 214th Meeting of the National Security Council, Denver, September 12, 1954," *Foreign Relations of the United States 1952–54* 14:618 (hereinafter, *FRUS*). The participants at this meeting also discussed whether United Nations authorization would make it easier to obtain, or even bypass altogether, congressional authorization (620, 621). I am grateful to Marc Trachtenberg for his generous advice in locating and deciphering various materials in the recently declassified Eisenhower papers that are periodically referred to in this article.

gressive formalization of a presidential first-use policy. Nor is it necessarily the case that impeachability, even if in force, would inhibit
a president if longstanding strategic habits (such as those provided
for in the U.S. flexible response doctrine) and the structure of technology itself appeared to require presidential action. Four months
after Eisenhower made the previously cited statements, he changes
from saying he will avoid initiating a strike *because* it is an impeachable act, to saying he will do it, if necessary, *even though* it is an
impeachable act. The National Security Council Record for January
21, 1955 reads, "The President said that all might be sure of one
thing—namely, that he would do in an emergency whatever had to
be done to protect the vital interests of the United States. He would
do this even if his actions should be interpreted as acts of war. He
would rather be impeached than fail to do his duty."[4]

Just as impeachability may fail to inhibit, so, far from inhibiting,
it may actually prompt or invite the act. During his own impeachment
proceedings,[5] Richard Nixon said to a group of Congressmen, "I can
go into my office and pick up the telephone and in 25 minutes 70
million people will be dead." Impeachment—by being the path from
the chief public officer to a private citizen (a demotion to the purely
personal)—makes manifest the kinship between the personal concerns
in looking at a family photo and worrying about getting fired. In
some way, Nixon's boast (or perhaps it was only an observation, the
production of a picture of himself on the telephone), and Bush's good-
natured gesture of reaching into a wallet to produce a treasured
photograph are deeply alike: the basic arrangements of a contractual
society are designed to prevent the situation in which a personal
decision is made. If the fate of five hundred galley slaves is dependent
on the personal decision of a ship's tyrant, no one can lightly dismiss
the issue of that individual's goodwill, kindness, or humanism. One

4. U.S. Department of State, "Memorandum of Discussion at the 233d Meeting
of the National Security Council, Washington, January 21, 1955, 9 A.M.," *FRUS*,
1955–57 2:94. Similar language is used in the September 12 meeting, without any
explicit reference to impeachment or the bypassing of congressional authorization:
"The President suggested . . . that everyone could be sure of one thing, and that is
that the vital interests of the U.S. in that area will be protected, and if we think
that those interests are in danger we will take appropriate action to help our friends
out there" (*FRUS*, *1952–54* 14:623).

5. As Eisenhower's vice president, Nixon was present at the National Security
Council meetings cited previously and had reinforced Eisenhower's own belief that
solitary action would make him impeachable. See *FRUS*, *1955–57* 2:92–93.

does not only *not* dismiss it. One actually wishes for it, urges it—
and must be grateful to the wife or woman whose *picture in the mind*
prevents his cruelty, and that, like the fear of losing office, acts to
brake rather than incite fatal actions. But how in a contractual republic should we have so abased ourselves as to be in a state of petition
or gratitude for humanism that stays the hand (rather than eliminating
the arrangements that keep us frozen in this posture of petition)?
And if it is not we who are the galley slaves but the citizens of other
republics—that is, if it is other populations and not we ourselves who
will be injured—the same question arises: how did we so abase ourselves that we left the fate of other populations up to a small number
of individuals and the accident of how they feel about a photograph
in a pocket? The grant of power by the population to the executive
government was never a grant of power to give or retract the lives
of millions of people, our own or other populations'. Not even the
most benign and generous leader can make contractually tolerable a
national arms policy that holds out to other populations this kind
of threat—the threat of annihilation to be restrained by purely personal (rather than transpersonal and legal) inhibitions on violence.
Family photographs too easily fall away: "When violence becomes
the characterizing gesture of a culture (the way it keeps its promises),
inscription is an intolerable burden in the lonely heart."[6]

This essay looks at the way language works, the way "representation" works—the way pictures come before the mind—in the
congressional declaration of war (in the five wars in which the United
States has had such a declaration: the War of 1812, Mexican War,
Spanish-American War, World War I, and World War II)[7] and then
seeks to contrast it with the way language, representation, and picture
making work in a presidentially executed war.

On one level, the photograph Sakharov invites us to contemplate—especially if seen at a distance and pushed out of focus so
that individual features (the Bush genetics) were blurred, vastly mul-
tiplied, generalized—might seem an appropriate address from the
populations of the earth to the handful of world political and military

    6. Allen Grossman, "*Summa Lyrica,*" *Western Humanities Review* 44 (Spring,
1990): 73.
    7. On the question of whether the country had a constitutional declaration
against Iraq in the Gulf War, see Michael J. Glennon, "The Gulf War and the
Constitution," *Foreign Affairs* 70 (Spring, 1991): 84–101.

leaders empowered to annihilate them. The transgenerational faces would seem like small shells, lining the cliffs and coastlines of the world, traces of a life form found on one of Darwin's journeys, that cannot be effaced, and, if they disappear from mind, are in the next crash of the wave uncovered once more, looking out from the ground of photograph and cliff, urging nothing, but bearing in their act of looking an absolute claim on our attention. But this is not the photograph that the U.S. president showed the Soviet dissident; and its transgenerational content was framed by an excruciatingly personal gesture, the opening of the wallet, the accompanying narration, "This is my family, my wife, children, grandchildren. I don't want them to die. No one on earth wants that." The final sentence—which seems for a moment to say that the populations of the world are united in their shared concern that the Bush family not die—must be understood to assert this only by a grammatical accident: surely the speaker means that no one wants his or her own family to die. But most people's concern about nuclear weapons is not restricted to family love. The grammatical accident is made possible by the unrelentingly personal framework. The president speaks not as a representative of the earth, not even as a representative of the population of the country over which he presides, but as the representative of the family to which he belongs and which he has sired; and though family love is very great and very noble, it is not the basis for political obligation, whether that obligation has a domestic or a foreign referent.[8] Locke's central project in the *Second Treatise*, for example, was to decouple political and paternal power; contract theory, in general, assumes the unknowability, rather than the familial intimacy, of the persons with whose fate one aligns one's own. Bush offered his photograph as a "guarantee," but, as Sakharov's question and the president's silence made clear, it was precisely not a guarantee.

Later parts of this essay will identify three structural attributes of the congressional declaration of war that enable it to function as a guarantee, both to its own and to foreign populations. Those attributes entail linguistic representation and, hence, also the phenomena of linguistic "substitution" and "substitutability." But the analysis

---

8. Although political obligation is traditionally understood as an "obligation" to one's own country, Joseph Nye extends the concept to include our "obligation to foreigners" in *Nuclear Ethics* (New York: Free Press–Macmillan, 1986), 27–41.

must begin where the congressional declaration of war itself begins, with the designation of the speaker of the declaration.

> *Be it enacted by the Senate and House of Representatives of the United States of America, in Congress assembled,* That war be and the same is hereby declared to exist.[9]

The most striking feature of the designated speaker is, as will quickly become clear, its nonsubstitutability. The consequences of this non-substitutability (both for issues of nuclear arms and for a general theory of linguistic representation)[10] will be slowly unfolded in subsequent sections of this essay.

I. The Wrong Speaker of the Speech Act

The first-use policy may be said to entail a presidential appropriation of the performative declaration by the Congress. Legally, it cannot be appropriated or delegated: the declaration of war is Congress's constitutionally stipulated obligation. But it also cannot be appropriated in the sense that, on some very literal level, it cannot be performed by the incorrect speaker. In *How To Do Things With Words*, J. L. Austin talks about the "necessary conditions" enfolded into a performative speech act, conditions that, if not met, do not merely impair or mar or make imperfect the speech act but, rather, disable it altogether so that it never occurs. That is, of the "unhappy" or "infelicitous" circumstances and features, some merely damage it, some prevent it from happening at all.[11] The enunciation of the performative act by the wrong speaker is in the latter group; when the wrong person speaks, the sentence (in Austin's oddly appropriate

---

9. The italicized phrasing that opens the 1812 Declaration of War ("Deliberations for the Declaration of the War of 1812," *Annals of Congress*, 12th Cong., 1st sess., [1812], 298, 2322 [hereinafter "Deliberations for the 1812 Declaration"]) recurs in the later declarations of war, as well as in many other genres of congressional action.

10. Embedded in discussions of both linguistic and political representation is the issue of the safety of persons and populations; it is, therefore, not surprising that a nuclear arms policy that imperils, achieves that imperilment by abridging constitutional as well as linguistic paths of representations.

11. J. L. Austin, *How to Do Things with Words*, 2d ed., ed. J. O. Urmson and Marina Sbisà (Cambridge, Mass.: Harvard University Press, 1962), 16.

phrase) "misfires." Austin's concept of "necessary conditions" is close
to what Howard Warrender, in his work on Hobbes, calls the "val-
idating conditions" of an obligation, a contract, or a covenant. For
Warrender, too, an inappropriate speaker makes the contract invalid
or inoperative.[12]

If, in Austin's familiar sequence of examples, a person already
married utters the marriage vow, the speech act simply does not
take;[13] no marriage occurs. If a spectator at a cricket game cries "out,"
it is not a good call or a bad call but not a call at all. If a person
walking along the coast sees a boat and says "I christen this boat
Mr. Stalin" or if a newspaper reader pronounces a judgment of guilt
or innocence of a person currently on trial, no boat has been christened and no verdict has been rendered.[14] Each of these (the marriage
vow, the game call, the christening, the delivery of a verdict) is, like
the declaration of war, a contractual act: it is what Habermas summarizes (in part to differentiate Austin's concerns from the much wider
class of speech acts with which many other philosophers are concerned) as an "institutionally bound speech act."[15] In each of these
instances, the speech act is inoperative; it misfires.

In these other performatives, the verbal action—if spoken by the
wrong person—never takes place and, hence, neither do its effects.
In fact, the same could be said of war in the long centuries of
conventional war: a population had the choice to ignore a president
who invalidly uttered a war declaration,[16] just as the audience or

12. Howard Warrender, *The Political Philosophy of Hobbes: His Theory of
Obligation* (Oxford: Clarendon Press, 1957), 14–17. Austin's conception of the speaker
tends to be exclusive (*no one* can successfully utter the speech act *except* the designated
speaker) while Warrender's conception tends to be inclusive (*everyone* can successfully
utter the speech act *except* people explicitly disqualified by, for example, "immaturity"
or by "insanity").

13. Austin says of the marriage, it "does not come off, is not achieved" (*How
to Do Things with Words*, 16).

14. Austin, *How to Do Things with Words*, 23, 59, 43.

15. Jürgen Habermas, *The Theory of Communicative Action*, vol. 1, *Reason
and the Rationalization of Society*, trans. Thomas McCarthy (Boston: Beacon Press,
1984), 321. See also John Searle's analysis of the "differences between those acts that
require extralinguistic institutions for their performance and those that do not"
(*Expression and Meaning: Studies in the Theory of Speech Acts* [Cambridge: Cambridge University Press, 1979], 7). Searle observes that Austin "sometimes talks as
if he thought all illocutionary acts" required extralinguistic institutions, but of course
many of the acts Austin is talking about *do* have that requirement. This is the genre
of speech acts that particularly interests Austin.

16. The Korean War and the Vietnam War both lacked congressional decla-

players at a tennis match have the choice to ignore a spectator who
starts hooting out loud calls. But with nuclear weapons this changes.
In presidential first-use, the absence of a verbal declaration does not
prevent the injuries from taking place. The performative is disabled;
it misfires; yet millions of persons die. The president has the technological power to bring war into being through instant materialization at the precise moment that any claim to authority for the
verbal declaration has ceased. Thus, there is a major distinction
between the invalidly uttered declaration in the nuclear era and all
other performative speech acts.[17] In the Austin examples, it would
be as though language had a demonic binding power regardless of
the speaker. Imagine, for example, that a nonminister—someone with
no authority to marry—were suddenly to pronouce two people married; the community received his words as though a curse, something
so potent that the couple now had to live together even though at
the same time their illicit status would require that they be shunned;
this would be like meeting a sentence at a crossroads that did not
apply to you; yet you had to forever live out the consequences of
what it describes.[18] Or we can imagine a tennis game with a voice-
activated scoreboard that registers calls whether they are made by
the referee, by a spectator, or even by someone wholly outside the
playing field crying "love" or "deuce" for wholly other reasons. Of
course, the players in this illustration are still free to ignore the
scoreboard. Let us say, instead, that voice sensors in the scoreboard

rations; the second was openly designated an invalid war by large parts of the
population.

17. In other words, the existence of nuclear weapons deforms the linguistic
category of the performative.

18. Accusations sometimes appear to work this way: the taint sticks even where
the person making the accusation is widely perceived as uncreditable. Here, an
allegation has the force of a verdict, despite the fact that the sentence has been spoken
by one who is not only *not* the designated speaker, but is not even a credible
undesignated speaker. (Strictly speaking, performative speech probably does not allow
for the category of the "credible undesignated speaker," since creditable or uncreditable, the sentence simply does not take.) The odd names incurred by children as a
result of the accidental naming of an older sibling can also be taken as an example.
Everyone may see that "Seaweed" is not a good name for the newborn baby, and
everyone may see that a two-year-old brother should not be naming his sibling
(an appropriation of the parental performative of naming; simultaneously, an invalidation of the performative that, in Warrender's terms, comes about when the words
are uttered by someone "immature" or not yet of age). Yet somehow the name sticks
or stays.

not only register the score, but, at the end of each game, they automatically upend the floor, tipping the two halves toward each other
so that the players are forced to change sides.

Because these other peformatives provide structural parallels to
the declaration of war, they allow us to see it with fresh eyes. At
the same time, because marriage, games, verdicts, and christenings
entail much smaller communities and much less lethal outcomes, there
is a somewhat painful tonal discrepancy in the sequence of analogues.
But in the end, that very discrepancy works to clarify and vivify
what is at stake.

Let us say that a president in the midst of watching the Rose
Bowl game on television at the White House should, at a controversial
moment when the game has stopped, call the stadium and give his
judgment; let us say also that his judgment is accepted. (One can
imagine how this would be reported in our homes: the television
announcer would say, "Wait a minute, apparently folks, President
Reagan has just called and is on the line with the umpires now, we're
awaiting his call; it looks like that last play was indeed offside.) Or
picture the president in the White House calling Wimbleton during
a tennis match. (The shift from the United States to Britain is not a
problem, since his appropriation of the British referee's sentences is
no more infelicitous than his appropriation of the U.S. referee's.
Indeed the crossing of national boundaries is relevant here since it
is often the claim of populations in such countries as Sweden and
Switzerland that their own contracts are subverted by the U.S. policy
of presidential first-use.) Or suppose a president should decide two
people ought to marry: perhaps they were strangers at a White House
dinner party, or perhaps they never inhabited the same space prior
to the president's decision. Perhaps the president would pronounce
them man and wife; perhaps he would do so during his state of the
union speech. Suppose he began to break bottles over ships and name
them. Suppose he slipped babies into water and christened them.
Suppose, during a trial, he announced the verdict of guilty or innocent. Suppose he did this for trials going on in France.

To imagine any of these is fantastic, and also deeply discrediting
or dishonoring of the U.S. presidency. Acts even close to these usur-
pations of the performative—as when Idi Amin set up the front page
of the daily newspaper; or when Reverend Moon or Reverend Jones
arranged marriages among their believers—are ordinarily scorned as

the ludicrous acts of petty tyrants. The inappropriate usurpation of
the performative could be said to be *the very sign of a tyrant; the
flag of a noncontractual society.* Yet (remarkably) the most momen-
tous performative act within a contractual society, the declaration of
war, has for several decades been assumed by the president in our
formal strategic doctrines of flexible response and presidential first-
use almost without protest. It is "invalid" in Warrender's sense, and
"unhappy" in Austin's sense, as well as in the sense of the many
millions of people who have never heard of Austin.

II. The Non-Delegability of the Speech Act: Authority in a Declaration of War is Transmissible but not Delegable

In the preceding illustrations, the invalidation of the speech act
occurred because one person "took" or "appropriated" the position
of the authentic speaker. But it is also true that it becomes equally
invalid if it is "given." This point is crucial, for the arguments that
follow will often speak of "transmissible authority" and this must be
kept wholly distinct from "delegability." We can say that an action
is *delegable* if it can itself be passed onto other persons so that the
body originally obligated to carry out the action instead carries out
the very different action of choosing the person(s) who will perform
it. In *transmissible authority*, in contrast, the designated actors perform the action, which will now radiate outward in its consequence,
because it permits and creates the conditions under which many other
actions can take place. There is no transfer or transmission of the
original act, except that its performance enables others to act on it
(performing parallel, duplicate, or derivative actions that give it a
wider materialization).[19] Everything therefore depends on the *point*

----

19. It is precisely to permit others to act—hence to permit transmission—that
the law of nations, according to Grotius, requires that a just war be "duly and
formally declared, and declared in such a manner, as to be known to each of the
belligerent powers." What makes the declaration necessary is not the need to eliminate
"clandestine dealings" (though that may be a secondary effect), but the need to identify
the source of actions: "the necessity that it should be known for CERTAIN that a war
is not the PRIVATE undertaking of bold ADVENTURERS, but made and sanctioned by
the PUBLIC and SOVEREIGN authority on both sides; so that it is attended with the
effects of binding all the subjects of the respective states" (Hugo Grotius, *The Rights
of War and Peace including the Law of Nature and of Nations*, trans. A. C. Campbell,

of origin remaining stable. The distinction is important because the declaration of war, as well as many other performative speech acts, precisely does entail transmissible authority[20] and precisely does not permit delegability.

While a member of a church congregation cannot "take" it upon

---

introd. David Hill [Washington: Dunne, 1901], 317, 321).

Austin explicitly uses the word *transmissible* in comparing the special way the phrases "I know" and "I promise" allow others to act and to rely on those spoken words (J. L. Austin, "Symposium: Other Minds II," in *Logic and Reality: The Symposia Read at the Joint Session of The Aristotelian Society and the Mind Association at Manchester, July 5th–7th, 1946,* supplementary vol. 20 [New York: Johnson, 1946], 171, 172). But the analysis and taxonomy of speech acts can be understood as centrally addressing the issue of "transmissibility" even if the term is not explicitly used. It is present, for example, in John Searle's attention to "the way the speaker gets the job done" (*Speech Act: An Essay in the Philosophy of Language* [Cambridge: Cambridge University Press, 1969], 61), to the level of "illocutionary force" that differentiates various sentences (Searle, *Expression and Meaning*, p. 2) and to the distinction between speech acts that "commit the speaker . . . to some future course of action" and those that enlist the hearer into a future action (Searle, *Expression and Meaning*, pp. 13, 14; also see Habermas, *Communicative Action* 1:319, 320).

20. In the case of the declaration of war, the lines of transmissible authority move in three directions. The declaration is addressed to a *first-person we* (the population of the home country who now perceive themselves in a fundamentally different way and collectively take hundreds of thousands of actions that reflect that change), *to a second-person you* (the foreign country now formally designated "the enemy" and whose government and population now collectively undertake hundreds of thousands of small actions including those of self-defense), and *to a third-person they* (third-party countries that are not at present on either side of the conflict but must take many actions, such as avoiding waters that have ceased to be neutral as well as actions to ensure their own continuing neutrality or that instead break that neutrality, replacing it with an alliance).

While it is accurate and useful to think of all three forms of address taking place simultaneously, historical evidence suggests that the *primary* recipient of the declaration has varied from one period to another. In his 1848 treatise on the law of nations, Archer Polson identifies 1763 as a dividing line between second-person and first-person forms of address. "The custom," Polson writes,

of making a declaration of war to the enemy, previous to the commencement of hostilities, is of great antiquity, and was practiced even by the Romans. . . . [E]arlier jurists . . . generally consider a war, undertaken without this previous declaration, to be contrary to the law of nations. . . . Since, however, the peace of Versailles, in 1763, such declarations have been discontinued, and the present usage is for the State with whom the war commences to publish a manifesto within its own territories, communicating the existence of hostilities, and the reasons for their commencement. The publication of this manifesto was looked on as so essential, that nations have demanded a restitution of everything taken before such a publication. (*Principles of the Law of Nations, with Supplementary Essays on the Law of Blockade and on Contraband of War* [London: Griffin and Co., 1848], sec. 6, pt. 3, 38).

himself or herself to utter the words "I now pronounce you man and
wife," neither can the pastor replace his or her words, "I now pronounce you man and wife" with the words "I now pronounce the
bride's uncle the person empowered to pronounce them man and
wife," or "I now designate the Prince of England, who has surprised
our congregation with his presence this morning, to perform the
marriage ceremony." Nor in all the other instances contemplated earlier, could that which could not be "taken" be "given away." The
referee, for example, cannot replace the "call" on a particular play
with a "call" designating the person in row 4 seat 20 (who has an
excellent vantage on that part of the playing field) the person to make
the call on the play. Nothing in the authority to do the one enables
the referee to do the other.

The Constitution distributes different performative speech acts
to different branches of the government, and the designated office
cannot (or at least ought not to be able to) replace the verbal act
with a verbal act of delegation.[21] The president cannot, at the moment

---

21. In the *Second Treatise of Government*, Locke insists on the nondelegability
of legislative acts. "The legislative cannot transfer the power of making laws to any
other hands; for it being but a delegated power from the people, they who have it
cannot pass it over to others" (sec. 141; see also secs. 212–19 on the dissolution of
the government that occurs "when the legislative is altered" by either the appropriation
or delegation of its legislative powers; *Second Treatise of Government*, ed. and intro.
C. B. Macpherson [Indianapolis: Hackett, 1980], 75, 107f.).

The current congressional habit of delegation has been severely criticized by
people on both the Left and the Right. Both John Ely and Justice Rehnquist, for
example, have urged the revival of the nondelegation doctrine. Ely argues that it
helps "ensure that decisions are being made democratically" and also "reduce[s] the
likelihood that a different set of rules is effectively being applied to the comparatively
powerless" (*Democracy and Distrust: A Theory of Judicial Review* [Cambridge,
Mass.: Harvard University Press, 1980], 131–34, 177). In the 1980 benzene case,
Justice Rehnquist rejects "uncanalized delegations of legislative power," and with these
words echoes Justice Cardozo's analysis of delegated powers "not canalized within
banks" in the landmark 1935 *Schechter* case (Industrial Union Department,
AFL-CIO v. American Petroleum Institute, 448 U.S. 607 [1980], reprinted in S. G.
Breyer and Richard Stewart, *Administrative Law and Regulatory Policy: Problems,
Texts, Cases*, 2d ed. [Boston: Little, Brown, 1985], 93). Rehnquist invokes a long
tradition of arguments against delegation, citing John Locke as well as the 1892 case,
Field v. Clark: "That Congress cannot delegate legislative power to the President is
a principle universally recognized as vital to the integrity and maintenance of the
system of government ordained by the Constitution" (Industrial Union in *Administrative Law*, 92). For a rigorous analysis of the arguments against congressional
delegation to the executive, see Paul Gewirtz, "The Courts, Congress, and Executive
Policy-Making," *Law and Contemporary Problems* 40 (1976): 46–85; as well as David

he is empowered and required (by Article II, section i, clause 8) to take the oath of office, instead announce, "I choose my brother to take the oath" or "I hereby designated Justice Rehnquist to speak the words." Nor can he replace his state of the union address with the verbal action of designating his daughter (who never got the break she deserved) or even his speech writer the one to deliver the address. (Under some extreme circumstances—namely the president's death or grave impairment—his verbal acts *can* transfer to another person, but so serious is this shift that the Constitution designates the permissible sequence of replacements ahead of time.)[22] Nor can the Supreme Court in a difficult decision about school integration announce, instead of its "decision," its "designation" of the president as the agent of the decision. So, too, with Congress. Imagine that,

---

Schoenbrod, "The Delegation Doctrine: Could the Court Give It Substance?" *Michigan Law Review* 83 (1985): 1224–90.

22. Crucially, the arrangements for first-use form a line of succession that is not the same line of succession the Constitution requires. Not surprisingly, it bypasses the Congress. Following the shooting of President Reagan, Alexander Haig's astonishing announcement, "I am in control here" was treated as a personal blunder. But, in fact, it exposed before the eyes of the nation—had we only understood what we were seeing—the extraordinary shift in the line of succession. The Twenty-Fifth Amendment to the Constitution requires that presidential authority move from the president, to the vice president, to the speaker of the House, to the president pro tem of the Senate, and then to the secretary of state. But the Reagan administration had also arranged for a military line of succession—or what Haig and others repeatedly referred to on the day of the shooting as a "crisis management" line of succession, renamed the "national command authority" a day later—that went from the president to vice president to (skipping the House and Senate, and even the civil cabinet member, secretary of state) the secretary of defense. In fact, some accounts indicate that the line goes directly from the president to the secretary of defense. Hence, there was a consciously designed split between constitutional or civilian lines of authority and military lines of authority. Evidence suggests a third line of succession for controlling the nuclear codes and, therefore, firing atomic weapons. As secretary of state, Alexander Haig was not "in control here" according to *any* of the three lines of succession; but the existence of three contradictory lines makes explicable Haig's own confusion about the matter. Press attention to Haig's "blunder" (and to his personal conflict with Secretary of Defense Weinberger) deflected attention from the far more astonishing and damaging revelation that secret, nonconstitutional lines of succession had been created that preempted the constitutional, popularly endorsed, and publicly recognized sequence. (For accounts of the shooting, Haig's announcement, and the constitutional and "crisis management" lines of succession, see the *New York Times*, March 31, 1981, and April 1, 1981. For nonconstitutional lines of succession authorizing the firing of nuclear weapons, see House of Representatives, Subcommittee on International Security and Scientific Affairs of the Committee on International Relations, *First Use of Nuclear Weapons: Preserving Responsible Control*, 94th Cong., 2d sess., March, 1976, 39, 42, 76, 79, 128, 213, 215).

at the moment of the roll call vote on a declaration of war, a member of Congress stepped to the microphone and, rather than performing the verbal action of "voting," instead announced that he or she was giving the vote to a neighbor who was particularly knowledgeable about Iraq-Kuwait relations (the neighbor might fairly influence the member's vote, but cannot himself or herself perform the vote). Neither can that same member of Congress step to the microphone and announce, "Mr. Speaker, I'm going to refrain from voting on this difficult matter and instead give my vote to the president, who has shown himself particularly knowledgeable." But now imagine that 40 different members of Congress, as their turns arose in the roll call vote, all gave their votes away to their neighbors. Or all gave their votes away to the president. That act, were it to occur, would surely be reported on national and international news as a disgraceful exhibition of subversion, an odd genre of revolution. But, in fact, by the nation's acceptance of the flexible response and first-use doctrines, we have watched not one member of Congress, or 40, but all 535 give their vote away to the president. The gravity of this collective abdication is apprehensible if we recall that Congress is required to continue functioning even when there is a vacancy caused by the death or disablement of one of its members. Unlike the office of the presidency (where a predetermined successor is installed within hours), there is no constitutional presumption of immediate succession. The constitutional substitute for a dead or disabled congressional representative is another, newly elected representative.[23] Com-

---

23. Vacancies in the House of Representatives remain empty until filled by election. Even in the Senate, where the number of members is comparatively small, the Seventeenth Amendment to the Constitution arranges for the election, rather than the predetermined succession, of a new senator: it stipulates that the governor (or other "executive authority") of the given state "shall issue writs of election to fill such vacancies." In some states (e.g., Kansas, Kentucky, Maine, Massachusetts, Minnesota, Nebraska), the governor arranges for the election to occur during the November period when general elections are normally held. In other states (e.g., Arkansas, Louisiana, Mississippi, Oklahoma), the governor arranges for elections in a month closer to the announcement of the vacancy: for example, South Dakota law requires that if the vacancy occurs more than six months before a regularly scheduled election, a special election shall occur between eighty and ninety days after the seat became vacant; and Vermont has a similar law.

The Constitution therefore anticipates that the House and Senate will continue to function during the interim period prior to the election while the seat remains vacant. In the case of the Senate, the Seventeenth Amendment permits, *but does not require,* the state legislature "to empower" the governor "to make temporary appointments"

prised of multiple members, Congress (like the Supreme Court) is treated by the Constitution as eternal and self-renewing and, therefore, unabsolvable from its obligations.

Finally, the mistaken sense that constitutionally designated acts of verbal performance can be shifted among branches is perhaps heightened by the belief that such shifts are reciprocal—that an action by the Congress might be given to the president, but so the president can let the Supreme Court do his or her work. But a transfer from one branch to the next is not made more appropriate by reciprocity. This is no more plausible than believing that a referee at Wimbleton on a Sunday afternoon can permit a minister in the audience to make a call, providing the minister, in turn, permits the referee to administer the Eucharist on Sunday morning. The "misfires" in speech do not cancel out: they continue and are compounded.

This point has been elaborated at length because there sometimes exists a startling belief that although powers of the government cannot be taken, they *can* be given away. Here are two brief examples. A group of people have designed a lawsuit alleging that Article I section 8 is incompatible with the presidential first-use doctrine. The first version of the case, in which two members of Congress were plaintiffs, was turned down by a federal court in California. The court ruled that although the Supreme Court might well eventually have to rule on this issue, the case was at present not yet "ripe" for judgment. By "not yet ripe," Judge Vuhasin meant *not* that we are not yet close enough to a nuclear war, but that Congress as a whole has not yet expressed collective alarm about the presidential appropriation. The judge's opinion that an executive appropriation of Article I section 8 is constitutionally permissible if only 2 members of Congress protest (but might well be impermissible if 535 members of Congress one day protest) expresses an erroneous idea that Congress has the option of abdicating its obligation to oversee our entry into war.

---

until the vacancy can be filled by election. While many states (e.g., North Carolina, Ohio) have laws stipulating that the governor "shall" make such a temporary appointment, other states (e.g., New Jersey, North Dakota, South Dakota, Virginia) merely provide that the governor "may" make such an appointment; and still others (e.g., Arizona, Oklahoma, Oregon) omit the possibility of temporary appointment altogether (Committee on Rules and Administration of U.S. Senate, *Senate Election Law Guidebook 1990: A Compilation of Senate Campaign Information, Including Federal and State Laws Governing Election to the United States Senate* [Washington D.C.: GPO, 1990], 174, 200, 202, 204, 210, 215, 227, 236, 238, 239, 240, 248, 257).

The historical record reveals that even a member of Congress may make this error. During the Taiwan Straits Crisis, for example, President Eisenhower's conviction that use of nuclear weapons would be unconstitutional if not authorized by Congress was verbally reinforced by his secretary of state,[24] by the vice president,[25] by the attorney general,[26] and by a representative of the British cabinet (the Brisith are described in these memoranda as "always very sensitive" about the subject of atomic weapons).[27] Remarkably, it is a member of Congress who appears in these records as disavowing congressional authorization. At this point in the record, Secretary of State Dulles has just been describing the British insistence that the president obtain the consent of Congress. Then, Eisenhower reports a phone conversation he has had with Speaker of the House Rayburn.

---

24. "Memorandum Prepared by the Secretary of State, Washington, September 12, 1954," *FRUS, 1952–54* 14:611. Here Dulles's notes on the need for congressional authorization are framed within explicit acknowledgments that "holding" or "defending" Quemoy would probably entail "general war with Red China" and "would probably lead to our initiating the use of atomic weapons." See also *FRUS, 1952–54* 14:615, 620, 621. Dulles argues that the president needs either congressional authorization or a United Nations authorization. A United Nations authorization may eliminate the need for a congressional act or may instead make obtaining such an act easier. Another document records Dulles's complaint that "some of the Chiefs [Joint Chiefs of Staff] did not seem to be at all familiar with the constitutional requirements relating to the employment of U.S. Armed forces in hostilities." The document differentiates the military's ability (if empowered by a congressional authorization) to act on "the massive retaliation theory" from its ability (if waiting for congressional authorization) merely "to defend Formosa from invasion" (Douglas McArthur II, "Memorandum of Conversation," October 30, 1954, John Foster Dulles Papers, White House Memoranda Series, Box I, File "Meetings with the President 1954" (1), 4).

25. *FRUS, 1955–57* 2:92–93.

26. *FRUS, 1955–57* 2:92. "In some anxiety, the Attorney General inquired whether the President intended to change his plan to seek additional authority from the Congress. The Attorney General thought it still highly desirable to seek this authority. The President assured the Attorney General that he had not changed his ideas on this subject."

27. Dulles periodically summarizes the British reluctance: "The British fear atomic war and would not consider the reasons for our actions to be justified" (*FRUS, 1952–54* 14:619). Again, in the January 21 meeting, Dulles attributes the British Cabinet's unease with U.S. action on the offshore islands to the "British feeling that in order to make the commitment stick, we might be obliged to use atomic weapons. . . . The British were always very sensitive about this subject" (*FRUS, 1955–57* 2:90). See also Eden to Dulles, April 28, 1954, John Foster Dulles Papers, Subject Series, Box 3, File "Atomic Weapons and Proposal 1953–54, 55" (2).

[Mr. Rayburn] had said that the President had all the powers he needed to deal with the situation, and that whatever the President decided to do would be unequivocally backed by the House of Representatives. He believed, however, that a joint resolution [i.e., a declaration of war] at this particular moment would be unwise because the President would be saying in effect that he did not have the power to act instantly, and a filibuster could start in the Congress, causing dissension both in the Congress and throughout the country. Accordingly, it was the Speaker's advice that the President take whatever action he deemed necessary, and thereafter ask for Congressional approval of such action. Speaker Rayburn guaranteed that this approval would go through the House in 45 minutes, without a word of criticism of the President.[28]

---

28. *FRUS, 1955–57* 2:91. In fact, the Formosa Resolution—by which Congress on January 29, 1955, authorized (without a declaration of war) the use of armed forces—was an extraordinary act of delegation and abdication, as opponents, particularly in the Senate, vigorously argued. The resolution opened by authorizing the president to use the military "as he deems necessary" and closed by empowering him to dissolve the resolution which "shall expire when the President shall determine that the peace and security of the area is assured." Most dangerous was an open-ended clause in the center of the resolution licensing "the taking of other measures as he judges to be required or appropriate" (H. J. Res. 159, 84th Cong., 1st sess.). Thus, as various senators pointed out, "we are authorizing the President to do anything he wants to do with the approval of the Senate, and we are authorizing him to do it in advance" ("Deliberations on Formosa Resolution," *Congressional Record*, 84th Cong., 1st sess., January 28, 1959, 942). Senator Morse summarized the import of the resolution: (1) it is an act of "predelegation"; (2) it means the president, not the Congress, declares war; (3) it is "unconstitutional"; (4) with its passage, the government ceases to be "a government by law"; (5) it is an act of establishing "personal government" in the White House; and (6) it is being passed without, on the population's part, any awareness of its grave import. Morse argued that, at the very least, Congress should openly announce to the people that they were currently performing a predelegatory, unconstitutional act that dissolved the government and replaced it with a personal regime (841, 842).
It may appear that (unlike Rayburn's pointed conversation with Eisenhower, and unlike the presidential first-use policy that has come securely into place since the 1950s) the Formosa Resolution, however much it predelegated the act of war, did not predelegate authority for *atomic* war. But the congressional record registers evidence of precisely this understanding. At one moment, for example, an amendment was introduced that would eliminate the resolution's open-ended phrasing. One Senator worried that if the amendment were defeated (which it eventually was), the Joint Resolution might be seen as carrying "a directive to the President to make a preventive strike, using atomic weapons" (949; in the House, see Brooks at 664, Kilday at 672,

It is, of course, the precise point of Article I section 8 to allow dissension to arise in Congress and from there to spread throughout the country. Only if the reasons for war are fully persuasive will a declaration be possible. The imperative to go to war must be so great that it overrides the gates of dissent.

There are, to summarize, people who believe the president can take congressional powers if he chooses. A second group of persons would reject this presidentially initiated appropriation but would accept the idea that Congress can delegate its powers to the president. A third group would reject delegation, but might entertain the plausibility of a conditional declaration of war. During the deliberations for a declaration of war preceding both the Spanish-American War[29] and World War I,[30] the formulations on the floor at some point took the form of a declaration stating that if event X should happen, the president was empowered without further word from Congress to begin military actions. In both instances, the conditional wording was quickly rejected and replaced with an actual declaration. The 1991 congressional authorization of force in Iraq was, even in its final form, a conditional declaration of war.[31] Because there was no

---

Holifield at 674, and Rivers at 675). Several months after the passage of the Formosa Resolution, a new resolution was introduced in the Senate that would have called back from the president the military powers accorded to him in January: it explicitly prohibited the president from "construing" the Formosa Resolution as a license to use armed forces in dealing with Quemoy and Matsu. The preamble to this new resolution attributed the retraction in part to the danger of nuclear war: "Whereas there now is danger of United States involvement in atomic war with the Chinese Communists in the defense of the Matsu and Quemoy Islands . . ." (S. Con. Res. 21, *Congressional Record*, 84th Cong., 1st sess., April 1, 1955, 4218).

29. "Deliberations for the Declaration: Spanish-American War," *Congressional Record*, 55th Cong., 2d sess., 1898, 3777 (hereinafter, "Deliberations for the Spanish-American Declaration"). The purpose of the conditional was to give President McKinley more time for negotiation; but this apparently pacific motive did not keep it from being, in its construction, slippery and dangerously open-ended.

30. "Deliberations for the Declaration of War for World War I," *Congressional Record*, 65th Cong., 1st sess., 1917, 210, 214, 256 [hereinafter, "Deliberations for the World War I Declaration"). The phrasing gave Germany notice that a "willful violation of the rights of American ships and American citizens . . . is an act of war . . . and thereupon, *without further declaration or notice*, the President be, and he is hereby, authorized and directed to employ the entire naval and military forces of the United States and the resources of the Government to carry on war against the offending country; and to bring the conflict to a successful termination all of the resources of the country are hereby pledged by the Congress of the United States" (italics added). Again, the motivation for the conditional was benign, giving Germany one more chance, but the outcome is no less dangerous.

31. The authorization of force was conditional on whether or not Iraq complied

declaration preceding either the Korean War or the Vietnam War, Congress's act can be seen as a reclamation of much of the power it had formerly abdicated; nevertheless, the conditional phrasing was dangerous, since it enabled members of Congress to license the infliction of injury without full acknowledgment of their responsibility for that act.

Sometimes people argue that congressional funding for nuclear weapons licenses the president to use them *if* certain events arise. In other words, Congress appears to have made a conditional declaration. The Congress has explicitly prohibited interpreting an act of funding as an act of declaration: from the deliberations on the War of 1812 up through the 1974 War Powers Act, Congress has periodically reiterated that in no case can its military spending ever be taken for a declaration of war or even an authorization of force. This explicit prohibition makes overt what should be visible even without direct statement. We have seen that in its deep structure, "delegation" is only a slightly disguised form of shifting the speaker in a way that nullifies the speech act. In turn, a "conditional declaration" is a disguised form of "delegation," hence a delayed nullification of the speech act. If one sees the three verbal acts—the declaration, the delegation, and the conditional declaration—lined up, it becomes clear that no feature in the first permits it to be replaced by the other two.

> Be it enacted by the Senate and House of Representatives of the United States of America, in Congress assembled, That war be and is hereby declared to exist. . . .

> Be it enacted by the Senate and the House in Congress assembled, That the president is hereby named the person to declare War.

with UN resolutions by January 15, 1991 (for the full text of the resolution, see S. J. Res. 2, Authorization for Use of Military Force Against Iraq, *Congressional Record*, 102d Cong., 1st sess., Daily ed. 5403–4; also printed in the *New York Times*, January 14, 1991). According to Jonathan Winer, a legislative assistant for Senator Kerry, certain Democrats discussed in committee the plausibility of changing the wording from a "conditional" authorization to a straightforward declaration. However, the change was judged implausible because the Democrats would clearly be seeking to introduce a wording that they themselves would then vote against, and that was designed to increase the number of negative votes (telephone conversation with Jonathan Winer, February 1991). The fact that the predictable outcome of such a shift of wording would be to increase the negative vote underscores the way an overt declaration inhibits a positive vote by requiring those voting for it to acknowledge responsibility. The final vote on the conditional declaration (42 percent "no" in the House, 47 percent "no" in the Senate) was already so negative that the resolution would almost certainly not have passed if that phrasing were eliminated.

Be it enacted by the Senate and the House in Congress assembled, that should event X happen, our own obligation to declare war will be null and void and will be transferred to the president.

The constitutional grant of power obligates Congress to declare war, but nowhere empowers Congress to determine *who* shall declare war.[32] That is an arrogation of the Constitution's own power of distributing performative acts among the three branches of government.

The argument so far has focused exclusively on *who is speaking* the declaration rather than (as in the sections that follow below) on the linguistic features of the declaration itself. The identity of the speaker is critically important on both concrete and theoretical grounds. Concretely, it matters whether Congress or the president issues the declaration because of the scale of annihilating military power eventually released; and because, in the meantime, the sheer existence of a presidential first-use policy (even prior to its actualization) dissolves Article I, section 8, the section that Joseph Story called the "cornerstone of the Constitution." Thus, we have a deformation of our social contract in the present and the possibility of actual annihilation of humankind in the future.

Simultaneously, the problem of the speaker's identity can be generalized to a set of theoretical descriptions that ultimately circle back to clarify the concrete problem. What emerges as a general principle is the utter nonsubstitutability of the speaker in a performative speech act. The prohibition on substitution in performative speech becomes clearer when it is contrasted with the substitutability of the speaker of a descriptive sentence. That substitutability takes its most clear form in science, where a sentence describing the world will be true only if it is true regardless of the speaker. The validity of an experiment depends on it being "replicable"; the validity of a sentence depends on its speaker being "substitutable"; in other words, its validity depends on its being independent of the features of the person uttering it. The speaker of the declarative sentence *must* be substitutable, whereas the speaker of the performative sentence *cannot* be substituted. This difference follows from the relation each type of

---

32. Locke's prohibition of delegation turns on this distinction: "The power of the *legislative*, being derived from the people by a positive voluntary grant and institution, can be no other than what that positive grant conveyed, which being only to make *laws*, and not to make *legislators*" (*Second Treatise*, 75).

sentence has to the material world. The descriptive sentence "represents," or aspires to represent, the world as given. The performative sentence bypasses (hence, derealizes or annihilates) the material reality as given in order to bring new sets of arrangements into being. Because this derealization is inherently dangerous, the only way to minimize the danger is to exercise restrictions on who can speak the sentence: someone chosen by the electorate in one instance; someone theologically educated in another; someone trained in coordinating the landing of airplanes in another; someone with visual acuity in tracking flying tennis balls in another. All the aspirations for "representation" contained in the sentence itself in the case of the descriptive must, in the case of the performative, be contained in the speaker instead. Material reality exercises referential control over the *content* of the sentence in the one case and over the *speaker* of the sentence in the other. Even performative speech where no harm is likely—for example, the sentences in a novel—must be relentlessly tied to an identified speaker (the author). How much more important it is when the power of literal global annihilation is at stake. In this sense, the presidential first-use policy—and the shameful harm it appears to license—is the extreme instance of the danger of the uncontrolled performative.

The arguments that follow turn from the speaker of the declaration to the language of the declaration in order to identify three major structural attributes.[33] The three are: first, the exact repeat-

33. There are, of course, many other subordinate linguistic features not attended to in this account. Though the major speech act is the declaration, the deliberations are studded with many assisting forms of speech act: the morning prayer, formal messages from the other house, roll call votes on subordinate issues, and so forth. So, too, there are informal linguistic features that vary from one congressional war deliberation to the next. For example, World War II has highly charged language, not found in the other deliberations, that was almost certainly prompted (not excused) by the fact that the country had just been attacked at Pearl Harbor. This charged language takes two forms. First, an astonishingly unrestrained racist idiom used for the Japanese; the European enemies, in contrast, are described in a language consonant with the idiom used in the four earlier declarations ("Deliberations for the Declaration of War for World War II," *Congressional Record*, 77th Cong., 1st sess., 1941, 9523, 9530, 9531, 9532; see 9530 for an exceptional moment when the language describing Hitler approximates that used for the Japanese [hereinafter "Deliberations for World War II Declaration"]). Second, a falsely poetic, or mock poetic, form of speech: the day of the Pearl Harbor attack is repeatedly referred to as "yesterday morn" rather than "morning"; "yon" recurs rather than "yonder" or "that" or "over there"; and there is repeated talk of the fact that soldiers will have to "don" their uniforms (9521, 9528, 9530, 9535).

ability of the declarative sentence that thickens and gives substance to the verbal performative; second, the pressure to dismantle the performative act by deconstructing "the enemy"; and, third, the inlaying of material persons and objects into the verbal act that anchors the performative to the material world.[34] *What gradually becomes visible across these three features is the precise process by which the referential control over the speaker (the Representatives) shapes or is transferred to the linguistic content itself.*

A performative sentence, as noticed a moment ago, lacks the material restrictions on content imposed on a descriptive sentence by the very material world to which it aspires to be true. But we will see that although the performative cannot acquire the attribute of materiality through the accurate representation of an already existing material world, it does indeed acquire it through a set of three adjunctive features that follow from the nonsubstitutable speaker. This portrait of materiality will be interrupted by a section entitled "The False Form of Materiality." The feature described in this section complicates, but does not deform, the true form of materiality achieved by the performative through the nonsubstitutability of the speaker, exact repeatability, the dismantling of the object, and the inlaying of the material world.

---

34. These three structural attributes will be contrasted with linguistic features of presidential deliberation. The population's legal power to stop presidential first-use comes from the fact that it is constitutionally prohibited rather than from a reasoned argument about the unique deliberative powers of the congressional assembly. Whether a call in a game can be determined by the referee or by the spectator in the stand does not turn on the phenomenological attributes of the two calls: if one could show that the spectator's seat permitted a more reliable angle of vision, that would be an argument that the referee's seat should be changed, not an argument that the accidental occupant of the seat should be given the obligation. So, too, if a spectator has a particular optical genius, that is an argument for why he or she should seek to become a referee, not an argument for why the spectator should be permitted to make calls. Similarly, a president's great knowledge of foreign affairs or brilliant ability to assess material dangers is not an argument for why he should be permitted to wage war single-handedly, but an argument for why he should address the Senate and House on the floor of Congress where he can openly make an argument to his congressional colleagues and persuade them to wage war. The Congress, as the subsequent argument will show, has linguistic features that make its process of deliberation far more appropriate than the president's. Though it is its constitutionality and not a demonstration of its features that legally protects us, it was clearly some apprehension of those attributes that made it the site chosen by the founders, and that should now dissuade us from ignoring this crucial section of the Constitution.

III. Exact Repeatability

The constitutional requirement that not the House acting alone, nor the Senate acting alone, but the total assembly oversee war means that the sentence

> *Be it enacted by the Senate and House of Representatives of the United States America, in Congress assembled,* That war be and the same is hereby declared to exist...[35]

has to, in order to become a declaration, have more than five hundred voices enfolded into it. Each person is required, in the presence of all others assembled, to agree to the sentence, to disagree, or abstain and so withhold his or her voice.[36] This enfolding of hundreds of voices within a sentence or a set of sentences is crucial on two overlapping grounds—exact repeatability and the coinhabitation of multiple voices—that (to use a term that emerges from the deliberations themselves)[37] *thicken* the performance.

---

35. As noted earlier, the wording for the 1812 Declaration ("Deliberations for the 1812 Declaration," 298, Appendix, 2322) has close equivalents in the other wars; the variations are described in the fifth section of this essay.

36. Only with a majority assenting will it become a declaration. The vote for the War of 1812 was 79 to 49 in the House, 19 to 13 in the Senate; for the Mexican War, the vote was 174 to 14 in the House, 40 to 2 in the Senate; for the Spanish-American War, 325 to 19 in the House, 67 to 21 in the Senate; for World War I, 373 to 50 in the House, 82 to 6 in the Senate; for World War II against Japan, it was 388 to 1 in the House, 82 to 0 in the Senate; against Germany, 388 to 0 in the House, 88 to 0 in the Senate; against Italy, 399 to 0 in the House, 90 to 0 in the Senate. The conditional authorization of force in Iraq was 250 to 183 in the House (42 percent negative vote) and 52 to 47 in the Senate (47 percent negative vote; data from "The Vote to Authorize War With Iraq: Never Before Has Congress Been So Divided," Council for A Livable World, Washington, D.C.).

37. A senator watching the 1812 Declaration gradually gain credibility and the assent of more and more people said, "I understand that ever since the prospect of war began to thicken..." ("Deliberations for the 1812 Declaration," 273). The sense that verbal acts performed in Congress have, or eventually acquire, a material form is openly registered in various ways. Sometimes the acts of the voice (speaking, listening, or reading) are referred to their material counterparts, as when one speaker on the eve of World War I says, "We have submitted to the dictates of every first-class power on earth during the past four years. Do some of you new Members of Congress realize that you or I could not ship this reading stand to Norway, a neutral country, until we had received a permit from the British Embassy in this city to do

The term *exact repeatability* is used by poet Allen Grossman to describe poetic speech: "The source of the poetic quality is the risk of commitment . . . to an unalterably singular manifestation,"[38] and he analyzes "the exact repeatability of sentences" in their association with immortal, enduring things, or alternatively, those things that are in a society most potent. William Ivins, whom Grossman cites, writes "The only important things the ancients could exactly repeat were verbal formulae. Exact repeatability and permanence are so closely alike that the exactly repeatable things easily become thought of as the permanent or real things, and all the rest are apt to be thought of as transient and thus as mere reflections of the seeming permanent things."[39] The declaration goes from the proposal stage to the enactment stage by the sequential enfolding of voices: in the midst of what in some instances is hundreds of pages of sustained debate, this small set of sentences remains poised in front of the assembled group. Each by a positive vote says "Be it enacted by the Senate and House, . . ." or perhaps more accurately, "Let it be enacted by the Senate and House . . ."

This inlaying of voices is a remarkable phenomenon. It is ordinarily reserved for theological moments such as chant or prayer; in

---

so? . . . Do you realize that you could not send a pen or pencil to Switzerland, another neutral country, without first getting the consent of Great Britain in London?" ("Deliberations for the World War I Declaration," 318). Speech takes place in, and is subject to the physical obstructions of, the material world; just as in turn, those physical obstructions may themselves have been created by verbal acts of treaty making or legislation. Similarly, the attributes of the physical world may be annexed to the verbal sentences describing and evaluating that physical world. During the deliberations for the Mexican War, for example, the question of Mexico's invasion of the United States became a key issue. The reality of that physical act became conflated with the verbal acts of assessing the invasion. The issue of invasion actually entailed two questions: (1) has "it" been invaded; and (2) if so, is the "it" that has been invaded "ours." These questions, in turn, led various Senators to use the language of "debatable ground" and "undebatable ground," though at all times what was being talked about was the concrete earth: "I was under the impression that it was on the east side of the river, that it was to be limited to undebatable ground," said Senator Davis, and he continued, "But if it turns out that this territory is debatable ground, a serious responsibility rests somewhere, and presents the question of war in a very different aspect from what it would have possessed had the invasion been made within the acknowledged limits of this country" ("Deliberations for the Declaration of War against Mexico," *Congressional Globe*, 29th Cong., 1st sess., 1846, 786 [hereinafter "Deliberations for the Mexican War Declaration"]).

38. Grossman, "Summa Lyrica," 15.

39. William Ivins, *Prints and Visual Communication* (Cambridge, Mass.: MIT Press), 162, quoted in Grossman, "Summa Lyrica," 15.

a political situation, it would be dangerously hypnotic if not accompanied by, or steeped in, a surrounding argument. One arrives at the sentences not by the sensuous properties of poetic or communal speech (as would be true in theological circumstances). The Speaker of the House or President of the Senate does not chant the sentence and gradually hypnotize all others to join in (as the minister of an evangelical congregation might do). Instead, one lays one's voice into the declaration by means of a *conspicuously staged vote.* This means that one's own entry into the communal voice is marked by a highly formal, registered act. Although the individual voice only matters because it speaks in concert with the cumulative weight of the others, it remains, in terms of responsibility, always uniquely recoverable.[40]

This leads to a second major characteristic. While exact repeatability pushes the process toward verbal thickening, there is simultaneously a relentless attempt to dismantle the declaration, to thin it out, to dissipate it and make it disappear. This second feature, a kind of ambient will toward linguistic dissipation, provides a countermomentum to exact repeatability; only if the assembly can overcome that countermomentum will the declaration take place. While, then, the first feature can be said to "thicken the declaration" and the second to "thin it out," the second (like the first) contributes to the declaration's gradual acquisition of substance, since it constitutes a process of testing that anchors and makes responsible the attribution of otherwise highly volatile words such as *enemy.*

IV. The Dismantling of the Object: An Ethical Exercise

The antiwar arguments made by members of Congress during the deliberations for the country's five declared wars take many different forms. Yet underlying their many variations is a single, coherent structure of dismantlement. The prowar arguments inevitably entail the charge that country X has inflicted injury on the United States.

---

40. Thus, for example, Ms. Rankin's solitary vote of "No" in the World War II declaration against Japan remains recoverable not only for her contemporaries but for all subsequent history, as do all the yes votes ("Deliberations for World War II Declaration," 9537). Not even unanimity would jeopardize the recoverability of individual votes, just as a unanimous jury verdict is often followed by a formal, person-by-person polling of each juror.

This framing coupling—country X and the action of injuring—is decoupled in almost all variations of the brake-on-war speech.

The attempted decoupling takes place through one of two genres of argument. *One: country X did not perform action A.* This form occurs only rarely; it may entail, for example, the argument that actions performed by particular persons within a foreign country cannot be understood as actions performed by the foreign country itself. *Two: country X did perform action A but action A is not grounds for war.* This second genre is far more frequent than the first. It ordinarily entails the argument that *injurability* does not equal *warability.* The major way to show this is to rotate attention toward a second country that has also performed injuring action A but toward whom there are no war feelings. In the War of 1812, for example, the motivation for declaring war against Great Britain was weakened by the fact that the major actions held to be injurable— the infringement on the maritime rights of neutral countries during the Napoleonic Wars—was equally descriptive of France. Those opposing war detached the given action A (blockade of ships, impressing of seamen) from country X (here Britain) and then reattached it to country Y (here France). This genre of argument—decoupling the action from country X and reattaching it to country Y—resembles an ethical practice advocated by Bertrand Russell who recommended that when reading or hearing the daily news, we ought routinely to substitute the names of other countries to the reported actions in order to test whether our response to the event arises from a moral assessment of the action or instead from a set of prejudices about the country.[41] This form of testing, introduced into the War of 1812, recurs throughout later congressional debates. The World War I deliberations against Germany, for example, contain brilliant attempts to detach given actions from Germany and to reattach them to Britain.

A variant is that country Y, the country to which the attributed action will be reattached, is in some cases not a third-party nation but the United States itself. This is true of the Mexican War, where the repeated charge that by crossing the Rio Grande, Mexico had invaded the United States was countered with parallel descriptions of U.S. troop movements. It is again true of the World War I deliberations: the charge that Germany, in going to war, had violated its

41. Bertrand Russell, *Unpopular Essays* (New York: Simon and Schuster, 1950), 31.

contract with its own population was occasionally countered with the charge that a U.S. war declaration without the explicit authorization of the population would subvert our own contract. Remarkably, it recurs even in the deliberations for the World War II declaration against Germany, despite the rapidity and rabidity of that declaration: descriptions of unmotivated attacks by German submarines are redescribed as provoked attacks, and the U.S. status as a neutral country is redefined as a covert allied status with Britain achieved through Roosevelt's lend-lease arrangements.

The two linguistic features of the congressional declaration—the thickening of the sentences (through exact repeatability and the inlaying of voices) and the countermomentum to thin it out (by decoupling actions from one "enemy" country and reattaching it to a second, "friendly" country, whether a third party or instead the United States itself)—are not features characteristic of the presidential deliberations about war.[42] There is no attempt to dismantle the designation of

---

42. The conclusions that follow about presidential deliberation are based primarily on documents concerning the Taiwan Straits Crisis (1954) and the Berlin Crisis (1959), during both of which the Eisenhower administration contemplated the use of atomic weapons as well as the possibility of general war (with China and Russia in 1954, and with the German Democratic Republic and Russia in 1959). The repeated references to atomic weapons are unambiguous in the documents. Hence, the emerging scholarly literature is consistent on this point. The recently declassified papers about the Taiwan Straits, for example, have also been analyzed in Gordon H. Chang, "To the Nuclear Brink: Eisenhower, Dulles, and the Quemoy-Matsu Crisis," *International Security* 12 (1988): 96–123; H. W. Brands, Jr., "Testing Massive Retaliation: Credibility and Crisis Management in the Taiwan Straits," *International Security* 12 (1988): 124–52. For an analysis of the Berlin Crisis that takes into account the newly available archives, see Marc Trachtenberg, *History and Strategy* (Princeton: Princeton University Press, 1991), esp. 209–15.

It might be argued that the conclusions about presidential deliberation arrived at in the present study must be understood as tentative until a larger array of presidential administrations can be surveyed. Such a survey is, of course, seriously impeded by the unavailability of much of the evidence. The set of formerly classified presidential papers that have now been partly declassified only goes up to the early 1960s, except for patches such as the papers about Vietnam. While the conclusions reached here will be strengthened by subsequent studies of presidential deliberation, two factors strengthen the reliability of those conclusions in their present, incomplete form.

First, the unavailability or (where papers exist only in a small number of libraries) the impeded availability of presidential papers itself confirms the portrait of deliberation reflected in those papers that *are* available. Congressional deliberations on war are in some instances open to the public as they are occurring or, in other instances, are made available to the public as soon as the declaration has been voted

"enemy" by relocating it to an alternative geography: *hence there is no dissent.* Nor does the process of deliberation and decision making entail any enfolding of voices, nor even any clearly stated set of sentences to which everyone understands they are agreeing: *hence there is no explicit and self-conscious procedure for consent.* The absence of these two features from presidential deliberation can be assessed by looking at a moment of conversation that has the greatest claim to resembling one of those features, and then observing its distance from its counterpart in the congressional record.

The memoranda for the Taiwan Straits Crisis do not record any

---

upon. In contrast, the presidential deliberations have been consistently withheld from contemporary eyes (as the "top secret" designation still visible in the Eisenhower papers makes clear) and are only made available to the population decades later. The act of withholding the documents is consistent with the attitude toward "public knowledge" recorded inside the documents. Eisenhower, for example, expressed anger that the European press had reports of our "honest John Missiles" (1954) going to Europe. The record includes a key sentence: "The President commented that if the people who were responsible for publicity could not better control the situation, they should be replaced by people who could better handle it" (Douglas McArthur II, Memorandum of Conversation, October 30, 1954, John Foster Dulles Papers, White House Memoranda Series, Box I, File "Meetings with the President 1954" (1), 4). During the period of contemplating the use of atomic weapons in Germany, the record indicates how important it was to withhold our thinking from West Berliners as well as from East Berliners: "Senator Johnson's volunteered statement that Senator Javits had proposed a resolution for a seven-man committee to tell our story to the Berliners brought an unpleasant reaction from the President" ("Memorandum of Conference with the President, March 6, 1959, 10:30 A.M.," Declassified Documents Collection 1981/597B). As both examples suggest, presidential deliberations are not considered the business even of those populations directly put at risk by those deliberations. Not only enemies but allies and even, of course, the American people themselves are considered unworthy to overhear, let alone participate in, the deliberative process.

There is a second reason why conclusions about presidential deliberation should not require that we wait for all presidential papers to become available. If study of further presidential papers should reveal occasional instances of the two linguistic features described here as missing, that would not change the overall argument. If, for example, Eisenhower or Kennedy or Reagan at a certain moment asked those around the table to vote "yes or no" on a certain question, that would certainly be an instance of designating a certain set of sentences in which the counsellors now inlaid their voices, thus constituting an explicit moment of consent and "exact repeatability." But such an instance would *not* then show that "exact repeatability" is a structural feature of presidential deliberation. The feature would instead be only discretionary, depending on the choice and disposition toward voting of a particular president. Hence, we merely return to the photograph in President Bush's pocket, and to national arrangements that depend on the psychological accident of presidential dispositions. We submit to "a rule of men" rather than to "the rule of law."

debate about the status of "enemy," nor even any debate about the nature of "enemy action" or "injurable action." One brief query about U.S. interest in the region, however, approximates an act of dissent.

> Secretary [of the Treasury] Humphrey replied that it was still going to be hard to explain to the American people why we were finding it necessary to hold on to Quemoy. In some exasperation, the President said to Secretary Humphrey that he sat in this room time after time with the maps all around him, and a look at the geography of the area would explain why we have to hold Quemoy.[43]

Unlike congressional debate, where skeptical speakers develop their uncertainty or opposition at length, Humphrey's query is quickly silenced by the hierarchical pressures of presidential consultation. Despite its brevity, his expressed hesitation is striking because it is so rare. Ordinarily only the president himself introduces uncertainties; others tend to do so only if explicitly invited by the president.[44]

---

43. *FRUS, 1955–57* 2:94.

44. President Eisenhower's query about his own impeachability is an example. Observers of the Kennedy presidency have reported the same inhibitions on disagreement. Robert Kennedy wrote that the office "creates such respect and awe that it has almost a cowering effect on men. Frequently I saw advisers adapt their opinions to what they believed President Kennedy and later, President Johnson wished to hear" (Robert Kennedy, *Thirteen Days: A Memoir of the Cuban Missile Crisis*, intro. Robert S. McNamara and Harold Macmillan [New York: Norton, 1969], 112). The problem is compounded by the fact that those holding opinions contrary to the president's are sometimes excluded in advance from meetings by well-intentioned participants or advisors (117). According to both Robert Kennedy and Theodore Sorensen, President Kennedy consciously created situations—such as periodically leaving the room—designed to promote open discussion (Theodore Sorensen, *Decision-Making in the White House: The Olive Branch or the Arrows*, intro. John F. Kennedy [New York: Columbia University Press, 1963], 60). The recently released transcripts of the Cuban Missile Crisis confirm the possibility of a counselor persuasively contradicting a president ("October 27, 1962: Transcripts of the Meetings of the ExComm," transcriber, McGeorge Bundy, ed. James G. Blight, *International Security* 12, no. 3 [1987–88]: 48, 57, 61). However, a president's toleration, or even welcoming, of disagreement does not permit us to conclude that "disagreement" is a structural feature of presidential deliberation: like the features described in n. 42, these instances must be understood as discretionary and individually laudable rather than as structurally necessary.

It might well be that individuals with objections make arrangements to speak with the president privately, because it is "unseemly" to challenge the president openly in the meeting. But this confirms the crucial role of congressional deliberation, where

Had anyone chosen to support Humphrey following his humiliating
reprimand (no one did), the person could have pointed to the fact
that in the September meetings Eisenhower himself had said almost
the same thing:

> [The President] thought that Quemoy was not really important
> except psychologically.[45]

> The President said that he did not believe that we could put the
> proposition of going to war over with the American people at
> this time. . . . It will be a big job to explain to the American
> people the importance of these islands to U.S. Security.[46]

> The President said that we must recognize that Quemoy is not
> our ship. Letters to him constantly say what do we care what
> happens to those yellow people out there?[47]

Again, the memoranda for the 1959 Berlin Crisis do not contain
attempts to dismantle the attributes of the word *enemy*, or to detach
the designation from one country and reattach it to another; nor
does anyone appear to question whether the status of "enemy," however incontestable, itself warrants the use of nuclear weapons. At
one moment, however, a senator invited to the presidential conversation introduces a query about how trivial an action will license
our use of those weapons. As in the Taiwan Straits example, the
question swerves precariously close to the neighborhood of dissent,

---

the nonhierarchical nature of the participants ensures the possibility of an attack by
one speaker against any other speaker. Objections are not silenced by unseemliness.
This means, crucially, that both the arguments on behalf of the recommended action
and the opposition arguments are not merely voiced but heard and scrutinized by a
large number of people listening.

Finally, even if a presidency should occur in which the counsellors habitually
and vigorously altered and reshaped the deliberative process, they are (with the
exception of the vice president) themselves unelected officials, as Paul Gewirtz reminds
us ("The Courts, Congress, and Executive Policy-Making," 47, n. 2).

45. *FRUS, 1952–54* 14:616.
46. *FRUS, 1952–54* 14:621.
47. *FRUS, 1952–54* 14:622.

then quickly disappears. A situation is imagined in which the German Democratic Republic destroys the bridges and autobahn routes to West Germany; West Germany then begins to rebuild the routes; some German Democratic Republic soldiers then fire rifles at the bridge repairmen. At this point, the record reads:

> Senator Fullbright continued with his example. If the GDR fires rifles at the engineer company, do we then respond with the use of atomic weapons? The Senator admitted that he was somewhat lost on our sequence of actions. The President here admitted that our course of action is not entirely clear. What we do will depend on the actual events as they occur. He pointed out, however, that once a contingency of this type occurs, it is too late to approach the United Nations.[48]

The president has responded to the senator's imagined scenario with the answer, "Maybe." Far from anyone challenging the use of nuclear weapons under the most extreme provocation, the record instead shows a contemplation of their use under the most modest circumstances with no one expressing disapproval. Perhaps someone present was dismayed, disturbed, or angered to learn that atomic weapons might well be used in retaliation for rifle fire, but if so, the person did not voice those reactions.

Just as these presidential papers show almost no act of dissent, neither is there any easily identifiable act of consent. Nothing in the record provides a counterpart to the feature of exact repeatability in the congressional record. There is no process of voting or voicing agreement to a decision,[49] in part because there is not, overarching the discussions, a set of sentences that everyone understands to be centrally at issue. Although, as in the preceding discussion, an "absent attribute" is difficult to illustrate, the vacancy can be summarized by President Eisenhower's own observation to the Supreme Allied Commander that the meetings on Taiwan never entailed dis-

---

48. "Memorandum of Conference with the President, March 6, 1959, 5:00," Declassified Documents Collection 1981/597B.

49. As observed in n. 42, even if a thorough examination of the historical record were to show that presidents do sometimes overtly poll their counsellors, this act is still contingent on the individual's discretion and cannot be understood as a structurally necessary part of presidential deliberations.

agreements on substance ("there have never been any great differences within the Administration on fundamentals") only disagreements on language ("Most of the talks centered around the question of 'what can we say and how can we say it' so as to retain the greatest possible confidence of our friends, and at the same time put our enemies on notice . . ."); in fact, as Eisenhower goes on to correct himself, there have been no real disagreements even about language ("I suppose that many of those around me would protest that even in this field I am sometimes something of an autocrat and insist upon the employment of my own phraseology when I consider the issue important").[50]

The comparison between congressional and presidential deliberation is presented here not in order to say that the president's meetings should have a clear sentence to which they know they are all agreeing, that the agreement should be made explicit by a vote or clear sign, and that someone has the obligation to attempt to dismantle the deliberations to see if the arguments can hold up under the strongest counterarguments. It is instead to say that although the secret, solitary, nondivisive form of meeting may be precisely appropriate to the hierarchical business of presidents, it is also precisely the reason the presidency is not the arena in which the country's decisions about going to war can be made.

The nature of the congressional declaration will be further clarified once we encounter the third major structural attribute (section VI below), the inlaying of persons and objects. It is there that the declaration's acquisition of a material form and the operations of

---

50. "Letter From the President to the Supreme Allied Commander, Europe (Gruenther), [Washington,] February 1, 1955," *FRUS, 1955–57* 2:192. The autonomy and solitude of other presidents during the act of decision making has also been acknowledged. Often presidential decisions are admiringly described as *inscrutable*, a word that suggests not only that the decisions were made in isolation but that, even after the fact, they cannot be penetrated from the outside. Theodore Sorensen recounts assessments of both Roosevelt's and Truman's inscrutability. He cites Arthur Schlesinger, Jr.'s, summary of Roosevelt—"Once the opportunity for decision came safely into his orbit, the actual process of deciding was involved and inscrutable"— as well as Rexford Tugwell's sense that Roosevelt "allowed no one to discover the governing principle" of his decisions. He also quotes Truman's self-description: "No one can know all the processes and stages of [a president's] thinking in making important decisions. Even those closest to him . . . never know all the reasons why he does certain things and why he comes to certain conclusions" (*Decision-Making*, 9, 10). The inscrutability, hence unaccountability, of presidential decisions is one of the reasons that war making must occur in Congress, where the deliberative process is each day exposed and transcribed.

political and aesthetic representation become most overt, though these phenomena are already at work in the two features already examined. The weighting of the declaration, easily apprehensible in "exact repeatability," is also at work in "dismantlement." Although dismantlement is an attempt to "thin out" or dissipate the declaration, it directly contributes, as noted earlier, to the declaration's acquisition of substance by testing the accuracy of the assumptions on which it is based and by necessitating stronger arguments on its behalf. The process by which the declaration gains material substance will be returned to in section VI below, after first looking in section V at one way in which it does *not* gain material substance.

V. *The False Form of Materiality*

The declaration of war, as the rubric implies, declares that war exists. The phrasing can, and ultimately must, be understood as a self-conscious performative sentence, a sentence that initiates the state of reciprocal injuring it linguistically registers. The verbal act slightly precedes and is responsible for bringing into being the often vast material acts and consequences of war. It is possible to hear the sentence, however, not as a performative but as a descriptive sentence, seeming only to register a state of affairs that "already" exists. The country's first declaration reads:

> *Be it enacted by the Senate and House of Representatives of the United States of America, in Congress assembled,* That war be and the same is hereby declared to exist between the United Kingdom of Great Britain and Ireland and the dependencies thereof, and the United States of America and their Territories. . . .[51]

The World War I resolution reads:

> *Resolved [by the Senate and House of Representatives of the United States of America, in Congress assembled,]* That the state of war between the United States and the Imperial German

---

51. "Deliberations for the 1812 Declaration," 266, 298, and Appendix, 2322.

Government *which has thus been thrust upon the United States* is hereby formally declared; . . .[52]

And the wording for World War II is:

Resolved [by the Senate and House of Representatives of the United States of America, in Congress assembled,] That the state of war . . . *which has thus been thrust upon the United States* is hereby formally declared. . . .[53]

The "which" clause in both the World War I and the World War II declarations works to separate the physical act of war and the verbal act of the declaration and make the physical precede the verbal. The declaration presents itself as a replication of an already existing material reality.[54]

The self-camouflage as a description of an already existing reality rather than a performative intervention (a creation for which the speaker's own responsibility must be acknowledged) is even more emphatic in the grammatical structure of the declaration for the Mexican War in 1846 and the Spanish-American War in 1898. In the first of these, the usual announcement that the performative act is about to come—"Be it enacted by the Senate and House of Representatives of the United States of America in Congress assembled"—is (quite remarkably) preceded by a "whereas" clause. "Whereas, by the act of the Republic of Mexico, a state of war exists between that Government and the United States: *Be it [therefore] enacted by the Senate*

---

52. S. J. Res. 1, "Deliberations for the World War I Declaration," 305; second italics added.

53. S. J. Res. 116, "Deliberations for World War II Declaration," 9505, 9537 (Declaration against Japan); second italics added.

54. In the debates on the declarations, a perceptual rather than a verbal idiom is sometimes used: Roosevelt requests from Congress its declaration against Germany and Italy by asking Congress "to recognize" a state of war between the United States and those countries ("Deliberations for World War II Declaration," 9652; see also "Deliberations for the Mexican War Declaration," 793, 796). Precisely the same ambiguity is involved as in the verbal idiom. Ultimately, the "recognition" is a formal performative act: the recognition of another country or of the existence of war helps bring it into being while seeming to be an act made possible by a preexisting fact. For a philosophic study of recognition, see Axel Honneth, *Kampf um Anerkannung* (Frankfort am Main: Suhrkamp, 1992).

and House of Representatives of the United States of America in Congress assembled..."[55] The declaration has a preamble asserting that war exists; the assertion is given a temporal location in the space prior to the verbal action of the bill.[56]

The declaration for the Spanish-American War is even more remarkable. If each of the other four asserts that the material form of war exists at least one second prior to itself (so that the declaration is merely a verbal replication of what already exists), the Spanish-American declaration engages in an act of actual backdating.[57] It takes place on April 25, and reads:

---

55. "Deliberations for the Mexican War Declaration," 795, 804. The declarations for both World War I and World War II had preambles asserting that the other country had committed repeated "acts of war" or "unprovoked acts of war," but not asserting the war to be already in existence (S. J. Res. 1, "Deliberations for the World War I Declaration," 305; S. J. Res. 116, "Deliberations for World War II Declaration," 9505).

56. The title of the bill reflects the same division: "An act providing for the prosecution of the existing war between the United States and the Republic of Mexico," where the gerund makes the war's existence prior to its prosecution. The entire debate during the deliberations for the Mexican War (far more than for the other four wars) became a sustained analysis of whether a declaration of war is a descriptive sentence or a performative sentence. The debate was necessitated by the preamble and gerund forms.

The final vote in the Senate was preceded by a vote on whether to eliminate the preamble: eighteen voted yes; twenty-eight no. The final vote had forty yes votes and seven votes expressing various forms of resistance to the preamble, two persons saying "aye except preamble," two voting no and three remaining silent at roll call on the express ground that the preamble made the act of voting impossible ("Deliberations for the Mexican War Declaration," 804). The preamble, therefore, determined the shape of the vote. It also shaped the discussion by causing extensive debate about which of two committees would consider it, Military Affairs (if the declaration merely says the United States will repel invasion and prosecute hostilities) or instead the Committee on Foreign Relations (if it is a declaration of war) (784).

57. A small number of other performative speech acts also *appear* to introduce the possibility of backdating. For example, should marriage vows that confer legitimacy on an already conceived baby be understood as an act of backdating the marriage? Legally, at least in the United States, no backdating has occurred since the term *legitimate* refers to the marital status of the parents at the moment of birth rather than at conception. So, too, in states where it is possible through marriage to legitimate a child after birth, the child is a "nonmarital legitimate" offspring; hence, again, there is no backdating (see Harry D. Krause, *Child Support in America: The Legal Perspective* [Charlottesville: Michie Law Publishers, 1981], 105, 112). Annulment would appear to be a stark performative act of backdating, but there are some signs that the annulment cannot be understood as retroactively happening in the same temporal space as the enunciation of the marriage vows, such as the fact that,

*Be it enacted by the Senate and House of Representatives of the
United States of America, in Congress assembled,* First. That
war be, and the same is hereby, declared to exist, and that war
has existed since the 21st day of April, A.D. 1898, including said
day, between the United States of America and the Kingdom of
Spain.[58]

Another version was introduced (and rejected) in both the House and
the Senate that would have backdated the war to February 15,[59]
backdating not by four days (at which time Spain had broken dip-
lomatic relations) but by more than two months. In the case of World
War II, Roosevelt's request to Congress for a declaration of war
entailed the same act of backdating: "I ask that the Congress declare
that, since . . . December 7, a state of war has existed between the
United States and the Japanese Empire."[60]

In all these instances, the inherent ambiguity of the three word
declaration "that war exists" (an act of origination or instead only
a description of what already exists) is pushed toward the descriptive
by *grammatical structures* (the "which" clause in World War II), by
a *preamble* that places the war in an antecedent linguistic space (in
the Mexican War), or by a *stark act of backdating* (as in the Spanish-
American War). The last of these—the action of backdating[61]—is a
subgenre that overtly exposes what actually occurs in *all* the other

---

in many states, a child conceived between the marriage and the annulment is legitimate
(Krause, *Child Support*, 111). A judge's or jury's verdict is another area where a
question about backdating can be raised: does a guilty verdict mean "guilty starting
at the moment the word is formally pronounced in court" or instead "guilty starting
at the moment of performing the action for which the person is being tried"?

58. H. Res. 10086, "Deliberations for the Spanish-American Declaration," 4244,
4254.

59. H. Res. 246 and S. Res. 158, April 25, 1898, "Deliberations for the Spanish-
American Declaration," 4231.

60. "Deliberations for World War II Declaration," 9505.

61. It may be that the action of *postdating* is the structural counterpart of
delegation, since delegation can be understood as an act of *predating*. During the
passage of the Formosa Resolution, for example, Senator Morse repeatedly referred
to the bill as an act of predating, since it gave the president authority to use the
military in advance of any facts that warrant that use ("Deliberations on Formosa,"
841, 955). Delegation can, in general, be understood as authorizing outcomes prior
to the existence of the very facts required to motivate those outcomes. This emphasis
on the temporal complication of delegation makes its kinship to "conditional declaration" clearer (see the second section of this essay).

subgenres and thus it provides an overarching description: a performative sentence that masquerades as a descriptive sentence backdates the material reality that it is itself bringing into being.

All these variants seek to make the declaration appear merely a verbal replication of an already existing state of affairs. The explanation for this is partially provided by the genre of "performatives" rather than the specific case of war declarations. Austin's discussion of performatives moves almost at once to the observation that performatives habitually sound like constantives or statements of fact: their "humdrum" verbs and their "masquerade" or "disguise" or "aping" of the descriptive is, Austin argues, what explains the failure of grammarians and philosophers to see that they are "operative" rather than "recitative" sentences. However characteristic of performatives in general, the inhibition on acknowledging the fact of origination is likely to be especially marked in war, where what is being originated is injury and bloodshed.[62]

---

62. The original model for disguising the performative as the descriptive may well be Patrick Henry's speech in the Virginia Assembly supporting the militia on the eve of the War of Independence. His "Give Me Liberty or Give Me Death" speech, the most remembered speech on liberty in the United States, is a brilliant feat of moving language from the performative to the recitative. This act of linguistic relocation occurs across three stages: the distant future (hence, a stoppable war); the immediate future (hence, an unstoppable war); and the present (hence, a war already happening). The Revolutionary War was *not* yet happening; Patrick Henry's speech (March 23, 1775) occurred several weeks before the gunfire at Lexington and Concord (April 19, 1775).

The transition from the first stage to the second is marked by the words: "The war is inevitable—and let it come! I repeat sir, let it come!" At this moment, war has changed from something deliberative and preventable to something inevitable. What is wholly unexpected is that, precisely at this moment, Henry shifts the war from something undesirable to something desirable: "Let it come! I repeat, sir, let it come!" In other words, while the war's inevitability should bring with it a suppressed sense of agency, the shift to the optative (let it come) and the strong assertive repetition (I repeat, sir, let it come) restores agency, though it has now been reattached to the heroic energy of national self-defense. It is the rhapsody of energetic defense that follows in the transition from the second to the third stage, as Henry moves from the optative ("let it come!") to the descriptive ("The war is actually begun!") and, hence, to the complete erasure of the performative: "Gentlemen may cry, peace, peace,—but there is no peace. The war is actually begun! The next gale that sweeps from the north will bring to our ears the clash of resounding arms! Our brethren are already in the field! Why stand we here idle?" This then leads to the climactic set of sentences known to and passed down across successive generations of the country's population.

Patrick Henry's cadence is audible in every subsequent war assembly: "The war

Ultimately, as the argument that follows will show, the assembly does indeed acknowledge the full weight of its responsibility for the war it is itself creating, does acknowledge that if there is a separation between verbal proclamations and material enactments, the second follows rather than precedes the first. But along the way, it is by demoting the verbal action that it becomes possible to perform that verbal action. On a second level, the backdating of material reality can be seen not as a falsification or diminution but as an amplification of the powers of the performative. The performative has the ability

is upon us; we simply declare it" (Senator Hardwick, "Deliberations for the World War I Declaration," 249), where the congressional agents are now only the object of a preposition, the recipient of an event placed cumbersomely on top of us. Or again, "War is here, if it is here, by the act of Spain" (Senator Lodge, "Deliberations for the Spanish-American Declaration," 3783). "War is a fact, sir," announces Senator Cass in the Mexican War ("Deliberations for the Mexican War Declaration," 800). "We behold . . . on the side of Great Britain, a state of war against the United States, and on the side of the United States, a state of peace towards Great Britain" (President Madison, "Deliberations for the 1812 Declaration," 1630).

One might argue that the assertion that "the war has already begun" occurs in some wars because—as in World War II—the United States has been subjected to an attack that incontestably precedes the declaration. The shift from the performative to the descriptive in the formal declaration—"Resolved, that the state of war . . . which has thus been thrust upon the United States is hereby formally declared" ("Deliberations for World War II Declaration," 9505 [against Japan]) is improvisationally echoed in the congressional deliberation. Repeatedly and appropriately, the war is described as "thrust upon us" (9523), "hurled into our very teeth" (9525), "thrown down to us" (9526), "forced upon us" (9532, 9524). The declaration does "nothing more than recognize the existence of a situation thrust upon us" (9532); it is "merely the statement of an obvious and patent fact" (9528); thus even before the vote on the declaration, there occurs the repeated phrase "We are at war" (Representative Scott, 9529); "We are at war" (Representative Angel, 9525).

But two factors make it clear that this is not an accurate or appropriate explanation for the language. First, the trope "the war is actually begun" or "war is a fact, sir, we merely declare it" occurs universally in these assemblies, if less insistently and less heatedly. It is not confined to World War II, the one war where the country was directly and unequivocally attacked.

Second and more crucial, even where (as in World War II) hostilities or severe levels of injury exist, the infliction of injury is radically distinct from constitutionally authorized war. Though the five deliberations have crudities here and there, the level of debate is high. All five of the assemblies affirm the fact that physical hostilities cannot themselves constitute war, that injurability does not equal warability, that "war" in a contractual state means and can only mean a constitutionally authorized congressional declaration. No act of an enemy, no act of one's own soldiers, no act of a president on either side places the United States at war. Only the declaration of war can do that. (For the most eloquent articulations of this point, see Calhoun's speeches in "Deliberations for the Mexican War Declaration," 784, 785, 796, 798; also see Moorhead and Archer, 784; Allen, 785; Lucid, 793).

not only to bring wars into being but to bring them into being retroactively, before its own announcement.

The argument below shows the way the declaration creates a material replication of its own already existing verbal action. It predicts the reality that it then brings into being; it issues a prophecy of war that it then fulfills. Insofar as it works "descriptively," it does so in the opposite temporal direction than originally thought. It precedes material reality while also identifying its point of origination after the fact. It therefore takes open responsibility for the fatal events it tried to disown. By leaving a clear signature, it identifies the agent, establishes and stabilizes the referent. The handprint of the national assembly will now be recognizable in the actions of soldiers, the swerving of ships, the movement of troops, the speeches of the president. Without the congressional signature, these events remain ambiguously and fatally poised between the spheres of individual and national action.

VI. The Inlaying of the Weight of the World

The linguistic space between the proposing of the declaration and the final passage of the declaration is occupied by arguments for and against the declaration. But there also occurs there, seemingly incidentally and parenthetically, a constant inlaying of persons and material objects. In the days between April 2, 1917 (when the declaration of war against Germany was proposed) and the April 5, 1917 vote (when both senators and representatives inlaid their own voices into those sentences), Congress begins to dig a thirty-five-foot deep channel in the East River and Long Island Sound for the passage of ships moving in and out of the navy yard;[63] it votes appropriations to clear back military debts, thereby reestablishing the country's credit;[64] it debates the relative merits of the universal draft and voluntary enlistment and the ability of each version of conscription to meet the distributional requirements of a democracy;[65] it spends $210,000 for the making and transporting of artificial limbs, as well for "appliances"

63. "Deliberations for the World War I Declaration," 121; see similar appropriations, 131.
64. "Deliberations for the World War I Declaration," 159, 161, 165; of the $62 million budget, $38 million is in war debt.
65. "Deliberations for the World War I Declaration," 138, 209, 223, 357, 402.

and "trusses" for disabled soldiers;[66] it reviews the country's light-houses;[67] it acknowledges that it will soon "provide for an Army" of between 190,000 and 500,000 men,[68] as well as to provide the equipment and training so that those men will not be butchered;[69] and it prints Field Regulations.[70]

Like the act of declaring war, the acts arranging for artificial limbs and the digging of channels for naval ships are themselves verbal acts, awaiting successive levels of enactment and material realization. In some cases, the bill is voted upon; in others, it is only introduced or referred to a committee. But in the specificity of these details, the monolithically unitary act of "making war" begins to be broken down into what will eventually be its hundreds of thousands of component parts; in this sense the enactment is already underway. Further, in the very particularity, the concreteness of the object world it introduces—East River, Upper Bay, Hell Gate, trusses, appliances, artificial limbs, field regulations—and in its obligation to begin to count (the number of men, the number of dollars, the number of limbs, the number of days and weeks for training), the verbal declaration begins *to thicken*. These objects are rhythmically enfolded, inlaid, into what might otherwise be hours of unanchored debate. This continual "enfolding of persons and things"[71] is a structural feature common to all the declarations.

Its occurrence is not, of course, strictly confined to the space between the proposed declaration and the accepted declaration; it spills outside the frame in either direction. In the days preceding the country's 1898 declaration of war, for example, the House of Representatives passed a bill for pensions for soldiers from earlier wars, another bill "to encourage enlistments by veterans of the late war during the coming war with Spain," and another providing for a "better organization of the line of the Army."[72] The final frame, too,

66. "Deliberations for the World War I Declaration," 272.
67. "Deliberations for the World War I Declaration," 278.
68. "Deliberations for the World War I Declaration," 284.
69. "Deliberations for the World War I Declaration," 285–92.
70. "Deliberations for the World War I Declaration," 158.
71. The coupling of "persons and things" implies that things are extensions of persons (as is perhaps most straightforwardly the case in the detail of the artificial limbs). On this continuity, in both war and peace, see Elaine Scarry, *The Body in Pain* (New York: Oxford, 1985), 108–13, 117–23, 281–307.
72. "Deliberations for the Spanish-American Declaration," 3792, 3341, 4229.

can be passed over: in the day immediately following the 1812 declaration, President Madison transmitted to the Senate "the first copy
of an edition of 'Regulations for the field exercise, manoeuvres, and
conduct, of the Infantry of the United States'";[73] in close by days,
John Dickey's "newly invented shell was taken up, and referred to
the Secretary of the Navy,"[74] and Congress held deliberations on the
First Meridian, "an appendage, if not an attribute, of sovereignty."[75]
How much of the enfolding of persons and things occurs inside the
frame of the declaration is usually determined by the length of that
interval. The declaration for World War II, for example, took only
hours, but the enfolding of persons and objects took place throughout
the two years preceding the deliberations and again in the months
following.

But whatever the technical location of the enfolding (whether it
takes place in immediate proximity to the frame or literally inside
it), we can say that structurally it occurs during the passage of the
bill, attached to the framing actions of introduction and confirmation,
and that it works to secure a correspondence between verbal utterance
and material enactment. This relation to the material world is twofold.
It was earlier noticed that a performative sentence rather than reflect-
ing or representing already existing features of the material world,
brings them into existence. Certainly on one level, the enfolding of
persons and objects makes visible the way the declaration seeks its
own enactment, begins to produce the very war it is about to declare.
Simultaneously, a very different account holds true. As will be argued
below, the enfolding of persons and objects *stabilizes and constrains*
the performative by placing material limits on this form of speech.
In other words, while the performative, unlike the descriptive, does
not "represent" the world (and hence, unlike the descriptive, is not
constrained by already existing features of the world), it has adjunctive features that assure the introduction of material constraints.
While the war—about to be declared—does *not* already exist, the

---

(The declaration of war is both introduced and passed on April 25, but earlier weeks
have a series of interventions declared and it is here, starting on April 13, that the
House passes these bills.)

73. "Deliberations for the 1812 Declaration," 321.
74. "Deliberations for the 1812 Declaration," 1490.
75. "Deliberations for the 1812 Declaration," 1577.

population—about to be put at risk—*does* already exist. Enactment
therefore entails a built-in requirement for acknowledgement.[76]

This inlaying of objects and persons weights the declaration
because it populates it. It imagines a population—it imaginatively
situates the country's population—in the interval between the proposal and the passing. When, immediately following President Polk's
address to Congress in 1846 or again President Wilson's address to
Congress in 1917, a senator arranges for the printing of 20,000 copies
of the speech,[77] the act acknowledges the existence of other minds,
other minds who are, if only as readers, enlisted into the Congress's
own verbal and auditory acts of speaking and listening. To picture
a population that reads is to picture a population that needs to be
addressed and persuaded. The fact of acknowledging a people's existence is therefore only a half-step away from acknowledging its capacity to resist. The material details credit the possibility of the
population's resistance, the possibility of their psychological or moral
hesitance, or more generally, the simple cumbersomeness of moving
embodied persons around. The instances cited above, for example,
acknowledge the capacity of today's soldier to notice that the pension
of yesterday's soldier has not yet been paid; they also acknowledge
the fact that sailors, even if they are willing to fight (that is, even if
they are not disgruntled by the unpaid pensions of yesterday's sailor)
cannot move in and out of the navy yard if there is no river channel
that is as deep as their ship is thick. Ships and soldiers and citizens
are thick. By acknowledging their thickness, the declaration repro-
duces that attribute, if only mimetically. "A soldier is not made in
a day," argued a brilliant rhetorician, Senator Bayard, in 1812;[78] it

---

76. Because any performative sentence introduces a new set of circumstances
into the world, it has what Hegel and others observed as the annihilative power of
a creative act, its inevitable destruction or disturbance of what is already given. In
the performative of war, of course, this annihilation becomes not just a secondary
or tertiary attribute of the act but its central content and direction. The congressional
deliberations habitually entail a verbal recognition of what stands to be annihilated,
in contrast to the arrangements for nuclear first-use, which permit enactment with
no sustained registration of the people and worlds to be destroyed.

77. "Deliberations for the Mexican War Declaration," 783; "Deliberations for
the World War I Declaration," 158. Curiously, the 20,000 figure occurs in both
Congresses.

78. "Deliberations for the 1812 Declaration," 291; see also Senator German,
277: the different geographies, climates, and customs of the civilians will slow down
the transformation into a soldiery.

takes, according to his reckoning, fourteen months "to form a soldier of a recruit." Incorrigible civilians become corrigible only in five seasons. So, too, as Bayard continued, it takes time to establish a numerical aggregate: "These are not the days of Cadmus. It will require great patience and industry, and a considerable length of time, to collect twenty-five thousand men."[79] It may be the 25,000 of the 1812 army, or the 200,000 of the 1917 army,[80] or the 100,000,000 of the 1917 citizenry, or the 130,000,000 of the 1941 citizenry, since it is alternatively the population as army and the population as citizenry whose approval in these declarations is needed and whose numerical aggregate is recited: "We know full well that if the 100,000,000 people constituting this great Republic act in unison of mind and heart . . ."[81]

The attention to numerical aggregates, the congressional act of census taking to which this intermediate space is devoted, is key. The war does not have an existence antecedent to the declaration, but the population *does*. It provides the anchoring material reality that diminishes the chances of unanchored performative intervention. Numbers and names—not narratives, not anecdotes—become the main form of populating the declaration. When the members of Congress introduce numerical aggregates, they do so either by very exact registrations or instead by mystifying adjectives. The deliberations for the War of 1812, for example, alternate between numerically specific phrases ("997 citizens of Vermont" or "a memorial of three hundred and ten of his constituents")[82] and diffuse numerical adjectives ("sundry inhabitants of Vermont," "a petition of sundry inhabitants of New Bedford").[83] At one moment in the Spanish-American War, a member of Congress describes a petition as "signed by a large number of solid citizens of Milwaukee"; a reading of the letter specifies the actual number as twenty-four persons.[84] Although both genres of numbers occur in the five declarations, the pressure over

---

79. "Deliberations for the 1812 Declaration," 291; see Senator German, 272–74, who slowly rotates his attention across the geography of New Orleans, New York (Bedlows and Ellis Island), Rhode Island (from "three to five thousand men can defend that island"), Boston ("perhaps, the only secure place of considerable consequence on the seaboard"), and so on to Maine, Detroit, and Albany, imagining the aggregate required for defense.
80. "Deliberations for the World War I Declaration," 284.
81. "Deliberations for the World War I Declaration," 207.
82. "Deliberations for the 1812 Declaration," 1490.
83. "Deliberations for the 1812 Declaration," 1515, 1570.
84. "Deliberations for the Spanish-American Declaration," 3451.

successive declarations appears to move in the direction of both precision and inclusion. In the World War I deliberations, at least fifty thousand persons are included by direct letters, petitions, or votes introduced into the congressional record. Because the people named and counted often originate the sending of the letters, they can be said to authorize their own appearance in the congressional deliberations.

The acts of naming and numbering are reflections of one another. Naming petitioners or signers is a way of establishing a count and conversely, the count is a count of persons all of whom, by having names, can be presumed to have personal histories even though those histories are absent from the record. Numbering, naming, and the omission of narrative will be returned to after briefly contemplating two exceptional, nonnumerical ways in which the population enters the record. Both are more overtly embodied: the one is imagistic (and therefore, though verbal, has more explicit sensory content than do numbers); the other entails the population's actual bodily presence in the galleries of Congress. Although each form of inclusion is itself nonnumerical, each enables us to see more clearly precisely how the numerical functions.

The first, the imagistic, is the phrase "blood and treasure." It occurs in the *Federalist Papers*, in the deliberations for the War of 1812, the Civil War, World War I, and World War II.[85] Because the phrase is so resonant, it sounds, when uttered, as though it must have a prehistory in European wars or in the language of pirate life. But it appears that it has no such prehistory, that the term is instead postrevolutionary, originating with either the French or the American Revolution.[86] Because the phrase "blood and treasure" expresses the participation of and cost to the people, it is unlikely to have occurred even in seventeenth-century Europe, where war was still "the King's

85. The phrase "blood and oil" used by American protestors during the 1991 war with Iraq is a transformation of "blood and treasure," or a deformation since it expresses the idea of exchanging blood for unneeded treasure, rather than a population giving *both* blood *and* treasure in exchange for some third thing warranting so profound a commitment. The phrase is often, of course, invoked in these earlier contexts precisely to question whether that third thing *does* warrant the spending of the people's blood and treasure.

86. For this speculation on the date of origination, I am indebted to the insightful suggestion of historian Peter Burke, Institute for Advanced Study, Berlin, April 1990. (My observation about the absence of the phrase in earlier European wars is tentative, as all statements about "absent" phenomena must be.)

War." Almost this same logic explains the numerical recitation of names throughout the postrevolutionary war deliberations: attention to "how many" signatures a petition or letter has requires a democratic context.[87] While we cannot be certain that "blood and treasure" was never uttered prior to the French and American revolutions, what is certain is that the phrase is used with a postrevolutionary meaning in U.S. deliberations. It expresses both the weight and the waste of warmaking, the heavy freight of bodies that will attend either victory or defeat. In *Federalist Paper* No. 6, Hamilton places the "blood and treasure" of the nation in opposition to the personal motives of leaders in going to war.[88] Those deliberating the War of 1812 pronounce the term frequently, often attaching it to the casualties and costs borne by their "Fathers" in the War of Independence.[89] Although its iteration in World War I sometimes has the jaunty bravado of a pirate idiom, it is usually invoked to announce the Kantian principle that only the people who "pay" for war should determine whether it will be fought. "That matter I prefer to let the people determine. If they want war, . . . if they feel that the offense justifies war, since they must pay the price in *blood and treasure*, in the name of God let them settle that question for themselves."[90] The context is always democratic. The phrase—in its continual reappearance in U.S. war deliberations— expresses not simply the fact that war is bloody and costly but that it is the population's (not the government's) blood that bleeds, the population's (not the government's) money that will soon be spent.

The population—bodied forth in names, numbers, and the

---

87. For the association in Europe between a new interest in counting signatures and an emerging idea of democracy, I am grateful to Peter Burke, Institute for Advanced Study, Berlin, March 1990.

88. Federalist No. 6, *The Federalist Papers*, ed. Clinton Rossiter (New York: Mentor, 1961), 55.

89. "Deliberations for the 1812 Declaration," 1554, 279, 281, 283, 292, 1638, 1655. For a sustained use of the term, see Mr. Taggart's speech in the House reprinted in the *Virginia Gazette;* while the phrase seems casually introduced, it provides the underlying structure of the long speech, three pages of which are about blood and three about treasure (1657–63).

90. "Deliberations for the World War I Declaration," 209, italics added (quoting Senator Vardamen); see also 212. For its occurrence in a later war, see for example, "Deliberations for World War II Declaration," 9668. During the Civil War, Jefferson Davis used the phrase in his November 1864 address to the Confederate Congress at Richmond (cited in *The Civil War: An Illustrated History*, narrative by Geoffrey C. Ward, based on documentary filmscript by Geoffrey C. Ward, Ric Burns, Ken Burns [New York: Knopf, 1990], 334).

imagery of blood and treasure—has actual bodily presence in one literal way. People occupied the galleries of Congress in the deliberations for both the Spanish-American intervention and the World War I declaration.[91] Those assembled in the galleries may appear to resemble a theatre audience: on April 4, 1917, for example, the House was concerned about the fair distribution of tickets to the relatives of congressional representatives for the following day, the day on which they knew the declaration was likely to occur.[92] A theatrical audience, however, can express its consent or dissent through the auditory means of clapping. In contrast, a formal rule makes it "a breach of order for any manifestation of approval or disapproval to be given by the galleries" (as the assembly on April 5, 1917, was reminded). A public recitation of the sentence prohibiting "manifestations of approval or disapproval" is repeated whenever applause occurs.[93]

The logic underlying this curious prohibition is worth unfolding. A "sample" of the population is present in the galleries. But the rule repressing their consent or dissent precisely works to prohibit them from acting as a "sample." It prevents them from "standing for" the population. Given the extraordinary efforts that the members of Congress make to record the voiced judgments of the population (long hours may be devoted to reading petitions that, even if unread, will be formally entered into the record), this suppression may at first seem strange. But the underlying logic is coherent. The sense that the congressional deliberations are a kind of theatrical performance is heightened by the spatial split between performers and watchers, and by the fact that the watchers are ticket holders. It is not, however, the members of Congress, but the people in the galleries, who are in danger of functioning like a theatrical illusion. The members of Congress do not merely seem to be the representatives of the people (as in a play, a particular actor seems to represent Othello). They actually do, by a vote, represent the population. They are their

91. The others took place behind closed doors.

92. "Deliberations for the World War I Declaration," 156, 208, 216, 262–63, 265, 283. The galleries had been full since the opening of the deliberations; their applause, according to the House record, occurs even during President Wilson's speech.

93. For example, "Deliberations for the World War I Declaration," 307, 317, 349.

constitutionally designated selves; and (unlike the actor playing Othello) their representation outlasts the meeting in the assembly. The gallery of live persons, in contrast, is in actual danger of functioning like illusionistic theatre. In the charged atmosphere of debate, the accident of their preferences may seem to stand for the entire population's preferences. The hall is divided into the space of congressional members and the space of the population. Those present in the second space may appear to exhaust the category of population. Paradoxically, the members of Congress *are* representatives of the people; the people in the galleries are *not* representative of the people, though they are themselves people.[94] Put another way, the hall appears to be split between the representatives of the population (the members of Congress) and the population represented (the gallery occupants). The first actually are what they seem, whereas the second are not.

---

94. In both the Spanish-American War and World War I, the applause occurs at moments when speakers have urged a declaration of war ("Deliberations for the Spanish-American Declaration," 3780, 3781, 3784; "Deliberations for the World War I Declaration," 119), even though petitions and polls in various regions suggested the population opposed the war by 10 to 1. An exchange between Mr. Britten and Mr. Glass provides one emphatic instance (House, April 5).

> Mr. Britten: The truth of the matter is that 90 per cent of your people and mine do not want this declaration of war, and are distinctly opposed to our going into that bloody mire on the other side. There is something in the air, gentlemen, and I do not know what it is, whether it be the hand of destiny, or some superhuman movement, something stronger than you and I can realize or resist, that seems to be picking us up bodily and literally forcing us to vote for this declaration of war when away down deep in our hearts we are just as opposed to it as are our people back home.
> Mr. Glass: How do you know our people do not want it? [Applause on the floor and in the galleries.] (317)

Two explanations seem plausible. It may be that the deliberations on the declaration would attract prowar people, or that the deliberations create their own urgent momentum toward that declaration. A declaration of war is what they have come to see; a nondeclaration is a nonevent.

A second explanation is that the pressure to express consent comes precisely at those moments when the thing described is so costly that it requires consent, that it provides every reason for presuming hesitation, and that, therefore, nonhesitation (if it exists) must be overtly and vigorously expressed. So during Wilson's address to the Congress on the eve of World War I, "It will involve.... It will involve.... It will involve the immediate full equipment of the navy.... It will involve the immediate addition to the armed forces.... It will involve ... taxation" (119). Each time Wilson recites an entailment, applause follows. This is crucial because it is of course here that consent is required. Precisely where the government cannot go on without the population, the population expresses its willingness to come along.

Only if it were clear that the gallery occupants merely *represent* the population represented rather than *are* the population represented could their "manifestations of approval and disapproval" be safe.

In contrast to the dangerous mimesis of *exhaustibility* in the galleries, no *one* petition or letter on the floor is ever in danger of seeming to exhaust the category of "the people": each is framed by scores of other letters and petitions articulating other positions; further, most specify the extent of, and conditions for, their own representativeness. The number of signatures in letters or petitions introduced into the midst of the World War I deliberations was, as mentioned earlier, at least fifty thousand. This count consists only of people who actually signed their name or who directly voted in a town meeting; a much larger figure, at least a hundred thousand occurs if one accepts the representational claims of the signers. Many of the letter writers identify themselves as a citizen of X, where X is a county, a congregation, a state assembly, a gender category, or a club. In some cases, they (like the members of Congress) have been explicitly authorized by the group to represent them; more often, they claim a bond of allegiance or residential identification with the group and, on that basis, generalize from their own position on the war to the position of the group. Because the letters are addressed to persons who are themselves representatives, and because a major ongoing issue on the floor of the debate concerns the obligation toward representation, the population's claims about, or theories on, slippages in representation are of particular interest.

The descriptions conform to four categories. The first entails a one-to-one correspondence between the number of persons signing and the size of the group represented: the signers of the letters or petitions claim to speak only for themselves. A telegram signed by 451 women, a letter signed by 10 persons, another by 35 persons, another by 71 persons, another by 23, another by 21, by 10, by 13, a unanimous town meeting of 2,000, another in Wisconsin of 4,000, a petition signed by 7,555 persons in California, and so forth.[95] The majority of the letters have this stabilizing precision.

The remaining letters illustrate lapses from this one-to-one correspondence and can be seen as falling into three genres of representational slippage. Occasionally the letter entails an act of

---

95. "Deliberations for the World War I Declaration," 132, 133, 261.

unanchored, or unexplained, self-magnification: I stand for 3,000 people. No context, no narrative, no explanation is specified. What underlies the leap from "me" to "the many I represent" seems to be the speaker's confident assessment of his or her own normality. The tone of this genre, therefore, alternates between modesty and swagger. A letter from a man in Mississippi instructs his representative to give the president the declaration he has requested and adds: "I feel safe in saying that 95 per cent of the people are with him."[96] In a second, more common genre of slippage, the magnification is achieved across a sequence of two numbers. Rather than saying "I stand for 3,000 people," the person will say, "I am part of a church of 300 in a community of 3,000 worshippers." For example, "Delegates [we are not told how many] from 51 clubs representing 300,000 automobile owners of Ohio" presented a "unanimous" resolution.[97] Or again, three signers of a letter provide a title under their names indicating they are themselves members of a "Committee [whose size is unspecified] Representing 90 percent of the Voters."[98] The double act of belonging (in the first example, 51 clubs, 300,000 car owners; in the second example, a committee, 90 percent of voters) allows a rapid upward leveraging of numbers. A third, closely related genre of slippage comes about by an apposition structure, which permits the number of signers to become conflated with the size of the member group.

> Dear Sir: At the annual meeting, held March 21, 1917, of the Harvard Club of Boston, Mass., an organization of 4,500 members, the following resolutions were unanimously adopted . . .[99]

Unanimity seems achieved by 4,500 persons rather than by the unspecified number present. Or again,

> Vancouver Lodge, No. 823, with membership of 650 patriotic Americans, have passed today the following resolutions . . .[100]

---

96. "Deliberations for the World War I Declaration," 136.
97. "Deliberations for the World War I Declaration," 258.
98. "Deliberations for the World War I Declaration," 256.
99. "Deliberations for the World War I Declaration," 141.
100. "Deliberations for the World War I Declaration," 259. The second and third genres of representational slippage bear a resemblance to what are normally considered legitimate forms of representational magnification, as when a member of Congress claims to speak for a district of 7 million, only 3 million of whom voted and 1.8 million voted for him.

But the majority of letters conform to the one-to-one model. The concern to include the population is evident throughout each of the war assemblies; but it becomes especially explicit in the World War I deliberations because a major grievance against Germany (introduced in Wilson's presidential address and returned to throughout the debate) was Germany's entry into war without any consultation of her population. The constant enumeration of persons becomes a way of certifying the contractual vitality of the United States.[101] To include narratives—rather than names or numbers—would wrongly deflect concern away from the population's collective fate onto an inappropriately individual fatality.

In World War I, constant attempts were made to assess what the constituents thought about going to war, and to document what they thought. The senators and representatives present themselves as second-order beings who must speak and act on behalf of others to whom they are responsible. Wilson, too, is repeatedly described as elected by a population who did not want war. The reverse form of representation occurs in World War II. The members of Congress feel at liberty to speak authoritatively on behalf of the 130 million Americans who stand united in wanting to go to war. The direct attack on the United States preempts the issue of whether or not to put the country at risk. "[N]othing else will be enough except an answer from 130,000,000 united people that will tell this whole round earth . . .";[102] "Just as I felt for the past 2 years that over 80 percent of our people were opposed to being involved . . . I feel at this very hour that the same 80 percent of our people are united in full support of war resolution";[103] "the Japanese have aroused 130,000,000 Americans to a resolute determination to crush forever these arrogant Asiatic assassins";[104] "By this declaration we place behind our armed

101. Two congressmen even formally poll their constituencies and report the vote ("Deliberations for the World War I Declaration," 362, 366). The many other acts of voting—in churches, clubs, and town halls—are, as noted earlier, initiated by the citizens themselves (see, for example, 129, 130–36, 140–55, 186–88, 225, 242, 254–61, 305, 365).

102. "Deliberations for World War II Declaration," 9505 (Vandenberg).

103. "Deliberations for World War II Declaration," 9523.

104. "Deliberations for World War II Declaration," 9525. This shift may be completely fair: it is in part why the Constitution has different procedures in the case of attack. Prescience, guessing the will of the people, is permissible in the extraordinary circumstance of direct attack. The very permission in the Constitution

forces on sea, on land, and in the air the marshaled might of our 132,000,000 people."[105]

The representatives feel empowered not only to speak on behalf of the population's judgments and sentiments, but to give away the lives of that population. The second is perhaps always entailed in the first since, by commiting the country to a path of war, Congress puts lives at risk. But here members of the assembly make a direct offering, like Aztec kings commiting the lives of sacrificial youths. A primary model is that of giving the lives of one's children. One representative gives her sons: "I am willing to give my sons to their country's defense. I am 100 percent in favor of avenging the wrong."[106] A representative from Pennsylvania gives his only son; then the constituents in his Pennsylvania district; then all the people of Pennsylvania as a whole.[107] Often the representative offers his or her entire community without going through the intermediate step of children: "I want to be on record before this great body, on behalf of 2,000,000 American citizens living in the American Territory of Puerto Rico. . . . On behalf of these 2,000,000 American citizens of Puerto Rico I can pledge the fortunes, the lives, and the honor of my people to fight and to die for this great country."[108] Perhaps the most uncomfortably magisterial gesture of all is those who compensate one sacrificial group with the promise that another group will also be sacrificed. "Those who don the uniform on the field of battle or on the high seas may rest assured that full and supreme sacrifice of those at home, in the fields, in the factories, the mills, the mines, the forests, the offices, from town, country, and city . . ."[109] Least

for the president to act without Congress when the country is invaded is precisely that kind of presumption of knowledge about the population's will.

105. "Deliberations for World War II Declaration," 9534 (Jennings).

106. "Deliberations for World War II Declaration," 9521 (House, Mrs. Byron); see also 9531.

107. "Deliberations for World War II Declaration," 9532. Representative Scanlon, who himself served in World War I, describes his "only son" as "ready to serve his country in whatever military or naval capacity he is needed" and then attributes this same readiness to the larger population: friends and constituents "have called me seeking advice whether to enlist or await the call under the draft machinery . . . set up by Congress. These people are typical of every citizen in the Thirtieth Congressional District of Pennsylvania. I know that *every person in that district*, I might even say that *everyone in the great Commonwealth of Pennsylvania*, will back up the votes that my colleagues and I make" (italics added).

108. "Deliberations for World War II Declaration," 9528.

109. "Deliberations for World War II Declaration," 9525.

magisterial and most plausible is the contractual exchange of military sacrifice for political and civil rights by blacks and other groups not yet fully enfranchised.[110]

The final weight of the declaration comes from three sources, the thickening that comes about through the enfolding of voices and the exact repeatability of sentences, the testing that comes by overcoming the attempt to dismantle the enemy object against whom the declaration is spoken, and, finally, the inlaying of persons, objects, and geography in the space between the declaration's introduction and its final acceptance, between the preliminary sketch and the final engraving. The vote is repeatedly weighed by the members of the war assemblies. Not all, but many, of the representatives become emptied of their individuality and attempt to body forth the scale of population they represent: "[W]e are intrusted with and are holding the power vested in 100,000,000 of American people. . . . The members of this Congress and the President of the United States are holding in their hands the destiny of 100,000,000 of people."[111] "[The member] may possibly be signing the death warrant of hundreds of thousands of his fellow citizens, bringing sorrow and distress to hundreds of now happy homes, and burdening posterity with a debt which will sap the moral and mental" life.[112]

One additional manifestation of the weight of the vote becomes visible in inverted form. Those who, for some reason, miss the vote feel compelled to give detailed narratives of their movements to account for their absence. One speaker explains, "I then proceeded via American Airlines to Washington, reaching the Capital Airport

---

110. "Deliberations for World War II Declaration," 9525. Representative Mitchell

pledge[s] the unbroken and continued loyalty not only of the First Congressional District, which I represent, but that of the 15,000,000 Negroes in America. . . . [T]he Negro proposes to give and will give all he has, including his life. . . . In view of the sacrifices which my group has always made and in view of the sacrifices which we are bound to make in this struggle, let me remind the Congress and the Government that the Negro expects the same treatment under our so-called democratic form of government that is accorded all other citizens.

For a discussion of the fusion of military and civil rights in the United States, see Scarry, "War and the Social Contract," 1301–9.

111. "Deliberations for the World War I Declaration," 219. Deliberations for the other declarations also include expressions of the weight of both the individual's and the assembly's vote (see, for example, "Deliberations for the 1812 Declaration," 287, 291, 1638, 1678).

112. "Deliberations for the World War I Declaration," 208.

at 1:28 Monday afternoon, five minutes ahead of the plane's regularly scheduled arrival."[113] Another begins his narration at 7:10 on the morning of December 8 and continues, "After calling Speaker Rayburn twice from Knoxville I chartered a plane but could not get it off the ground because of Civil Aeronautics Authority orders to ground all civilian pilots. At 10:05 we got clearance, and although we made it in less than 3 hours the vote on the declaration of war against Japan was completed before I could get to the House Chamber. That is how fast democracy works once it is severely shaken."[114] He wired the clerk, we then learn, to say he would vote yes if he were there. A member of the House in the World War I deliberation gives an inappropriately long story about his wife's need for an operation and her refusal to be operated on without him, thereby necessitating his absence from Congress.[115] These autobiographies seem awkward and starkly out of place, yet their very ungainliness, their tone deaf quality, itself becomes a sign of the weight of the vote, which must occasion such inappropriately individual, hence self-abasing, personal narrative in the midst of debates whose idiom is nonpersonal, whose diction is impersonal and politically inclusive.[116]

But this odd little genre of travel narratives reminds us that personal narratives and autobiographies are often prompted by failure. It is failure that is also signaled by the autobiographical narratives of presidents rehearsing the possibility of impeachment or looking at family photos. No solitary person can, like a full assembly, conjure forth the full weight of the population it is about to put at risk. It is because, in the country's nuclear policy, our government has lost the ability to imagine both its own and other populations—has lost

---

113. "Deliberations for World War II Declaration," 9531.
114. "Deliberations for World War II Declaration," 9537.
115. "Deliberations for the World War I Declaration," 322.
116. The World War II deliberations have two genres of exclusion—hence two lapses from the inclusive and impersonal—not characteristic of the other deliberations. The first is the extreme racist idiom noted earlier. The second is a self-interested iteration of obvious arguments: because the assembly is close to unanimous, the speeches seem (unlike those in the other deliberations) less arguments intended to enlighten or persuade than recitations of the self-evident intended to put the speaker on record as having correct sentiments. Such passages have the tone of personal anecdotal narratives, though they are very different in content. The recitation of the obvious, however, while not admirable, is not wholly without merit, since it ensures that the common understanding is, indeed, the common understanding. Certainly, the assembly's overall act of putting itself on record is crucial, even if the individual ambition to "be on record" is personally driven.

even the inclination to imagine them—that we have, like the faces
in the family photo, become a story that is left cliff hanging.

The bypassing of the constitutional requirement for a congressional declaration of war has called attention to a general set of
differences between performative and descriptive speech. Descriptive
speech achieves its responsibility to the world by the constraints on
it to "represent" the materially given world. Performative speech, in
contrast, achieves its responsibility to the material world by constraints on the speaker. Although its content originates rather than
replicates events in the world, the requirement for "representation,"
far from disappearing, has simply been relocated from what is spoken
to who is speaking. In description, the sentence represents; in a speech
act, the speaker represents. In this sense, our concepts of "linguistic
representation" and "political representation" can be understood as
necessitated by the need to account not for two different spheres of
human action but for two different types of speaking.

As was noticed throughout this essay, a descriptive sentence
tolerates and sometimes even, as in science, requires a substitutable
speaker, while a performative sentence requires a nonsubstitutable
speaker.[117] A descriptive sentence replicates materiality, while a performative sentence, on one level free of the constraint of material
replication, achieves adjunctive forms of materiality through the representational requirements on the speaker (Congress in the case of
the declaration) that are then transferred to the linguistic center of
the sentence (in the case of the declaration, exact repeatability, dismantlement of the object, and the inlaying of persons and objects).
Because so many descriptive sentences have failed to represent the
world accurately and because so many performative sentences have
been spoken by the wrong speaker, it sometimes seems that a general
skepticism has arisen so that we no longer aspire to have descriptive
sentences that are true and performative sentences constrained by the
authorization to speak. But to lose this aspiration imperils our world.
It takes away the ground from which we can criticize language that
has ceased to be true and resist speakers who oblige us to live outside
the rule of law.

117. It may at first seem that conversely, a performative sentence tolerates, even
requires, substitutable content while a descriptive sentence insists on (or aspires to)
the nonsubstitutability of its content; but, as the foregoing argument has shown, the
performative sentence achieves high constraints on its content through the constraints
on the speaker.   .

Violence under the Law:
A Judge's Perspective

Patricia M. Wald

The subject of this lecture series is Law's Violence, a concept provocatively surveyed by Robert Cover in 1986.[1] Professor Cover
reminded us that, for all of the current emphasis on law as an articulation of society's norms or as an interpretative exercise on the judge's
part or even as a creative dynamic between the law giver and the
law receiver, law is fundamentally different from other kinds of communication: there *is* an iron fist in the velvet glove. When judges
speak, people don't just listen, things happen; someone acts and
someone or something gets acted upon. There can be the threat of
violence if parties do not comply.

Yet judges in our culture are supposed to be men and women
of peace, of reflection, of deliberation, the antithesis of warriors,
presidents, or even corporate CEOs. They are theoretically selected
for qualities of intellectual agility, dedication to enduring values,
compassion and care for others, and their ability to step away from
the battles of the day and to articulate the principles of a rational
and orderly society. Often, by the time the most controversial and
violence-fraught disputes reach the courts, they have been sanitized
into doctrinal debates, dry legal arguments, discussions of precedents
and constitutional or statutory texts, arcane questions of whether
the right procedural route has been followed so that we can get to
the merits at all. A historian would do poorly to gauge the flavor
of our society by reading its legal tomes. Judges too easily think of

---

1. Robert M. Cover, "Violence and the Word," *Yale Law Journal* 95 (1986):
1601–29.

themselves as Platonic Guardians in charge of a Peaceable Kingdom of Law.

But, as Professor Cover reminds us, a society is defined by its ability to enforce communal decisions—by force, if necessary. And the judge in our society is often the one who decides when, how, and whether to apply that communal force in the name of the law, when to let violence out into the open, when to suppress it, against whom it may be directed, where and how it can take place.

Judges live in a paradoxical proximity to violence. The courts are generally regarded as the alternative to fighting in the streets, yet, inherent in many of our decisions is the probability, even the certainty, of violence; we affirmatively sanction yet try to control and channel that violence to attain the law's ends.

In this essay, I will discuss several areas of the law in which judges encounter violence daily, look at the doctrines that we use to handle violence, and venture some tentative, not always original, thoughts about how judges can wield their harsh powers more responsibly.

The Violence of the Criminal Law

Death Penalty Jurisprudence

Professor Cover's primary example of the Law's Violence is the grim

> red-robed magistrate pronouncing a death sentence and to the sobs and piteous cries of the defendant and his family, ordering sternly that the prisoner be removed from the courtroom and taken to the execution chamber.

One of the great bonuses in my own judicial career, I might say parenthetically, has been the absence of death penalty cases in the District of Columbia, where I sit; my peers on other benches tell me these cases are agonizing. In capital cases, judges cannot avoid an acute awareness of the direct and lethal consequences of their action: the eve-of-execution pleas for stays, the newspaper headlines and television soundbites, the candlelight vigils all underscore the violence of their role.

And yet the way in which the courts currently impose the law's ultimate violence is a national shame—both critics and supporters of the death penalty agree. While two Supreme Court Justices, Brennan and Marshall, for decades declared their belief that it was never constitutionally legitimate for the state to kill a defendant, no matter how heinous the crime, the majority of the Court ruled otherwise. It is now well established that a death sentence is not cruel and unusual punishment so long as it is imposed under a law that gives the judge or jury reasonable (that means not too rigid, not too loose) discretion as to whether to impose it in a particular case and as to what mitigating and aggravating factors they may consider, and so long as the judge or jury is provided with an opportunity to hear all the relevant information about the defendant and the crime beforehand, and so long as the sentence of death is not disproportionate to the gravity of the offense (rape, for instance, has been held not to warrant death, but first degree murder may). This is true even for minors or retarded persons. Substantial statistical evidence showing black defendants are more likely than whites to be given the death sentence has been rejected by the Court as a reason for challenging its validity.[2]

Accepting, then, the constitutionality of the death penalty for some crimes, the failure of our legal system to act responsibly in selecting those on whom it should be imposed is still inexcusable. Basically, our death penalty jurisprudence is characterized, at the beginning of the case, by inadequate expenditure of legal resources to insure that all of the appropriate challenges to the conviction or to the propriety of the death sentence are properly raised and decided at the original trial, and, at the end, by round after round of habeas corpus petitions, pursued through successive tiers of state and federal courts, culminating in desperate pleas for stays on the eve of execution. The biblical tale of the marriage at Canaan—the best wine saved for the last—comes to mind. The best lawyers and winning arguments are often saved to the last. But, in the final analysis, the long waits on death row and the emotional, last-minute pleas essentially denude both the law and the prisoner of any dignity in death.[3]

2. Penry v. Lynaugh, 492 U.S. 302 (1989); McClesky v. Kemp, 481 U.S. 279 (1987); Godfrey v. Georgia, 446 U.S. 420 (1980); Coker v. Georgia, 433 U.S. 584 (1977); Woodson v. North Carolina, 428 U.S. 280 (1976); Gregg v. Georgia, 428 U.S. 153 (1976).

3. See, e.g., Walt Harrington, "How Can Anyone Do Anything Else?" *Washington Post Magazine*, January 6, 1991, 15: "The people who end up on death row

Efforts to reform the legal process in death cases have accelerated recently. The most promising would limit the number and timing of federal habeas corpus petitions in exchange for a requirement that states provide competent and fairly paid attorneys for trial, appeals, and collateral challenges. Automatic stays of execution would be in place while the allowable number of habeas proceedings ran their course. Some proposals would allow states to opt into such a quid pro quo system—others would make it mandatory.[4]

But the reformers themselves are bitterly divided about how much money a state should be required to spend to insure adequate counsel for a defendant faced with the death penalty, how long after conviction a habeas petition can be filed, and under what circumstances a new issue, even a worthy one that might invalidate the death penalty, can be raised. Because the reformers could not agree among themselves, all reform bills failed during the 1991 session of Congress.

As it stands now, the law too often imposes violent death on a wrongdoer without affording adequate counsel to insure that it is being legally imposed. Then it takes the prisoner back and forth through years of successive appeals before finally executing the poor devil. In

are always poor, often black. And almost always they had bad lawyers—real estate lawyers who never handled a capital case and who had to be dragged screaming into the courtroom." Also see Paul Marcotte, "Snoozing, Unprepared Lawyer Cited," *A.B.A. Journal* 77 (February, 1991): 14–16 (83-year-old white lawyer, former imperial wizard of Ku Klux Klan, who "slept a lot," appointed to defend black accused in capital case); Richmond v. Lewis, 921 F.2d 933 (9th Cir. 1990) (prisoner spent sixteen years on death row).

4. Title II of what would have been the Violent Crime Control and Law Enforcement Act of 1991—the famous "1991 Crime Bill" that ultimately failed to pass the Senate—was to be called the "Habeas Corpus Reform Act of 1991." The proposed reforms would have required states that have the death penalty to provide qualified attorneys to represent indigent defendants during habeas proceedings. See House Conference Committee, *Violent Crime Control and Law Enforcement Act of 1991: Conference Report to Accompany H.R. 3371*, 102d Cong., 1st sess., 1991, H. Conf. Rept. 405, 18–22. Prior proposed reforms include S. 1970 (*Congressional Record*, 101st Cong., 2d sess., May 23, 1990, S6805-7; the Thurmond-Specter bill) and S. 1757 (*Congressional Record*, 101st Cong., 1st sess., October 16, 1989, S13474-75; the Biden bill). See generally Ronald J. Tabak and J. Mark Lane, "Judicial Activism and Legislative 'Reform' of Federal Habeas Corpus: A Critical Analysis of Recent Developments and Current Proposals," *Albany Law Review* 55 (1991): 1–95; Ad Hoc Committee on Federal Habeas Corpus in Capital Cases," (The Powell Committee), "Report on Habeas Corpus in Capital Cases," *Criminal Law Reporter* 45 (1989): 3329-45; American Bar Association, Criminal Justice Section, Task Force on Death Penalty Habeas Corpus, *Toward a More Just and Effective System of Review in State Death Penalty Cases* (Chicago: American Bar Association, 1990).

many ways, Professor Cover's grim, sentencing judge, who hands the prisoner over directly to the executioner, is more merciful. If a society adopts the death penalty, it has the responsibility to insure that the process—trial and sentencing—is conducted fairly and in a way designed to raise, at the earliest possible stage, all the relevant arguments, pro and con, affecting both guilt and the appropriateness of the death sentence. No judge should be asked to preside at a trial in which death may be imposed without adequate counsel provided and paid, by the state if necessary,[5] with investigative resources to do the job. Our society has not yet fulfilled that responsibility.

The Depersonalizing of the Sentencing Function

Fortunately, death penalty cases are relatively rare. But a sentence for any extended length of time in a cramped, desolate prison cell away from family, friends, and all rudiments of ordinary social life also represents an invocation of the law's violence. As a generality, judges have traditionally given great care to sentencing—weighing an offender's past record, the seriousness of the crime, the injury to the victim, the potential danger to the community if he or she is released, the rehabilitative potential of the defendant—all in an effort to come up with a just sentence. Over the years, however, it became apparent that sentences imposed by different judges for similar crimes were too widely disparate; in adjacent courtrooms, Judge X would impose ten years, Judge Y probation, for the same crime. As a result, in both the federal and local systems, criminal law reform of the 1980s focused on sentencing guidelines—restrictive criteria governing the sentence a judge could impose for any particular crime. The guidelines movement reached its zenith in the form of the Federal Sentencing Guidelines enacted by Congress in 1984, which are, in fact, not guidelines but compulsory rules that sentencing judges must follow in almost all cases. The federal law establishes a three-member

---

5. Ruth Marcus, "Lawyer's Victory on Court Fees a Small One," *Washington Post*, January 25, 1991. Fees for death penalty representation at the Supreme Court were capped at $5,000, which amounts to $17 per hour. A *National Law Journal* survey of indigent capital clients in six Southern states showed their appointed counsel were 3–46 times as likely to have been disbarred or suspended; for over half, it was their first capital case and, in some, as little as fifteen minutes of court time was spent before the death sentence was imposed.

Sentencing Commission, appointed by the President for six-year terms, that promulgates immensely detailed standards binding on the nearly 800 federal judges in individual sentencing proceedings. Under the guidelines—bear with me—a judge finds a "base offense" number on the vertical axis of a 258-box grid derived from the crime of conviction and surrounding circumstances or other related crimes. He or she then consults a horizontal axis based on the offender's criminal record and, where the two axes intersect, determines the sentence. For instance, a first-time offender convicted of selling 5 grams of crack would receive a mandatory sixty-three months in prison.[6] The judge is allowed to move up or down the scale from the base offense level only for predetermined reasons, that is, if the defendant cooperates with the government, take off some points; if the defendant has inflicted aggravated cruelty on the victim or been a manager in a criminal enterprise, add some on. The judge may depart from the guidelines only if he or she finds some factor the guidelines did not articulate that makes the sentence truly unjust, and then he or she must explain his or her reasons and hope to prevail when the government appeals. The judge can no longer individualize sentences to the characteristics of the offender—his or her youth, intelligence level, social or educational status, or family responsibilities. And the judge most definitely cannot take into account his or her own impression of the rehabilitative potential of the defendant or the effect a long prison stay will have upon him or her. The inability to tailor the law's violence to fit the offender is the reason many federal trial judges frankly abhor and, in some cases, actively resist the guidelines. At least one has resigned from the bench in protest.

The federal guidelines system is an example of a development in the jurisprudence of law's violence that profoundly distances the judge from the violent consequences of the sentence. It strips the process of any personal dynamic between the deliverer and the recipient of that violence. The sentencing commissioners never see individual defendants during trial; they only read about the unique facts of their cases or lives in cold print. And the judge who does see and hear

---

6. United States Sentencing Commission, *Guidelines Manual* (Washington, D.C.: U.S. Government Printing Office, 1991), 78, 280; 18 U.S.C. § 3553 (1988); 28 U.S.C. §§ 991–98 (1988). See Steve Y. Koh, "Reestablishing the Federal Judge's Role in Sentencing," *Yale Law Journal* 101 (1992): 1109–34.

the defendant is constrained as to what punishment to impose. The imposition of law's violence has been depersonalized.

Principles of uniformity, proportionality, and just desserts have—at least in theory—replaced appraisals by the sentencing judge of blameworthiness or salvageability of individual wrongdoers. Some prisoners may benefit as well as suffer from the change: there were "maximum Johns" and "hanging Hannahs" as well as "compassionate Charlottes" in our old system. Overall, however, it appears more criminals spend longer terms in prison under the new guidelines system.[7] In a retributive era, many citizens may regard this result as salutary, but that, I think, is not the point. What we must ask ourselves is whether a mathematical grid, where the judge has little discretion and, accordingly, little direct responsibility for the sentence he or she fixes, is the optimal setting for imposing law's violence.

At the time Professor Cover used the grim, sentencing judge as his paradigm of law's violence, that judge was making an individual decision about what type of sentence fit the crime and the defendant. The sentencing guidelines movement has largely wiped out such discretionary power. That is a profound ethical and policy result for a society to reach without—it is evident in retrospect—much debate or input from the ethicists, moralists, philosophers, or sociologists. Is the law's violence more justly administered personally or impersonally? Many trial judges I talk to feel that as many, if not more, injustices occur now, through the imposition of similar punishments on dissimilar defendants, as through the old imposition of dissimilar punishments for similar crimes. There is a widespread belief that a midcourse correction is needed—a revamped sentencing structure that begins with general principles of sentencing in the form of presumptive guidelines, but allows for more liberal departures by sentencing judges based on their intimate knowledge of the facts applicable to individual defendants. Judges need to retain the humanizing sense of accountability for imposing law's violence on individual defendants.

---

7. Katherine Oberlies, "Reviewing the Sentencing Commission's 1989 Annual Report," *Federal Sentencing Reporter* 3 (November–December, 1990): 152–54 (more than 80 percent of prisoners sentenced under guidelines receive prison sentences; sentences confirm "tremendous projected growth in Federal prison population"); Sharon LaFraniere, "U.S. Has Most Prisoners Per Capita in the World," *Washington Post*, January 5, 1991 (one million prisoners, or 426 per every 100,000 U.S. residents, are incarcerated; this is twice as many as in 1980).

Judicial Activism and Prison Conditions

In his treatise, Professor Cover suggested that a wise judge, in deciding on a violent punishment, would do well to take account of how others would execute his orders. Otherwise, he warned, the "interpreter sacrifices the connection between understanding what ought to be done and the deed, itself."[8]

Does a good judge, then, need to understand the way the police department or the prison system works—what inhibitions or incentives impel its actors to violence—in order to mete out a just punishment? If, for example, the judge knows that a young, vulnerable prisoner will quite likely be gratuitously beaten or sexually violated if sent to prison, should he or she take that into account, insofar as the judge has any discretion, in setting the term of confinement, or, perhaps, in avoiding incarceration altogether? If the judge ignores it altogether, a prisoner is subjected to two kinds of violence—the law's sanctioned violence and the unlawful violence committed in the course of the legal sentence.

This dilemma has produced a strident debate over judicial activism in remedying prison conditions. In the 1960s and 1970s, a succession of federal trial judges, at the behest of prisoner advocacy groups, issued orders laying down minimum conditions and rights for prisoners, relying sometimes on the Constitution, sometimes on state statutes, and occasionally on the courts' inherent powers to sentence offenders to institutions. Often these judicial decrees were highly detailed, spelling out dietary regimes, the minimum size of a prisoner's cell, hours of outdoor exercise, rules under which internal discipline could be imposed, or the frequency of contacts with the outside world. They also created a variety of innovative mechanisms—monitoring committees, human rights committees, masters—for reporting to the court how its orders were carried out. The reaction to these decrees was mixed; some commentators applauded the judges for enforcing standards of human decency when other sectors of the government had failed, others complained that notions of the separation of powers, executive power particularly, were being undermined by an obsessively managerial judiciary seeking to extend its day-to-day control over the entire machinery of justice.

---

8. Cover, "Violence and the Word," 1612.

In defense of those activist judges, I would say that they usually acted only after hearing firsthand tales of true horrors perpetrated on hapless prisoners. Their decrees contained detailed protocols for institutional life because they were understandably skeptical of what would happen if they merely enjoined prison administrators to sin no more. Contrary to Professor Cover's thesis that judges' words and deeds are inevitably separated, these judges were insisting on maintaining some control over the manner in which the law's violence was carried out.

The Supreme Court has not been particularly supportive of these efforts. The leading Supreme Court case on conditions of confinement, *Rhodes v. Chapman*,[9] provides few protections to prisoners and instructs courts to accord substantial deference to prison officials. In *Rhodes*, the trial judge found that the practice of "double bunking" in an Ohio maximum security prison (i.e., assigning two prisoners to a single cell) constituted cruel and unusual punishment in violation of the Eighth Amendment. The trial court found that inmates in the prison were serving long sentences; the prison population far exceeded the prison's designed capacity; the size of the cells was below "contemporary standards of decency" (a deficiency that was exacerbated by the fact that prisoners spent most of their time in their cells); and double bunking was a permanent rather than a temporary condition at the prison.

The Supreme Court, however, held that there was no violation of the Eighth Amendment. The Court said that only if punishment either involved the "unnecessary and wanton infliction of pain" or was "grossly disproportionate to the severity of the crime warranting punishment" could a federal court intervene. The Court stated that "the Constitution does not mandate comfortable prisons," and courts must show substantial deference to the judgment of prison authorities about acceptable conditions of confinement.

During the 1991 term, in *Wilson v. Seiter*,[10] the Court imposed an even stiffer requirement on prisoners alleging overcrowding, excessive noise, insufficient locker storage space, improper ventilation, unclean and inadequate restrooms, unsanitary dining facilities and food preparation, and housing with mentally and physically ill inmates. The Court held that to prove a violation of the Eighth

9. 452 U.S. 337 (1981).
10. 111 S. Ct. 2321 (1991).

Amendment, the prison conditions not only had to be sufficiently serious so as to deny "the minimal civilized measure of life's necessities," but also that the prison officials had to have acted or failed to act with "deliberate indifference" to those conditions, a well-nigh impossible burden to meet.

As of now, only prison conditions so egregious as to result in "unnecessary and wanton infliction of pain" or deprivation of the "minimal civilized measure of life's necessities" that are maintained by callous or malevolent officials may justify judicial intervention. It is disheartening that, in a follow-up case to *Rhodes* in our court of appeals, a prison designated by the District of Columbia's own expert consultant as "unfit for human habitation" did not warrant condemnation.

While I agree that judges should not act as "roving commissions" on prison conditions, I do believe that, when trial judges are presented with evidence of prison conditions that fall markedly below professionally endorsed standards for humane confinement, they should be able to mandate the correction of these conditions, on constitutional grounds if necessary. Prisons will never be popular objects for legislative largesse, but this fact of political life should not lessen the judge's responsibility for insuring that defendants are not sentenced to more punishment or violence than the law intends—or that due process has authorized—to infestation, disease and contagion, or physical brutality at the hands of fellow inmates or guards. For the law's violence to be legitimate, it must have roots in the law itself— not in the law's refusal to stop lawless violence inflicted in its name.

The Violence that Precedes the Word

Finally, there is, in our criminal law, the so-called Ker-Frisbie doctrine, which holds that a court can take jurisdiction and try a defendant even if he or she was arrested illegally or was brought into the state or country by illegal force. *Ker v. Illinois* involved a defendant kidnapped from Peru to Illinois,[11] and *Frisbie v. Collins* concerned a defendant kidnapped from Illinois to Michigan.[12] Both defendants were tried and convicted on murder charges. Justice Black's opinion for the Court in *Frisbie* explained the doctrine's rationale.

11. Ker v. Illinois, 119 U.S. 436 (1886).
12. Frisbie v. Collins, 342 U.S. 519 (1952).

[T]he power of a court to try a person for crime is not impaired by the fact that he had been brought within the court's jurisdiction by reason of a "forcible abduction." . . . [D]ue process of law is satisfied when one present in court is convicted of crime after having been fairly apprised of the charges against him and after a fair trial in accordance with constitutional procedural safeguards. There is nothing in the Constitution that requires a court to permit a guilty person rightfully convicted to escape justice because he was brought to trial against his will.[13]

Frisbie was decided, however, on the threshold of the Warren Court's revolution in the rights of criminal defendants, and, even in 1952, it sat uneasily alongside a case decided just a few weeks before— *Rochin v. California*,[14] where the Supreme Court reversed a conviction for possession of morphine on the ground that the forced administration of a stomach pump on the defendant was "conduct that shocks the conscience," and that to condone it by upholding the conviction "would be to afford brutality the cloak of law." Doubts about the validity of *Ker* and *Frisbie* surfaced briefly in the Second Circuit's decision in *United States v. Toscanino*,[15] where the defendant allegedly had been kidnapped from his residence in Uruguay and brutally tortured by persons acting under the direction of U.S. narcotics agents before being brought into the United States for trial. Remanding for a hearing on the allegations, the court held that

we view due process as now requiring a court to divest itself of jurisdiction over the person of a defendant where it has been acquired as the result of the government's deliberate, unnecessary and unreasonable invasion of the accused's constitutional rights.

But the reach of *Toscanino* was short-lived. No other circuit followed it, and several explicitly refused to do so. Less than a year after *Toscanino* was decided, the Second Circuit limited *Toscanino* to situations involving "torture, brutality, and similar outrageous misconduct." And the Supreme Court, although never directly con-

---

13. *Id.* at 522.
14. 342 U.S. 165 (1952).
15. 500 F.2d 267 (2d Cir. 1974).

fronted with situations such as that presented in *Toscanino*, has, in general terms, continued to reaffirm Ker-Frisbie in recent years.[16]

The Violence of the Civil Law

Violence to Bodily Integrity

Professor Cover told us that "the court's physical control over the defendant's body lies at the heart of the criminal process."[17] Judges exercise a similar, less notorious, bodily control under the civil law as well. The role of the judge in ordering the cessation of "extraordinary" and violent efforts at keeping a comatose patient alive, the Nancy Cruzan case, is a recent example.[18]

It is a basic premise of law that a competent adult has the right to decide for herself whether to refuse medical treatment, even where necessary to sustain life. In 1891, the Supreme Court stated that "no right is held more sacred, or is more carefully guarded by the common law, than the right of every individual to the possession and control of his own person, free from all restraint and interference of others, unless by clear and unquestionable authority of law."[19]

---

16. The Supreme Court in 1992 decided the case of United States v. Alvarez-Machain, 60 U.S.L.W. 4523 (1992). *Alvarez-Machain* involved the kidnapping of a Mexican citizen who had been charged in a grand jury indictment with the murder of Enrique Camarena, a special agent with the United States Drug Enforcement Agency. On the authority of the Ninth Circuit Court of Appeals' decision in United States v. Verdugo-Urquidez, 939 F.2d 1341 (9th Cir. 1991), which held that the extradition treaty between the United States and Mexico prohibited the United States from kidnapping an individual for purposes of prosecuting him and that a defendant has standing to assert the treaty violation in challenging the trial court's jurisdiction to adjudicate the criminal charges against him, the district court in *Alvarez-Machain* dismissed the indictment. *Verdugo-Urquidez* had held that Ker-Frisbie is inapplicable, because the abduction was perpetrated at the request and on behalf of the United States government and because Mexico had explicitly objected to the abduction. The Supreme Court (6–3) decided that a person whom the government brings to this country for criminal prosecution by means other than those provided for in an extradition treaty has no right not to be tried in this country's courts.

17. Cover, "Violence and the Word," 1607 n. 17.

18. Cruzan v. Director, Missouri Dep't of Health, 110 S. Ct. 2841 (1990). See Symposium, "*Cruzan* and the 'Right to Die,'" *Georgia Law Review* 25 (1991): 1139–1326.

19. Union Pac. R.R. Co. v. Botsford, 141 U.S. 250 (1891). There are a few exceptions—some prisoners and children. See Washington v. Harper, 494 U.S. 210 (1990). Courts have, on occasion, also ordered compulsory cesarean sections for

When, however, an individual is not mentally able to give consent to a particular treatment or to life-sustaining procedures, courts are often called upon by hospitals, relatives, or state authorities to make the wrenching choice. On such occasions, a judge is, in effect, being asked to do violence to the patient, although judges seldom articulate their decisions in those terms. Yet listen to Justice O'Connor in the *Cruzan* case.

Feeding a patient by means of a nasogastric tube requires a physician to pass a long flexible tube through the patient's nose, throat and esophagus and into the stomach. Because of the discomfort such a tube causes, "many patients need to be restrained forcibly and their hands put into large mittens to prevent them from removing the tube."[20]

Justices Brennan, Marshall, and Blackmun were even more graphic in dissent:

The technique to which Nancy Cruzan is subject—artificial feeding through a gastrostomy tube—involves a tube implanted surgically into her stomach through incisions in her abdominal wall. It may obstruct the intestinal tract, erode and pierce the stomach wall or cause leakage of the stomach's contents into the abdominal cavity. The tube can cause pneumonia from reflux of the stomach's contents into the lung.[21]

---

pregnant women in order to save the child's life, or, in one recent case, a birth control implant for a convicted child abuser (see William Booth, "Judge Orders Birth Control Implant in Defendant," *Washington Post*, January 5, 1991).

Invading a person's body when there is probable cause to believe it contains evidence of crime is another exception to the rule of bodily integrity. Although in Rochin v. California, 342 U.S. 165 (1952), the Court held that stomach pumping went too far, commenting that "the struggle to open his mouth and remove what was there, the forcible extraction of his stomach's contents . . . is bound to offend even hardened sensibilities" (172), other courts have allowed body searches and even forcible use of emetics or laxatives to compel excretion of drugs. See Blefare v. United States, 362 F.2d 870 (9th Cir. 1966); but see Winston v. Lee, 470 U.S. 753 (1985) (surgical operation to remove incriminating bullet not permitted).

20. *Cruzan*, 110 S. Ct. at 2857 (O'Connor, J., concurring).

21. *Id.* at 2866 (Brennan, Marshall, and Blackmun, JJ., dissenting) (citations omitted).

At an earlier stage of the case, a state judge had said, "There is evidence that Nancy may react to pain stimuli. If she has any awareness of her surroundings, her life must be a living hell."[22]

Chief Justice Rehnquist's majority opinion in *Cruzan*, however, made no reference to those violent, life-sustaining procedures. While recognizing that freedom from unwanted medical attention was "a constitutional right deeply rooted in our country's traditions," the majority nonetheless held that a state may "decline to make judgments about the 'quality' of life that a particular individual may enjoy, and simply assert an unqualified interest in the preservation of human life" that can be overriden only by "clear and convincing" evidence the patient would have chosen to die rather than live on in a vegetative state.[23]

The dissenting justices strongly disagreed; they would have allowed the family's wishes to be followed where there was no conflict with prior indications of the patient herself, and no harm—as to a fetus—brought on by her death. According to the dissenters, "the state ha[d] no legitimate general interest in someone's life, completely abstracted from the interest of the person living that life, that could outweigh the person's choice to avoid medical treatment";[24] the only legitimate state interest was in safeguarding the accuracy of the determination of what the patient's own wishes were. Pointing out that, under Missouri law, no proof at all would be required to show that an incompetent person wished to continue treatment, they concluded that "just as a state may not override Nancy's choice directly, it may not do so indirectly through the imposition of a procedural rule" such as the "clear and convincing" test.

Both the majority and the dissenters agreed that the fundamental question was what would the patient have decided for herself. Clearly, we all submit throughout our lives to endless medical discomforts and indignities in exchange for the prospect of better health and long life. Thus, it may be legitimate for the law or a judge to presume the unconscious accident victim wants a transfusion in order to stay alive. But, as Justice Stevens asked in *Cruzan*, is it equally legitimate to presume that the patient wants to suffer interminable, demeaning,

---

22. Cruzan v. Harmon, 760 S.W. 2d 408, 429 (Mo. 1988) (Blackmar, J., dissenting).

23. *Cruzan*, 110 S. Ct. at 2853.

24. *Id.* at 2870 (Brennan, Marshall, and Blackmun, JJ., dissenting).

and painful invasion of her body to no end but a persistent (and financially draining) vegetative state?

One other aspect of this unsettled area of the law is troubling: the legal concept of "substituted judgment" alluded to in Justice O'Connor's concurrence, where she referred to the patient's prior choice of someone she trusted to make decisions about her body should she become incompetent. This is unexceptionable, but, if extended beyond the designated proxy—to members of her family or her doctor, the state, even a judge—the doctrine of substituted judgment becomes more controversial and less palatable.

The concept of substituted judgment is what lawyers call a legal myth, useful sometimes, but capable of mischief as well.[25] Originally, in nineteenth-century English law, the concept of substituted judgment allowed the king to make property decisions for a lunatic who it was thought might become lucid again so that his lands should not be vested in the meantime. In the words of Lord Chancellor Eldon, "[T]he Court will not refuse to do, for the benefit of the Lunatic, that which it is probable the Lunatic himself would have done."

In twentieth-century U.S. law, however, the doctrine has emerged in a different guise, as a basis, for example, for deciding that a twenty-seven-year-old retarded man could, in his own "best interests," be required to donate his kidney to a competent older brother.[26] So applied, substituted judgment gives the decision maker a superhuman power over an incompetent person. In the words of one commentator, "The doctrine of substituted judgment allows the state to invade the bodily integrity of the incompetent without having to justify the

---

25. For a history of substituted judgment, see Louise Harmon, "Falling Off the Vine: Legal Fictions and the Doctrine of Substituted Judgment," *Yale Law Journal* 100 (1990): 1–71. See also Steven H. Miles and Allison August, "Courts, Gender and the 'Right to Die,'" *Law, Medicine and Health Care* 18 (1990): 85–95. In twenty-two appellate court decisions rendered in 1979–89, seeking to ascertain comatose patients' wishes and involving eight men and fourteen women, researchers found sharp differences in the way courts viewed past remarks by now-incompetent men and women: women's were more likely viewed as emotional, immature, and unreflective; men's as rational, mature, and decisive. In 75 percent of men's cases (as compared to only 14 percent of women's), the courts found such remarks adequate as a basis for allowing withdrawal of life support. In six of the fourteen women's cases, as compared to one of the eight men's, the court directed the decision to be made by a father or spouse.

26. Strunk v. Strunk, 445 S.W.2d 145 (Ky. 1969).

invasion."[27] It can be used to avoid the moral judgments that a judge ought to make consciously in approving the use of violence on an unconsenting individual. What overriding interest allows anyone other than the individual himself or herself to make critical decisions about the invasion of his or her body? What is the quality of the patient's life worth? How much suffering should any person (and his or her loved ones) be forced to endure and for how long? How many thousands of public dollars should be spent on preserving an individual in a permanent vegetative state? Such terrible decisions, if they are to be made by judges at all, it seems to me, should be made openly rather than in the shadow of such myths as substituted judgment. Professor Louise Harmon of Touro Law School has written that,

> with the doctrine of substituted judgment, the raw truth is: the judge and the puppet do not stand on equal footing; they are not both rational, autonomous human beings. Beneath the facade of equality, there is total power in the wielder of the words, and no power in his victim.[28]

The judge in a right-to-die case, then, must do his or her best to ascertain the patient's true intent about living on in his or her present state; when that is not possible, the judge must confront the violent reality of making a judgment that results only in preserving a life beyond consciousness or sensation.

Family Violence

We usually think of law's violence as emanating from orders of the court. But there may be equally violent consequences in the law's refusal to mediate certain disputes, leaving the parties to fend for themselves. By denying its offices, the law may affect the balance of power between individuals and, in certain circumstances, may actively encourage or legitimize violence by one toward the other. Where one disputant is at a significant disadvantage through age, economics, or social status, the law's abstention raises serious moral

---

27. Harmon, "Falling Off," 61.
28. Harmon, "Falling Off," 70–71.

as well as legal issues. Through our history, examples of this phenomenon have been the law's markedly different treatment of violence by owners toward slaves, husbands toward wives, and parents toward children.

There is no doubt that a healthy society encourages the development and respects the autonomy of a variety of institutions that help control the behavior of their members, resolve disputes among them, and minimize the need for resort to the formal processes of law: the family, churches, schools, unions—all fill such a need. And, indeed, our law has traditionally given these social units a wide measure of freedom in regulating their members' relationships; it has refused to interfere with the way parents raise their children, with corporal punishment in schools, with prison administrators' efforts to keep order, with churches' methods of sanctioning errant members. But that discretion is supposed to stop short of permitting physical abuse or violence by one individual of the group on another.

In recent decades, violent behavior within the family circle has become the focus of legal attention. Historically, courts were reluctant to interfere with the actions of husbands toward wives or parents toward children, presuming an authoritarian hierarchy within the family. The husband and father was authorized by common law to use "moderate correction" (translated, that meant physical punishment) toward members of his family as well as his servants. While a wife, child, or servant could complain that the correction was too severe, for understandable reasons they seldom did. As the common wisdom had it, all judges were males, police or prosecutors seldom responded, and wives invariably returned compliantly to their lords and masters.[29]

Recently, however, there has been a strong push, spearheaded by women's advocacy groups, toward a more punitive approach to abusive spouses, toward treating their violence just as one would treat violence between strangers. Last year, the chairman of the Senate Judiciary Committee asserted that, every week, 30 women in the United States were killed by their spouses and predicted that, in the six-week period between Thanksgiving and Christmas, 1990, 450,000 women would be violently abused in their homes. He proposed that spousal abuse become a federal crime (penalized by stringent pen-

---

29. See, generally, Lloyd Ohlin and Michael Tonry, eds., *Family Violence* (Chicago: University of Chicago Press, 1989).

alties) when state lines were crossed in pursuing a fleeing spouse and that financial incentives be offered to those states that actively prosecute spouse abusers.[30] Such legislation proceeds on the premise that the law's violence is needed to counteract the individual's violence. We know that batterers often move in social networks that emphasize male dominance in the family, and only a strong counterforce from the law will dilute that effect.

Social perceptions have changed considerably in regard to what level of violence is tolerable in private relationships; women's groups have accorded a high place on their agendas to criminalizing spousal violence; they want recognition that wife beating is about power and that the power of the law is a necessary antidote to the imbalance that other political, social, and economic institutions, even nature itself, have created between men and women. Women have begun to convince legislators and judges that the myth of family integrity should not be raised as a shield against the enforcement of the criminal laws in a violent household. Much creative work remains to be done in the use of legal sanctions to educate or treat abusers in those cases where the underlying marital relationship still has viability, but it is surely possible to say that centuries of experience with the law's refusal to invoke its violence in the case of battered wives has only resulted in greater, not less, violence inflicted on these hapless women.

Although our society has expressed more overt concern for battered children than for battered women, its reaction to child abusers has been, if anything, more ambivalent. Because of children's impotence, judges have been even more reluctant to sever the family bonds and to criminalize family violence in the case of children than of

---

30. "Domestic Violence is Target of Bill," *New York Times*, December 16, 1990. See also Tamar Lewin, "In Crime, Too, Some Gender-Related Inequities," *New York Times*, January 20, 1991: A Department of Justice study showed one-fourth of 2.5 million women robbed, raped, or assaulted are attacked by family members or intimates; violent crimes against women are six times as likely to be committed by intimates as violent crimes against men. Title II of what would have been the Violence Against Women Act of 1991 was to be entitled the "Safe Homes for Women Act of 1990." Among its various provisions, it would have provided for a minimum incarceration of three months (and a maximum of ten years) for anyone who travels across state lines and who, "in the course of or as a result of such travel, commits an act that injures his or her spouse or intimate partner" (S. 15, 102d Cong., 1st sess.; reprinted in Senate Committee on the Judiciary, *The Violence Against Women Act of 1991: Report to Accompany S. 15, as amended*, 102d Cong., 1st sess., 1991, S. Rept. 405, 17).

wives. This skepticism about law's ability to do anything meaningful for abused children infects others in a position to help them as well; only an estimated one-third of suspected child abuse cases are reported by neighbors, teachers, or health personnel; those refusing to report say they feel the law provides no satisfactory out-of-home alternatives for the abused child and intervention may only make things worse for the child at home. Most state laws require a "clear and present danger" of serious and lasting physical harm to the child before outside intervention is permitted.

Historically, the law has made a determined choice to withhold its criminal sanctions in favor of a social work approach. Reports of child abuse invariably go to a social agency, not to a prosecutor; a program of family therapy is instituted that includes the abuser and the victim, despite the dubious prospect that chronic abusers will stay in or benefit from such programs or desist from their violent behavior. One study shows that in only 20 percent of substantiated child abuse cases is the child removed from the home; in only 5 percent of such cases (usually involving homicide, torture, sexual pathology, or starvation) is a criminal prosecution brought.[31]

Three years ago, the nation's attention was drawn to the violent effects of these policies in the case of *DeShaney v. Winnebago County*.[32] There, a four-year-old boy—"poor Joshua," in Justice Blackmun's words—had been permanently paralyzed and brain damaged as a result of a series of brutal beatings, over a period of several years, by his father, who had custody. The county social workers knew about the beatings; the father had been repeatedly warned, told to get an abusive girlfriend out of the home, directed to attend therapy sessions, and to enroll Joshua in Head Start. The father did none of these and the boy was briefly removed from his father's custody but returned. The social worker assigned to Joshua kept detailed notes indicating that the beatings were continuing, but took no decisive action. She later told reporters, "I just knew the phone would ring someday and Joshua would be dead." Ultimately, Joshua's mother brought a federal civil rights action against the county, alleging that it had deprived Joshua of his constitutional right to safety by failing

---

31. These statistics are cited in Laura Oren, "The States' Failure to Protect Children and Substantive Due Process: *DeShaney* in Context," *North Carolina Law Review* 68 (1990): 659–731.
32. 489 U.S. 189 (1989).

to act in the face of overwhelming evidence that he was being abused. The case eventually reached the Supreme Court, where she lost. Writing for the Court's majority, Chief Justice Rehnquist held that government had no constitutional duty to protect any citizen from violence at the hands of another unless it had first deprived that citizen of his liberty by placing him in custody so that he could not take care of himself (thus differentiating Joshua from prisoners, mental inmates, or residents of children's homes whom the courts have held qualified for state protection).

Justice Blackmun, in dissent with Justice Brennan, accused the majority of retreating "into a sterile formalism which prevents it from recognizing either the facts of the case before it or the legal norms that should apply to those facts."[33] If, as in Wisconsin, Blackmun said, the law has decided on a response to child abuse that eschews removal of children from their homes in favor of family casework, it cannot then turn about and deny them protection. Joshua was a four year old; he could not fend for himself. For all practical purposes, he had been committed to the custody of his abusive father by the state's inaction. Blackmun analogized the Court's decision to the antebellum judges who refused to intervene to protect slaves from the violence of their masters because, in the eyes of the law, the slaves were "property."

DeShaney dramatizes the unsettled state of the law dealing with violence against children. The law is understandably protective about parental authority and reticent to let the state—especially in the form of "do-gooder" social workers—undermine that authority. But we know family privacy can mask violence and oppression against innocent and helpless victims. As with spousal abuse, weak and ineffective state intervention on behalf of abused children does double damage. It reinforces the abuser's instinct to attack the child, and it offers no viable threat of deterrance.

There has thus been, in the past several years, a belated recognition that spousal and child abuse are crimes of oppression by the strong over the weak and deserve more, not less, attention from the law. The law's violence is a resource that should not be arbitrarily withheld on the basis of shattered myths about family autonomy.

---

33. DeShaney, 489 U.S. at 212 (Blackmun, J., dissenting).

Violence and the First Amendment

Another dilemma in applying law's violence centers around what a judge should do when he or she can foresee violence erupting as a result of a decision, but must balance that risk against damage to other, preeminent values in our society.

The First Amendment guarantees freedom of expression for all points of view, no matter how controversial. Some of those viewpoints, we know, can be so provocative that almost certainly they will produce a violent response among listeners. Yet the courts have been reluctant to remove them from First Amendment protection unless they fall within the narrow exception of "fighting words"— "those which by their very utterance inflict injury or tend to incite an immediate breach of the peace."[34]

Governments do, however, regularly require demonstrators to obtain a permit to march or picket or assemble in public and put conditions in the permit as to time, place, and duration. These conditions, the courts have said, must be reasonable and not based on the content of the message. Issuing permits is necessary to allocate public space fairly and to allow the life of the rest of the community to go on uninterrupted during the demonstrations. Thus, for example, local authorities may have some say in specifying parade routes for demonstrators so long as they insure visibility for the demonstrators.

Washington, D.C., as you can imagine, is a uniquely desirable location for marches and rallies. The White House, the Washington Monument, and the Capitol make an impressive backdrop for the sought-after 6:00 news soundbite. For decades, the traditional parade route for demonstrators has started at the Washington Monument, moved down Constitution Avenue to Pennsylvania Avenue and up the hill to the Capitol for a climactic rally. ERA backers, pro- and antiabortionists, Iranian students, the handicapped, civil rights marchers, and war and peace demonstrators have all followed that route.

In October, 1990, the Ku Klux Klan sought a permit to march. Washington, with its predominant black population, was predictably anti-Klan, and feelings ran high. Threats of violence were posted all

34. Chaplinsky v. New Hampshire, 315 U.S. 568 (1942).

over the city. Indeed, there had been a violent episode a year earlier, when Klan marchers had to be rescued by the local police from the bricks and stones of onlookers and escorted in cars to their rallying place. But the Klan wanted to come back, it said, to show that it would not and could not be denied the right to march along the same route as other groups. This time, however, an understandably anxious District of Columbia government insisted on a permit curtailing the normal parade route on the ground that the district simply could not provide the necessary police protection for the usual route. The Klan, backed by the ACLU and the Justice Department, took the District of Columbia government to court on Friday—two days before the scheduled Sunday afternoon march.

The Klan argued that curtailing the traditional route because of the fear of reactive violence would amount to a "heckler's veto" over the speech of peaceful demonstrators. The ACLU argued that the distastefulness of the Klan's message did not justify such a gag, citing the recent Supreme Court decision upholding flag burning as a permissible form of expression, despite its likelihood of inciting viewers to violence.

The District of Columbia government, on the other hand, argued that it had a right to limit the Klan to a section of the traditional route that it could reasonably protect without stripping the rest of the city of essential police services. It proposed to limit the march to four blocks along Constitution Avenue instead of the usual eleven.

The trial judge who heard the evidence on both sides refused to permit any limitation of the route, expressing confidence that the city police, aided by the federal Park Police, could contain any violence. An emergency appeal from that ruling was taken on the Friday night before the Sunday parade. A panel on which I sat heard the appeal. My two colleagues voted to stay the march, and remanded the case to the trial judge for more detailed findings on the city government's capacity to police the march. With some apprehension, I dissented, expressing my concern that allowing the city to curtail the usual parade route would open the way to similar or greater curtailments of other controversial marchers in the future.[35]

On Saturday night, the district judge made new, detailed findings, reaffirming the right of the Klan to march the full route, and, on

35. Christian Knights of Ku Klux Klan Invisible Empire, Inc., v. District of Columbia, 919 F.2d 148 (D.C. Cir. 1990).

Sunday afternoon, twenty-seven bedraggled Klansmen marched the full eleven blocks guarded by 3,125 police in riot gear who, at various points, were hammered with bottles and rocks hurled by some of the 1,200 protestors lining the parade route. One policewoman suffered a fractured neck; 13 others were injured; some 40 counterdemonstrators were arrested. Building and car windows along the route were smashed. The Capitol, the National Gallery, and one Metro station had to be closed during the march. The cost to the city was estimated at $800,000. Predictably, the protestors claimed the police officers had used excessive force in guarding the demonstrators.

Was it worth it? What should a judge do when faced with the real threat of violence along a parade route? The Supreme Court has never actually told us. Many such constitutional crises come down to very particularized fact finding and prediction making on the part of the trial judge. From past experience, everyone knew that there would be violence when the Klan marched in the District of Columbia. But the judge had to choose which police expert to believe—the city's, who said the police force could not handle the full fourteen blocks without taking away necessary protection from the rest of the city, or the federal government's, who said that "on the facts . . . presently known to the federal government, the applicable case law simply does not permit curtailment of the First Amendment rights of a controversial group solely on the basis of the strident, disruptive and even potentially violent reaction that may be provoked in counterdemonstrators."[36]

In this case, the trial judge found there was not a threat of violence "beyond reasonable control," and the extreme efforts required to police the march were justified by the value of the First Amendment right involved. "The public," he said, has an interest in establishing "that no mob can rule seven blocks of Constitution Avenue."[37]

Unlike family violence, where the risk is that judges will retreat from the violent facts into abstractions about family life, the challenge for a judge in First Amendment cases is the opposite—to hold the

---

36. Defendant United States' Opposition to Plaintiffs' Application for a Temporary Restraining Order and Motion for a Preliminary Injunction (filed D.D.C. October 25, 1990) at 18.

37. Christian Knights of the Ku Klux Klan v. District of Columbia, 751 F. Supp. 216, 217 (D.D.C. 1990).

principle of free speech apart from the message of the speaker. Here, history provides an ironic footnote. In affirming the right of the Klan to march, the trial judge had come full circle from Judge Frank Johnson's 1965 decision to allow a second Selma-to-Montgomery civil rights march after the first march had been violently disrupted by Klansmen (among others), rejecting the government's plea that it was unable to provide adequate police protection for the fifty-mile march.

Judges faced with these decisions are aware that there may come a point when the likelihood of widespread violence is so great that the balance tips against unfettered First Amendment rights. The Supreme Court has told us thus: It simply has not yet marked out that divide. The judge can order the police to do their best to prevent the violence of counterdemonstrators; in the Klan march, the police used shoulder-to-shoulder barricades, moving scooter patrols, and shields; in many situations, they have resorted to tear gas. But, in the final analysis, violence may occur and innocent people may be hurt. Were the judge to curtail the march, that violence might be avoided. But at what price? How much anticipated violence is tolerable as the quid pro quo for free speech is an issue a judge now decides case by case without the sure guidance of the Supreme Court. In the Klan case, we ruled, ultimately—and I believe correctly—for free speech. But I will tell you, I felt a deep sadness watching, on television, that young policewoman being carried away on a stretcher, the casual victim of a brick thrown by a Klan protestor. She, too, was a victim of the law's violence.

Violence to the Environment

My final example of the law's violence deals with an area of relatively recent sensitivity: violence to the environment. At present, the law conceptualizes violence almost entirely in terms of how people treat one another or another's property. Through most of history, our human ethic has ignored violence against nonhumans. But we do not inhabit the planet alone. The human organism belongs to a larger ecosystem of land and air and water. We know it is possible to do violence to that ecosystem; indeed, uncurbed, such violence can eventually threaten human existence.

Even in earlier times, isolated voices were raised to challenge the law's preoccupation with human violence. Leonardo Da Vinci once predicted, "The time will come when men . . . will look on the murder of animals as they now look on the murder of man."[38] In our own time, radical environmentalists have melodramatically warned that we should "no more sink the blade of an ax into the tissues of a living tree than . . . drive it into the flesh of a fellow human."[39]

But building a jurisprudence around the rights of the nonhuman assets of our globe is a complicated exercise. Condemning such acts as cutting graffiti into a tree trunk or polluting water that kills wildlife is easy, but what about cutting down forests to build low-income housing, expropriating farmlands for highway projects, diverting rivers for hydroelectric dams? Just in the last few decades, we have enacted legislation requiring governments to minimize the deleterious effect of their activities on the environment. The National Environmental Protection Act (NEPA) requires an impact statement for all major federal activities. Of course, it is still humans who do the evaluating and who make the ultimate choices on which activities to go ahead with despite their environmental consequences. Even in the Endangered Species Act, the enjoyment and education of man is the ultimate end, rather than the right of species to exist on their own. The purpose of the act is to preserve species that are of "aesthetic, ecological, educational, historical, recreational and scientific value for the Nation and its people." It is not easy to avoid the mind-set of ourselves as the Rulers of the Universe. And this mind-set controls the way the law reacts to environmental violence in peculiar ways, such as who may legally complain of such violence in the first place.

In *Sierra Club v. Morton*,[40] decided by the Supreme Court in 1972, the Sierra Club sought to enjoin a ski resort development in the Sequoia National Forest because of the damage it would visit on wildlife and plants inhabiting the wilderness area. A majority of the Supreme Court held that the Sierra Club could not bring the suit because it had failed to allege any injury to its own members. To

---

38. Quoted in Roderick Nash, *The Rights of Nature: A History of Environmental Ethics* (Madison: University of Wisconsin Press, 1989), 173.

39. Edward Abbey, *The Journey Home: Some Words in Defense of the American West* (New York: Dutton, 1977), 208.

40. 405 U.S. 727 (1972). Before the case reached the high court, Christopher Stone, an ecologist, wrote an article entitled, "Should Trees Have Standing?—Toward Legal Rights for Natural Objects" (*Southern California Law Review* 45 [1972]: 450–510), which set out a legal theory on which the Sierra Club could represent other forms of life.

bring such an action—the Court said—the club must show harm to its members' "aesthetic, conservational and recreational" interests. A "special interest" in protecting the "Nation's heritage from man's depredations" was not sufficient; humans could not act as the spokesmen for the rest of the environment unless they were themselves at risk. In a lone dissent, Justice Douglas would have taken a broader approach.

> Those who hike it [the Forest], fish it, hunt it, camp in it, frequent it, or visit it merely to sit in solitude and wonderment are legitimate spokesmen for it, whether they may be few or many. Those who have that intimate relation with the inanimate object about to be injured, polluted, or otherwise despoiled are its legitimate spokesmen.[41]

Ironically, the theory of environmental guardianship is not unique. Artificial entities created by human beings—governmental units, estates, municipalities, universities, and corporations—are often recognized in the law as having enforceable legal rights of their own. But, so far, we have not seen fit to extend that recognition to living creatures and plants, except in those few instances, such as the Endangered Species Act, where the government is mandated by law to prevent their extinction.

There are, however, some hopeful signs that the law is beginning to accept the notion that environmental violence may be remediable in its own right. The EPA, in its risk reduction priority list, now looks at ecological damage as well as human health effects.[42] In damage law, increasingly, polluters are required to repair environmental damage rather than merely pay compensation for the economic harm to the owner. Thus, my own court has required polluters to restore or replace a seal rookery rather than simply pay the economic value of their pelts on the market. (Many plants and animals have no economic value to man.)[43] We still have a long way to go,

41. 405 U.S. 727 (1972), at 744–45 (Douglas, J., dissenting).
42. See William K. Stevens, "E.P.A. Moves to Change Environment Priorities," *New York Times*, January 26, 1991, § 1, p. 11 (Science Advisory Panel urges EPA to concentrate on protection of natural ecosystem).
43. See, e.g., Ohio v. United States Dep't of Interior, 880 F.2d 432 (D.C. Cir. 1989).

however, before the focus of our law on human interests is broadened to encompass unjustifiable violence to other, nonhuman elements of the environment.

The most ardent ecologists are waiting. They have sponsored a constitutional amendment stating that "all wildlife . . . shall have the right to a natural life," and some compare the sale or destruction of acres of old-growth forests to traffic in slavery. But for now, violence against the environment is only a fledgling idea in the law, implemented sporadically in practice primarily through a few laws designed to protect at-risk species or to make governments stop and think about the effect of their activities on the rest of the environment.

Conclusion

I have tried to survey briefly several areas in the criminal and civil law where judges must confront the fact that their decisions will authorize, or at least encourage, violence. I have pointed out some troubling trends in our modern criminal law that distance the judge from responsibility for the violence he or she authorizes or the way in which sentences are carried out, or even from awareness of how the defendant got before the judge in the first place. On the civil side, the danger that judges will not acknowledge the violence implicit in their decisions is greater still, as in the right-to-die cases. Family violence, on the other hand, illustrates an instance in which the law has withheld its violence and, by so doing, has encouraged powerful private parties to impose their own violence on vulnerable women and children. The law's violence must be rationed fairly and not denied to some individuals who need its protection. The case of demonstrators who incite violence in others by exercising their First Amendment rights provides an example of where a judge must balance the high risk of violence against such values as free speech that are enshrined in our Constitution. Finally, I have suggested that the law is just beginning to conceptualize the notion that other beings in this universe are deserving of protection in their own right from the violence of man.

I hope all this has served to flesh out a bit how Professor Cover's provocative, disturbing notion of law's violence translates into the everyday life of judges.

Reading Violence

Carol J. Greenhouse

Words and Violence

While, for the most part, evolutionary approaches to the anthropology of law have dropped from a long period of fashion, one of their central premises remains alive in new venues. From Sir Henry Maine's interpretation of the transition from status to contract in Roman law, through Durkheim's more tentative essay on the diffuse progress from mechanical to organic solidarity, and early anthropological classics on so-called primitive law—the roots of sociolegal scholars' concerns with law have been consistently nourished by the distinction they draw between social orders based on personal power and force and those "superior," "more advanced," or "more rational" orders based on the authority of words.[1]

I am grateful to the organizers and sponsors of the *Law's Violence* series at Amherst College for their invitation to participate, and for their generous hospitality while I was in Amherst. Students and colleagues at the colloquium provided constructive comments on the original version of this essay. For their individual readings and suggestions, I am particularly indebted to Alfred C. Aman, Jr., Brenda Bright, Kristin Bumiller, Rosemary Coomb, Thomas Dumm, Lawrence Douglas, Thomas Kearns, and Austin Sarat. That we each had a different reading of Cover's essay made this project an exciting and rewarding collegial enterprise for me.

1. Sir Henry Maine, *Ancient Law*, 10th ed. (London: John Murray, 1906); Emile Durkheim, *The Division of Labor in Society* (New York: Free Press, 1964); Max Weber, *Economy and Society*, ed. G. Roth and C. Wittich (Berkeley: University of California Press, 1978). Formative examples of anthropological writings on "primitive" law include Ralph Barton, *The Ifugao* (Berkeley: University of California Press, 1969); Bronislaw Malinowski, *Crime and Custom in Savage Society* (Paterson, N.J.: Littlefield, Adams, 1962); for synthetic assessments of early writing in legal anthropology, see also E. Adamson Hoebel, *The Law of Primitive Man* (Cambridge, Mass.: Harvard University Press, 1954); Leopold Pospisil, *Anthropology of Law: A Comparative Theory* (New York: Harper and Row, 1971).

This is not the place to detail the history of the literal concept of "the primitive" in ethnology and jurisprudence, nor its dismantling. Suffice it to say that the original evolutionary rationale for cross-cultural empirical sociolegal research organized around the distinction between force and words is now largely abandoned, but the distinction remains. Detached from its evolutionary matrix, the hierarchical distinction between force and texts as alternative normative bases still has a durable career.

That distinction provides some of the basic meanings of law as a social force, for both social scientists and others. For example, Montesquieu's eighteenth-century fictional Troglodytes (who discover the inefficiencies of a world run by force and so invent social contracts) and Posner's imaginary society based on vengeance are virtually identical creations.[2] This is not because the later one is a copy, but because both are substantiated by the cultural premise that violence and law form separate legal foundations, law representing a categorical advancement over force. Some of the positive aspirations implicit in this view of law's "progress" toward textuality can be found in White's conceptualization of law as "culture."

> [T]hrough its forms of language and of life the law constitutes a world of meaning and action: it creates a set of actors and speakers and offers them possibilities for meaningful speech and action that would not otherwise exist; in so doing it establishes and maintains a community, defined by its practices of language.[3]

Such examples illustrate one way in which the premise of the polarity between force and texts as alternative (even rival) bases of law forges a link between the Enlightenment and its modern heirs.

The premise of a polarity between words and force continues to shape the language and traditions of research practice in sociolegal scholarship. For example, modern cross-cultural research has lent support to the view (sometimes as a premise, sometimes as a finding)

---

2. Montesquieu, *Persian Letters* (New York: Penguin Books, 1973); Richard Posner, *Law and Literature: A Misunderstood Relation* (Cambridge, Mass.: Harvard University Press, 1988), 27–33.

3. James Boyd White, *Justice as Translation: An Essay in Cultural and Legal Criticism* (Chicago: University of Chicago Press), xiii–xiv.

that law displaces violence when law is successfully institutionalized.[4] Even where this idea is not proferred as such, its substance is encoded in familiar language. For example, anyone who reads sociolegal literature even casually knows that *social control, settling disputes, law,* and *justice* (to offer just a few examples) are terms that are generally supposed to signal reductions in the likelihood of violence both in interpersonal contexts and in social systems overall. Such usages and suppositions might reflect noble aspirations for the law, but they are largely untested (and untestable) ones.

The enduring presence of this intellectual legacy is to be valued without doubt. Whatever its theoretical defects, it does provide the world with one conceptual framework within which to imagine a global social order where the sanctity of human life is continually affirmed and enhanced. Some alternative would be preferable only to the extent that it preserves or improves the possibility of imagining human dignity in a flourishing, multicultural world. A search for such an alternative would also be useful in more immediate and modest ways in that the persistence of this distinction in its present form now unnecessarily vexes methodological debates in the sociolegal field. These methodological debates contain a strong ethical component. I refer to the tensions between interpretivists (defined subsequently) and others, who argue that interpretivists' concerns with symbols and meanings have little "real-world" relevance. In what follows, my aim is to strengthen the intellectual bridge across that divide.

We might begin with the observation that the sociolegal domain is a particularly appropriate one for some renewed scrutiny of the relationship of words and force. There is much common ground in the fact that most sociolegal research traditions view the law "itself" as involving a coercive element. Further, most sociolegal scholars acknowledge the law's textual aspects—in the unfolding of cases of dispute, the negotiation of outcomes, the improvisation and selection of terms of argument, the creation and use of legal documents and discourses, and so on.

Still, most recent reviews of legal anthropology sooner or later emphasize—with varying forcefulness—the current methodological

---

4. For classic elaborations of this view that were influential in sociolegal studies, see Donald Black, *The Behavior of Law* (New York: Academic Press, 1976); Klaus-Friedrich Koch, *War and Peace in Jalémó* (Cambridge, Mass.: Harvard University Press, 1974).

eclecticism in anthropology generally and legal anthropology specifically.[5] The intellectual tensions discussed in these reviews are along
a supposed axis dividing symbolic, hermeneutic, and interpretivist
approaches on the one hand from empirical studies of social action
(politics, economy, courts, and so on) on the other. Within anthropology, perhaps the clearest statement of this division and what is
at stake in it is Moore's.

> The hermeneutical domain is a fail-safe and interesting intellec-
> tual sanctuary in a world in which the coherent total cultural
> systems of earlier theoretical models are as hard to find as
> cannibals. . . . By deconstructing the scene into the meanings of
> particular concepts, icons, symbols, and practices, the social
> drama can be treated as if it were a temporary amalgam of
> cultural parts, and the serious consideration of many difficult
> larger-scale questions can be avoided. That there may be a polit-
> ical economy of cultural diversity beyond the focal range of the
> inquiry can be gently acknowledged. Such matters as "back-
> ground" can be recognized in an "out of focus" way without
> serious analysis. . . . "Interpretive" analysis is art, not method.[6]

5. See John Comaroff and Simon Roberts, *Rules and Processes* (Chicago: University of Chicago Press, 1981); Clifford Geertz, *Local Knowledge: Further Essays
in Interpretive Anthropology* (New York: Basic Books, 1983); Sally Falk Moore,
Social Facts and Fabrications: "Customary" Law on Kilimanjaro 1880–1980 (Cambridge: Cambridge University Press, 1986); June Starr and Jane Collier, eds., *History
and Power in the Study of Law* (Ithaca: Cornell University Press, 1989). For more
general reviews of legal anthropology, see Jane Collier, "Legal Processes," *Annual
Review of Anthropology*, no. 4, ed. B. Siegel (Palo Alto: Annual Review Press, 1975),
121–44; Sally Falk Moore, "Law and Anthropology," *Biennial Review of Anthropology 1969*, ed. B. Siegel (Stanford: Stanford University Press), 252–300; Laura
Nader, "The Anthropological Study of Law," *American Anthropologist* 67 (1965): 3–
32.
    6. Sally Falk Moore, *Social Facts and Fabrications* (Cambridge: Cambridge
University Press, 1986), 325–26. Compare to Rosaldo's recent critique of "interpretivism" and other textual approaches in postmodern anthropology, stemming from
his reassessment of his Ilongot study.
    [A]nthropology's classic norms . . . prefer to explicate culture through the gradual
    thickening of symbolic webs of meaning. By and large, cultural analysts use
    not *force* but such terms as *thick description, multivocality, polysemy, richness,*
    and *texture*. The notion of force, among other things, opens to question the
    common anthropological assumption that the greatest human import resides in
    the densest forest of symbols and that analytical detail, or "cultural depth,"
    equals enhanced explanation of a culture, or "cultural elaboration." Do people

The debates in anthropology (to which Moore refers) are gene-
alogically and rhetorically related to methodological debates in other
disciplines. In an essay that is similar in tone and substance to
Moore's, Cover—a lawyer—forcefully rejects what he calls "humanistic interpretation" or "literary interpretation" in the field of law.[7]
His position is anchored in the irreducible distinction he draws
between violence and language.

> [Pain] and death destroy the world that interpretation calls up.
> That one's ability to construct interpersonal realities is destroyed
> by death is obvious, but in this case, what is true of death is
> true of pain also, for pain destroys, among other things, language
> itself.[8]

The law, in Cover's view, is "played out on the field of pain and
death"[9]; it is violent, even when that violence is concealed by courtroom procedure, or simply by blinding habit.[10] He refers to the judiciary's "homicidal potential."

> The judges deal pain and death. . . . From John Winthrop through
> Warren Burger, they have sat atop a pyramid of violence,
> dealing. . .
>   In this they are different from poets, from critics, from
> artists. . . . Even the violence of weak judges is utterly real . . . in
> need of no interpretation.[11]

In terms such as these, Cover's essay elaborates his refusal to admit
interpretivists (though he never uses the word) to the legal arena.

---

always in fact describe most thickly what matters most to them? (Renato
Rosaldo, *Culture and Truth: The Remaking of Social Analysis* [Boston: Beacon
Press, 1990], 2, italics in original)
The reference to thick description—and, indeed, interpretivism—evokes Clifford
Geertz, "Thick Description: Toward an Interpretive Theory of Culture," in *The Inter-
pretation of Cultures* (New York: Basic Books, 1973), 4–30.
    7. Robert M. Cover, "Violence and the Word," *Yale Law Journal* 95 (1986):
1601–29.
    8. Cover, "Violence," 1602.
    9. Cover, "Violence," 1606–7.
    10. Cover, "Violence," 1613.
    11. Cover, "Violence," 1610.

There, he argues, the analogy of the literary text fails, both technically and ethically. The ethical charge is that interpretivists actually extend and increase the law's violence by disguising violence as art. I will return to Cover's argument, since it involves such a full statement of the fundamental and conventional distinction between language and violence that pervades so much contemporary sociolegal research.

Thus, while anthropologists and others concerned with the socio-cultural aspects of law have provided rich documentation of the impact of state law on everyday life, they do tend to divide at the point where some give their attention to the apparatus of power (state or otherwise) at the local level, as opposed to the negotiations of symbols and meanings that are evidence of some of the ways in which power is understood and felt in people's lives. While this difference is often felt as a division (in the more conflictual sense), the fact remains that both sides (though I hesitate to reify them as such) tend to downplay the extent to which the law might be implicated in the *circulation* of violence in social systems.[12] Further, both sides conventionally "read" texts as compositions in a language *other* than that of coercion, power, and violence. Both tendencies are part of the evolutionary legacy referred to previously.

The critical claims of Moore and Cover (and others) against interpretivist approaches to law rest on the distinction between a real-world domain of power and violence and an "imaginary" world of symbols that "operates" apart from it. This is a compelling and humane distinction. It focuses analytical attention on the different qualities of life of those people whom society harms, and whom it protects; no one would deny the importance of this dividing line. Even so, "interpretivists" and others who deal primarily with the law as text resist consigning symbols to the realm of "the imagination" if that means that they are thereby parcelled off from "the real world." Interpretivists examine the myriad ways in which social relationships, institutions, and cultural practices are invented, defended, and renewed through interaction, conversation, observation, and the interpretation of symbols—that is, in everyday experience.[13] This,

12. For suggestive critiques along related lines, see Pierre Bourdieu, "The Force of Law: Toward a Sociology of the Juridical Field," *Hastings Law Journal* 38 (1987): 814–53; Roger Chartier, *Cultural History: Between Practices and Representations*, trans. L. Cochrane (Ithaca: Cornell University Press, 1988); James C. Scott, *Domination and the Arts of Resistance* (New Haven: Yale University Press, 1990).
13. I use the term *interpretivist* in this essay, since it is a convenient way of

they say, is not a denial of the real world, but, rather, an assertion that symbols are real, too, in their capacity to mobilize and/or cure harm.

The world being what it is—this essay was written during the months of military buildup and fighting against Iraq in 1990–91— the claims of interpretivism's critics represent urgent and troubling charges. In the spirit of the times, the central question of this essay is this: Do textual approaches to law and social ordering necessarily trivialize or deny outright the world's violence and the law's role in it? If power and violence stand outside the domain of language, symbols, and texts, then the answer must be yes. On the other hand, if violence can be shown to have a textual, as well as a physical, reality, then there is some solid ground from which to defend the relevance of interpretive approaches to empirical sociolegal research.

In what follows, I propose to undertake this defense through three ethnographic case studies in which violence—in very different ways—not only plays a role in actors' visions of social order, but is also celebrated. I consider the cases in two stages. First, I explore the question of the textuality of violence on the basis of ethnographic evidence gathered among the Ilongot (by Rosaldo)[14] and the Kaluli (by Schieffelin).[15] These cases provide different sorts of evidence about the ways in which violence is understood culturally and scripted into narratives of various kinds. These provide the basis for a response to the general criticism of interpretivist approaches I have outlined.

---

referring to one set of voices in a methodological controversy. At the same time, I do not mean to suggest that interpretivists share some coherent ideology or practice, nor do I think there is much to be gained by searching for this term's boundaries, since they are, by definition, likely to be blurred (see, for example, Clifford Geertz, "Blurred Genres: The Refiguration of Social Thought," in Local Knowledge: Further Essays in Interpretive Anthropology [New York: Basic Books, 1983], 19–35). Elsewhere in the essay, I use the term interpretation to refer to what interpretivists do. Throughout, my intention is to focus on the issue of how the proximity of textual and physical forms of violence challenge the conventional distinction between "the real world" and the world of symbols—the distinction that is, I believe, at the heart of the current methodological debates to which I refer. For the eponymous key text, see Clifford Geertz, The Interpretation of Cultures (New York: Basic Books, 1973); see also Clifford Geertz, Local Knowledge: Further Essays in Interpretive Anthropology (New York: Basic Books, 1983).

14. Renato Rosaldo, Ilongot Headhunting 1883–1974: A Study in Society and History (Stanford: Stanford University Press, 1980).

15. Edward L. Schieffelin, The Sorrow of the Lonely and the Burning of the Dancers (St. Lucia: University of Queensland Press, 1976).

Cover goes further, though, in detailing an ethical argument against turning to the humanities for legal interpretive strategies.[16] He takes the position that legal interpretation is radically different from ordinary textual interpretation (he consistently refers to literary interpretation) in that law is constantly disruptive (dealing as it does in "pain and death"), while ordinary textual interpretation is integrative. In other words, the law "works" by constantly overturning meanings and creating new ones in its own language of violence; other texts "work" by revealing meanings held in common by "interpretive communities." Cover objects, on moral grounds, to deploying any interpretive approach whose premise involves shared meanings in contexts where meanings are not shared—hence his ethical objections to what I call interpretivist approaches to law (again, he refers primarily to literary approaches to legal interpretation). To do so, he argues, is to do further violence to the victims of the law's violence. This warning makes his argument against textual approaches to law particularly interesting and challenging.

Accordingly, in the second part of this essay, I turn to the question of whether a textual approach necessarily rests on the assumption that its meanings are revealed and shared among solidary interpretive communities. The ethnographic material in the second part comes from the United States, where a journalist's report of a current law case provides the basis for discussion. The conclusion of the essay returns to the general question of the contempory technical and ethical relevance of interpretivist approaches to law. Overall, my basic argument is that when interpretivists examine the ways in which people construe and construct their social worlds, they are not escaping from the world's misery, but, along with other empirical scholars whose intellectual and professional traditions they share, confronting it.

The Ilongot

The Ilongot live about eighty miles from Manila in the uplands of Northern Luzon, the Philippines.[17] Though their lands are relatively

---

16. Cover, "Violence," 1602, n. 2.

17. All references to the Ilongot are based on Rosaldo, *Ilongot*, esp. 1–60 and the extended description of the Butag-Rumyad feud, 61–106. Additional references are cited by page number, below. For his subsequent reflections on Ilongot head-hunting, see Renato Rosaldo, *Culture and Truth*, 1–21.

close to the national capital and the Ilongot have been in contact with Europeans since the first Spanish missions arrived in 1565, they have remained relatively unintegrated in—though not isolated from—the lowlands mainstream. The Spanish colonial strategy was to attract indigenous populations to the lowlands, and some Ilongot did move and were converted to Christianity. For the most part, though, except for occasional reciprocal raids involving Spanish soldiers, the Ilongot lived fairly independently in the highlands.

Ilongot autonomy grew substantially less secure in the early part of this century, when the United States assumed control of the Philippines as a result of the Spanish-American War in 1898. The United States began a major development effort that affected the highland areas; that impact probably would have been more extensive had the colonial administration not run short of funds in the early 1930s. The Ilongot remember the years before World War II as the *pistaim* (peace time)—roughly the years from 1919 to 1945.[18] Peace time ended for the Ilongot in June, 1945, when U.S. forces drove the Japanese into the Philippine highlands; one third of the Ilongot were killed amid general and profound disruption.

The Ilongot describe peace time in terms of two series of changes. The first of these is the movement of their own population: consolidating, dispersing, and then consolidating again. The second refers to the relative intensity of their headhunting activity. Until it was effectively banned by martial law in 1972, the taking of heads was an integral part of Ilongot feuding. The Ilongot remember peace time as initially involving intense headhunting activity, then the absence of headhunting, then its gradual intensification once again.

The external source of postwar headhunting—which reached its peak in 1959–60—might have been the "indirect result" of battles between the guerrilla movement and counterinsurgency forces.[19] At the same time, a major hydroelectric project outside of the Ilongot area brought change there by displacing other upland populations, some of whom moved into this part of the country. These developments, as well as a new U.S.-based evangelical mission, altered the shape of social relations in the uplands. Relationships between the uplands and the lowlands changed even more acutely: "Head-

---

18. Rosaldo, *Ilongot*, 40.
19. Rosaldo, *Ilongot*, 36.

hunting . . . became even more clearly than before the dominant symbol for Ilongot identity in the context of lowland/upland relations."[20]

Rosaldo's book on the Ilongot is an examination of their historical
narrative, and it is through these narratives that we can learn something of what headhunting meant to them and how it was bound up
in their sense of individual and collective identity. Headhunting was
a masculine activity; a man's first head was a valued and highly
visible sign of his personal effectiveness. Men of roughly the same
age in the same village tended to compete with each other both in
headhunting and in courting; the Ilongot say that the envy that
motivates men can have positive effects: " . . . everybody should move
in loosely coordinated fashion so that each one, energized through
healthy competition, will arrive at his or her equal share."[21]

The competitive activity of coresident male peers is inevitably a
collective concern, since the meanings and implications of headhunting go (or went) well beyond being some benchmark of masculine
expertise. The consequences of headhunting could be terrible; the
Ilongot tell of times when they were afraid to go to sleep for fear of
a raid in the night and of times when the scale of violence was
shocking to them, out of control (e.g., in June, 1945, as well as
subsequent occasions). Violence could relatively easily escalate beyond the senior generation's ability to contain it with alliances, since
a coresident group was collectively liable for an insult or attack
against an individual from another group. (The Ilongot themselves
contrast this form of liability with that of the police, who look for
a particular individual against whom to address their violence.)[22]

More preferably, the consequence of headhunting was an alliance
with the adversaries, and it was these alliances that provided young
men and women with their marriage partners. Marriages conventionally cross-cut lines of political tension. The political and ritual
energies of the senior generation were aimed at preserving viable
alliances against the risks of disruption. While excessive headhunting
could be disruptive from the Ilongots' point of view, headhunting
itself was not, terrifying though it might be.

Headhunting and marriage were conceptualized by the Ilongot
as reciprocal movements across familiar territory. Feuding and alli-

20. Rosaldo, *Ilongot*, 36.
21. Rosaldo, *Ilongot*, 58.
22. Rosaldo, *Ilongot*, 251.

ance, headhunting and marriage, dispersal and consolidation—these
continue to provide the Ilongot with their sense of history and with
their understanding of social change as a quick succession of moves
in the same direction by peer groups.

> Often imaged as spatial movement, the Ilongot sense of history
> can be represented, on the one hand, as a group of people walking
> in single file along a trail and, on the other, as an alternation
> between the focus of inward concentration and the diffusion of
> outward dispersal.[23]

Accordingly, Ilongot historical narratives include the recitation of long
series of place names, each one the emblem of the violence or some
other event that took place there.[24] Violence was at the core of Ilongot
textuality: "[The] concept of the feud is a cultural construct used
most often for looking back on events and making amends."[25] The
Ilongots see their social order as the product of constant improvi-
sations; headhunting and marriages were the improvisatory "moves"
that made their social life comprehensible to them and that made
narratives of social life possible and essential.

Though Rosaldo does not say so directly, actual violence (not
just narrated violence) also appears to have given Ilongots a sense
of their own lives' capacity to "make sense." Now, headhunting has
been suppressed, and the Ilongot sometimes say that they are no
longer Ilongot.[26] When Rosaldo left the field, Ilongots were beginning
to convert to Christianity in an effort (as the Ilongots explained) to
find some means of discharging the burdens of their wrath and grief
that now gnawed at them from within. It was too soon to know
whether Christian textual forms would be adequate to serve the
Ilongots' interpretive needs. At that time, Ilongots experienced the
cessation of headhunting, externally enforced, as in itself a disruptive
and consuming form of violence.

Ilongot historical narrative, which dwells on the sites of episodic
violence, juxtaposes violence with what the Ilongot say is its reciprocal—marriage alliances. The Ilongot preference for interpreting vio-

---

23. Rosaldo, *Ilongot*, 58.
24. Rosaldo, *Ilongot*, 128.
25. Rosaldo, *Ilongot*, 276.
26. Rosaldo, *Ilongot*, 60.

lence as a form of dispersal that is recovered by the in-gathering of
a marriage gives feuding its textual quality; indeed, Rosaldo himself
does not insist on a distinction between feuding and feud narratives,
so deftly do the Ilongot inscribe their raids on the social landscape.
At the same time, the Ilongot preference for understanding and referring to violence as one element of a larger equilibrium is sometimes
severely strained—sometimes past the breaking point—when they
face violence that is excessive or excessively constrained. For these
very reasons, the Ilongot offer a constructive example of the double
proximity of violence and narrative on the one hand, and, close by,
the social landscape and the physical landscape on the other.

   In the next example, the risks of violence breaking the bounds
of textuality are confronted in different ways. In the Kaluli example,
the proximity of violence and narrative becomes even tighter, to the
point where violence is part of the syntax of the narratives in question.

The Kaluli

The Kaluli live under the tropical forest on the slopes of Mount Bosavi
in Papua New Guinea.[27] Like the Ilongots, they are horticulturalists
with a long tradition of contact with other cultural and linguistic
groups; however, in the case of the Kaluli, the first contact with
Europeans came only in 1935. When Schieffelin began his fieldwork
among the Kaluli in 1966, their warfare and cannibalism had recently
been suppressed (in 1960) under pressure from administrative patrols.
Schieffelin collected narratives of warfare and cannibalism from
informants' recent memories; however, his principal aim in his book
on the Kaluli is to offer an exegesis of the *gisaro* ritual, which involves
various other forms of violence. I will return to the *gisaro* shortly.

   The Kaluli conceptualize their society in terms of reciprocal relationships among oppositionally formed groups. Indeed, their understanding of the natural world is in the same terms: while all life
forms were one at creation, speciation occurred as the result of differences analogous to human disputes.[28] The *gisaro* embodies the
principles of reciprocity that also pervade everyday life: the circulation of food, other wealth, and marriageable women across social

27. All information on the Kaluli comes from Schieffelin, *Sorrow*.
28. Schieffelin, *Sorrow*, 94–95.

space is conceptualized by the Kaluli as reciprocal exchange. Of these, the exchange of food is the dominant symbol of social integration and social health.[29] The idiom of reciprocity expressed in the *gisaro* celebrates these affirmative aspects of life, among others.

Kaluli concepts of conflict are similarly expressed in terms of reciprocity. Conflict in itself is not thought of as disruptive, since Kaluli ideas about creation make contest a neutral condition of existence. But some people—mostly men—are witches (the Kaluli term is *sei*); it appears to be witches that make conflict dangerous. Witches are responsible for all death (in this sense, all death is murder). Sometimes, a dying person will realize the identity of the witch and whisper his name; otherwise, the Kaluli have a number of divinatory means of discovering the identity of the witch. A witch may not realize he is one, but that is not an excuse. Kaluli talk about the recent days when witches were routinely executed in the course of retaliatory raids. When the identity of a witch was known, a raiding party would be drawn from those men who felt especially aggrieved by the death in question or from men who were looking for some excitement. The witch was attacked and killed in his house during the night. The attackers would smash his skull with a club and remove his body and an autopsy would confirm the identity of the witch; the heart would be kept for subsequent examination by the dead witch's relatives, and the body would be butchered and distributed to longhouses other than the raiders' own to deflect any future vengeance. The matter would be settled when and if the dead witch's relatives accepted compensation in lieu of a vengeance killing. An agreement of this kind would be celebrated by a shared feast and an overnight visit by the witch's relatives in the longhouse of his executioners.[30] Although the Kaluli no longer do these things, they still talk of them.

Kaluli define the danger of the witch not in his capacity to deliver harm, but in the fact that that harm is all out of proportion: "*Seis* [witches] are malicious, irrational, voracious, disgusting, dangerously violent, and tremendously strong. They are the incarnation of implacable evil."[31] In contrast, normal anger is carefully modulated in proportion to its context and cause. Kaluli say they fear other people's

---

29. Schieffelin, *Sorrow,* 71–72.
30. Schieffelin, *Sorrow,* 78–80.
31. Schieffelin, *Sorrow,* 101.

anger, though they also say that quickness to anger is a sign of normal masculine vitality.[32] When the Kaluli narrate episodes of conflict from the past, they stress episodic closure, even when the events in question form part of a much longer sequence of still-unresolved events. Importantly, it is the witch and the retaliation against the witch that permit this textual strategy. "For us, a person dies, and there is no way to resolve or make up his loss. For the Kaluli, there is the *sei*."[33] Schieffelin does not tell us what has happened to the Kaluli now that there is no longer "the *sei*" in the sense of bringing closure to death through retaliatory violence.

Schieffelin argues convincingly that the *gisaro* encodes a Kaluli view of the world as constructed in reciprocal oppositions, oppositions constantly renewed in the episodic closure narrative provides. The *gisaro* ceremony affirms social relationships—new or old—as ties of reciprocity. It is often performed at weddings or food distributions, but never at funerals. The *gisaro* involves male dancers from among the visiting longhouse group who volunteer to sing lyrics they have composed themselves that are addressed to their hosts. The songs are nostalgic in tone; they evoke the hosts' dead kinsmen or neighbors, desolation and waste, the passing of familiar and cherished things. The dancers' artistic goal is to make their hosts weep. The hosts, angered by the intrusion of memories of personal sadness, take revenge on the dancers by assaulting them with flaming torches, burning them extensively on the shoulders and back. After the dance, the dancers pay compensation to the men they have made weep, and the ceremony ends on a lively note. Kaluli say they find the ceremony "exciting, beautiful, and deeply moving."[34]

The songs themselves dwell on the contrast between the seen and the unseen, or, more accurately, the onstage and the offstage, so much so that they are sung in a neighboring language, not the Kalulis' own. These verses are from one song.

A *kalo* bird at Dubia Ridge is calling juu . . . juu.
The *kalo* calling there is calling you.
Go see the Walaegomono pool,

---

32. Schieffelin, *Sorrow*, 135.
33. Schieffelin, *Sorrow*, 147.
34. Schieffelin, *Sorrow*, 24.

Go see the fruited *gala* sago. . . .

Do you see the Galinti pool?
Do you see the crocodile?
The *beulin* tree up on top there at Gunisaweli, will it break?[35]

Schieffelin explains that, to Kaluli listeners, the place names identify familiar locations of abandoned houses or other signs of dereliction, the fruited sago has not been harvested in time, but left to bolt, and so on. "The entire beloved landscape seems about to be destroyed."[36]

The hosts of the *gisaro* experience these evocations as a form of violence for which they retaliate with violence of their own. The singers remain impassive and continue their performance as they are attacked with torches, or hugged, by their weeping hosts. Schieffelin describes the scene as one of "incredible pandemonium,"[37] but adds: "The violence of the audience does not disrupt the performance because it is absorbed and contained within it."[38]

The violence against the singers is no illusion. At the end of a performance, a singer's shoulders and back are covered with second-degree burns. Sometimes his skin sloughs off during the dance or a day or two later; usually, he takes three or four weeks to recover fully. Evidently appalled by this, the local administrative officer prohibited the burning of the dancers. Local constables put on their uniforms to supervise the next *gisaro*. Schieffelin reports that the ban on burning made the ceremony even more violent, as weeping men attacked the dancers with their fists or threw heavy objects at them. Shortly thereafter, the practice of burning resumed, burning being more appropriate to the Kaluli sense of scale.

For the Kaluli, the focus of the ritual is not on the burning alone, but on the songs that make them weep, the burning, and the compensation to the hosts. Taken together, these make the *gisaro* an occasion of exhilaration and intimacy.[39] Without the burning, the songs were unbearable: "To move a person deeply with the songs

---

35. Schieffelin, *Sorrow*, 179–80.
36. Schieffelin, *Sorrow*, 178–79.
37. Schieffelin, *Sorrow*, 192.
38. Schieffelin, *Sorrow*, 193.
39. Schieffelin, *Sorrow*, 206–7.

and then deny him the right to retaliate is to make him suffer help-lessly, unable to return his pain."[40]

The Ilongot and Kaluli cases bear similarities and differences. From both of them, we learn about logics of retaliation, and the embed-dedness of violence in concepts of gender, marriage, exchange, friend-ship, society, time, and place. We also learn from both about the importance of narrative—oral texts in which individual and collective experiences can be temporarily inscribed and reappraised. Both exam-ples show that it is not only "we" who are concerned to comprehend the violence in our lives and in our visions of society. The Ilongots and the Kaluli have their own articulate analyses of social order and its intrinsic risks. Violence is not uniformly disruptive in these exam-ples, though some of it is. The Ilongot and the Kaluli—in different ways—have a vocabulary of violence that distinguishes among its forms and scales; people in both cultures abhor and suffer from the disruptions of excessive violence.

The cases are also different in a way that may or may not be obvious (quite apart from the fact that these are very different cultures and societies). Among the Ilongot, there are feuds and also narratives of feuds. Among the Kaluli, antiwitchcraft raids have been sup-pressed, though they are remembered and retold. The *gisaro* involves other forms of violence, which appear in the song narratives not as subject, but as part of the very syntax of the text. Still, the native exegeses included in these ethnographies cross and recross whatever the distinction might be between "real" and "symbolic" violence (i.e., narrative violence) so readily that it is literally impossible to define it.

It would seem that violence does not stand outside literature for the Ilongot and the Kaluli; it is incorporated into their literary texts. Violence is not only the subject of Ilongot narrative, for example, but its very form. Violence is not only a response to the Kaluli *gisaro*, but part of the songs themselves.[41] In these examples, violence is not

---

40. Schieffelin, *Sorrow*, 205.
41. Further, the ethnographic examples illustrate the process by which violence can be absorbed and symbolically encoded in ordinary social practice. For example, the Ilongot juxtapose feuding and marriage as reciprocal moves; in a sense, they represent each other. For the Kaluli, some elements of the meanings of capital, gender, and food symbolically encodes them as reservoirs of violence.

outside the symbolic language of the community, but is central to it, as the theme, medium, and syntax of their narrative texts. Indeed, it appears that, to the Kaluli and Ilongot, these texts are in part legible because of the way they "speak" the violence of the everyday— as opposed to the violence that is unspeakable or unbearable, to which the Ilongot and Kaluli are also profoundly sensible.

Do the ethnographic examples support the critics' claim that violence and texts belong to two essentially mutually exclusive domains? I think not, for several reasons. The *gisaro* is a dramatic ritual performance in which physical attacks against the dancers become— literally—part of the song text. In an ordered society, the Kaluli say, a certain amount of violence is embedded in the social order, as the witchcraft narratives also show. This suggests that it is not violence in itself that is disruptive, but, rather, disruption that is experienced as extreme violence. I do not mean by this that everything is relative— far from it. The carnage is real. I mean that it is not violence in itself that "destroys the world that interpretation calls up"[42] for the Ilongot and the Kaluli, but, rather, other sorts of disruptions—of excessive violence, violence out of proportion, violence unilaterally denied a response, hunger, invasion, evil. In other words, it is not that violence is to be understood as art, but, rather, that the violence in the texts extends, circulates, modifies, or contains—or fails to do these things—the violence in the world.

Both ethnographic examples illustrate the extent to which cultural notions of proportion vis-à-vis violence are bound up in corollary notions of the textuality of social life. The Ilongot and the Kaluli do more than emphasize the centrality of violence in the narratives they compose to represent themselves to themselves and to the world. The central theme of Ilongot narratives is the feud; the feud provides both the narrative structure (as an alternation of dispersal and return) and the images themselves (series of place names where heads have been taken). Like the Ilongot, the Kaluli deploy place names as key emblems of social identity in time. Unlike the Ilongot, though, who use place names to validate the narratives' content as eyewitness accounts, the Kaluli use place names to evoke the unseen. It is the evocation of the unseen within the familiar that moves men to tears. The performance of such narratives is itself highly textualized, the dance,

---

42. Cover, "Violence," 1602.

the burning, and the payment of compensation being different forms of inscription. The dance, the burning, and the compensation also represent different modalities of the circulation of violence.

At the same time, the textuality of violence has limits—that is, not all violence is "legible" to the Ilongot and the Kaluli. At any given time, some violence surpasses—or falls awry—of the text. This is not experiened by them as a literary difficulty, but as an unbearable human emergency. Some Ilongot say they are no longer Ilongot, for example, because their grief can no longer be contained in traditional narrative. The Kaluli *gisaro* songs evoke another kind of textual limitation, and that is in their repeated gestures toward the immanence of the unseen future within the familiar. As the next example also shows, such textual limits are not fixed, but change with culture, consciousness, and context.

Within the limits of the text, interpretation—"understood as interpretation normally is in literature, the arts, or the humanities"[43]— does not preclude contact with real violence, because of the extent to which that violence is encoded in everyday life and the social order. As the next example shows, real violence in U.S. life also has an everyday quality that is accessible through law's texts (and, as that example also shows, the law must also manage the boundaries of the unspeakable). The frightening thing about the law's violence is not that it cannot be read or interpreted textually, as the critics claim, but that it can be read that way so easily.[44]

Any and all of the above points would seem to challenge the assumption that violence and texts belong to different domains, with

---

43. Cover, "Violence," 1602, n. 2.

44. Dumm makes a related point, which is relevant again in the second part of this essay.

The projection of an imagined future for law requires understanding the originary position of law, not as a unity, but precisely as a writing that precedes the word. This eliminates one source of the "specialness" of law, because one then realizes, if only with a nervous laugh, that the gap between perpetuator and victim of violence is all to[o] easily bridged, and that writing is itself only a replication of the gap between violence and the word, a replication that allows one to think of law's future . . . with some minimal measure of hope. That hope is embedded, not in the uniquely violent character of legal interpretation, but in the audacity of its most basic claim, to imagine a future and to project that future upon the present, and then to call the result reality. (Thomas L. Dumm, "Fear of Law," *Studies in Law, Politics and Society* 10 [1990]: 55)

Dumm's essay is devoted to a critical reflection on Cover's essay, addressing, in particular, Cover's view of law as a projection of the future in the present.

the important qualification that texts do not contain or express all of the violence that people are capable of unleashing on each other. In the next section, I will pursue the idea that an essential task of textual interpretation is to discover the contours of the text against the unspeakable that it claims to keep at bay. Attending to the law's textuality offers one means of holding the law accountable to something beyond itself—something like a connection between language and life. Viewed from that perspective, interpretation and the search for justice are related creative activities.

Violent Readings

Cover's critique of the literary interpretation of law texts involves the claim that textual approaches necessarily and falsely import an interpretive solidarity into the law's constant disruptions. As I noted earlier, his argument rests on his distinction between legal texts and literary texts (I have expanded his rather open-ended references to literature to refer to any nonlegal text). The image of a literary text that is at work in Cover's essay is one that he seems to share with the other scholars whose work he addresses—by such "law and literature" figures as Dworkin, Ferguson, White, and others. While Cover's views of literary interpretation are fairly implicit in his essay, the works against which he positions himself in developing his critique of the "literary interpretation" of law contain extended discussions of the nature of reading and literary/legal interpretation.[45] His disagreement with these authors is not over the way they characterize literary interpretation, but over the analogy they draw between reading literature and reading law. Cover's essay appears to be a response to a series of published programmatic statements by academic lawyers and others who advocate just such an analogy.

The attractions of literature for academic lawyers appear to be in the new vantage points literary criticism provides for questioning traditional understandings of what it means to read legal texts—

---

45. See Cover, "Violence," 1602, n. 2. In my subsequent discussion, I rely primarily on the sources available to Cover. For more recent developments in the law and literature field (and current bibliography), see Richard Posner, *Law and Literature: A Misunderstood Relation* (Cambridge, Mass.: Harvard University Press, 1988); James Boyd White, *Justice as Translation: An Essay in Cultural and Legal Criticism* (Chicago: University of Chicago Press, 1990).

precedents, statutes, and other documents. The traditional view is that reading law literally engages the interpreter (the advocate, the judge, et al.) in direct contact with the intentions of the documents' authors.[46] The very notion of an independent yet accountable judiciary in the United States depends, to some extent, on the idea that canonical understandings can be received in this way.

At the same time, there is a long tradition of doubt among legal scholars. Where the legal realists of the 1930s looked to the social sciences for strategies of reading the law as social process, some academic lawyers in the mid-1980s turned to the humanities for new approaches to reading law as cultural process.[47] Perhaps considering law texts as literature held open the promise of reading the law in a way that was simultaneously creative, accountable, and true to life—that is, one that acknowledged the subjectivity of reading without rendering the notion of justice relative to the point of meaninglessness. This aspiration rested on a particular understanding of what it means to read literature, or, for that matter, anything else; I will return to this point shortly.

What "law" means as an objective for these authors' interpretive projects varies considerably among them.[48] For example, Dworkin

---

46. For discussion, see Ronald Dworkin, "Law as Interpretation," in *The Politics of Interpretation*, ed. W. J. T. Mitchell (Chicago: University of Chicago Press, 1983), 249–70, esp. 251–52. Posner considers a broader range of causes for the recent flowering of the dialogue between law and literature, for which he credits the increased theoretical content of academic law and literature, the "growing politicization of intellectual life in this country [i.e., the United States]," the "general decline in the autonomy of scholarly disciplines," the collapse of the academic job market in the humanities, and the influx of humanists into law. An additional factor, in Posner's view, is that, "to law professors, literature offers a hope of redemption from a technocratic future. To literature professors, law offers a hope of redemption from social marginality" (Posner, *Law and Literature*, 11–12). This is an especially interesting statement, since it suggests that what is at issue in the distinction or integration of law and literature is not their respective texts, but, rather, the institutional hierarchies within which they operate. I return to this latter possibility in the conclusion.

47. See, for example, symposium on interpretation, *Southern California Law Review* 58, no. 1 (1985): 1–275 and 58, no. 2 (1985): 277–725; symposium on law as literature, *Texas Law Review* 60 (1982): 373–586. See also Robert A. Ferguson, *Law and Letters in American Culture* (Cambridge, Mass.: Harvard University Press, 1984); W. J. T. Mitchell, ed., *The Politics of Interpretation* (Chicago: University of Chicago Press, 1983); James Boyd White, *When Words Lose Their Meaning: Constitutions and Reconstitutions of Language, Character, and Community* (Chicago: University of Chicago Press, 1984).

48. Other key terms also have unsteady meanings, as Eagleton points out; see

refers to the interpretation of legal practice itself, not just "documents or statutes."[49] Fish refers to texts.[50] For White, "[law] is in a full sense a language . . . it is a way of maintaining a culture, largely a culture of argument, which has a character of its own."[51] Elsewhere, White describes law more broadly as "an art essentially literary and rhetorical in nature, a way of establishing meaning and constituting community in language."[52] Levinson turns the law-language relationship around, pointing to the "centrality of law to textual analysis."[53] Ferguson develops this idea empirically, in a study of lawyers' contributions to what he calls a "coherent" ideology and language in the United States in the eighteenth and nineteenth centuries.[54] Perhaps the largest landscape is the one Bruns points to when he writes that law is "exemplary of what it means to understand and interpret anything at all."[55]

For his part, Cover refers to the "legal decision" as the scholar's interpretive object,[56] but he also refers to legal interpretations themselves.[57] He also moves beyond the verbal text to the performance of the law: "We begin, then, not with what the judges say, but with what they do."[58] From there, his essay develops and mobilizes an opposition of law as the domain of violence and literature as the domain of art. His evocations of art seem to address particularly the formulations of White and Dworkin, who experimentally develops a critique of intentionalist interpretation on aesthetic grounds.[59]

Terry Eagleton, "Ineluctable Options," in *The Politics of Interpretation*, ed. W. J. T. Mitchell (Chicago: University of Chicago Press, 1983), 380.

49. Dworkin, "Law as Interpretation," 249.

50. Stanley Fish, "Working on the Chain Gang: Interpretation in the Law and in Literary Criticism," in *The Politics of Interpretation*, ed. W. J. T. Mitchell (Chicago: University of Chicago Press, 1983), 271–86.

51. James Boyd White, "Law as Language: Reading Law and Reading Literature," *Texas Law Review* 60 (1982): 415.

52. White, *When Words Lose Their Meaning*, xi.

53. Sanford Levinson, "Law as Literature," *Texas Law Review* 60 (1983): 377.

54. Ferguson, *Law and Letters*, 10.

55. Gerald L. Bruns, "Law as Hermeneutics: A Response to Ronald Dworkin," in *The Politics of Interpretation*, ed. W. J. T. Mitchell (Chicago: University of Chicago Press, 1983), 315.

56. Cover, "Violence," 1602, n. 2.

57. Cover, "Violence," 1611.

58. Cover, "Violence," 1609.

59. James Boyd White, *When Words Lose Their Meaning*, xi; Dworkin, "Law as Interpretation," 249–70. These authors mean different things by situating law in

Where these authors (Cover and the others) are more in agreement is on the question of what it means to read literature. For them,
literature, as I have already suggested, is charged with aspiration. It
would appear to be what they see as the affirmative aspects of literature itself that leads them to extend (or, in Cover's case, reject)
the literary model for the law's normativity. Each of these works
envisions an individual reader's interpretation of a text as occurring
within a consensual canon of some interpretive tradition. Accordingly, literature categorically emerges as world building and integrative while, at the same time, offering individuals the satisfaction of
a personally meaningful, socially responsive reading experience.

The attraction of literature to these legal scholars (except Cover)
would thus appear to be in its mediating quality—mediating between
the individual and the whole social order (that is, the largest viable
interpretive community). Viewed in this way, literature has a strong
normative dimension and takes on a positive legal character. It is the
vehicle of a (reading) tradition—while simultaneously being literally
recreational (re-creating and generative). Reading literature thus seems
to them to promise a rehearsal for some future time when the language
of law will be as unified and coherent as literary language.

We can hope that some future conjunction of author and reader
will provide a common language of constitutional discourse fit
for "a nation of supple and athletic minds," but for now we can
only await its coming and make do with the fractured and fragmented discourse available to us.[60]

Similarly, White defines the "integration" that literature makes available to a society as being about "tolerance" and "clarification of
diversity and difference."[61] His subsequent move from literature to
social relations suggests that literature, in a sense, provides a sur-
rogate for some larger global vision: "[T]he image of integration I

literature, or vice versa, but all of them, including Cover, equate literature with
language. As I have already explained, this is where Cover parts company with the
interpretivists, by situating law's violence outside the textuality of literary language.
While we have seen that violence can be expressed textually, Cover's reservations
about equating texts with all social experience are well placed.

60. Levinson, "Law as Literature," 402–3.
61. White, *Justice as Translation*, 3–4.

have been trying to get before us is an image of ... the relations between people and races and cultures."[62]

There are many issues here—and many paradoxes.[63] The one I want to focus on now is these authors' (including Cover) evident hope or expectation that literature accomplishes, through interpretation, something of what the law can do only through domination, that is, to create a real community in which individuals voluntarily participate, fully empowered by virtue of their common language and capacity to understand the tradition for which they are responsible as readers. Their assumption that a common language signals

---

62. White, *Justice as Translation*, 21. It is intriguing to consider the extent to which such understandings and aspirations for literature involve particular Western cultural propositions about the relationship between texts and social order. The implied connection between the primacy of the word and the social world in which the word is inscribed is a very ancient one in the West (Emile Benveniste, *Le vocabulaire des institutions indo-europeenes*, 2 vols. [Paris: Les Editions de Minuit, 1969]; Walter Ong, *Orality and Literacy* [New York: Methuen, 1982]). Similarly longstanding is the conventional construction of reading as involving a polarity between author and reader. The "author-reader dichotomy" represents reading as the reader's reception of a text whose meanings were established at some prior point in time by its author (Susan Noakes, *Timely Reading: Between Exegesis and Intepretation* [Ithaca: Cornell University Press, 1988], 214). This is, in Noakes's view, a fundamental misrepresentation of what reading involves, that is, the production of meaning by readers. In another vein, the view of literature I have been describing also involves the assumption that a community's coherence is in inverse relation to its diversity, i.e., that meaning— to be valid—must be held in common. This idea, too, touches on ancient (as well as modern) Western claims that sociocultural categories have their foundations in natural distinctions (see Louis Dumont, *Essays on Individualism: Modern Ideology in Anthropological Perspective* [Chicago: University of Chicago Press, 1986]).

As empirical claims, each of these propositions is highly problematic. Moreover, as recent scholarship by anthropologists, feminists, and others demonstrates, each of these propositions underscores the extent to which the particular visions of literature and society at issue here *themselves* involve forms of real and symbolic violence (see Marilyn Strathern, *The Gender of the Gift: Problems with Women and Problems with Society in Melanesia* [Berkeley: University of California Press, 1988], for a discussion of Western concepts of agency, individuality, gender, and society and the misreadings they proliferate cross-culturally).

63. Not least of the paradoxes is that these authors generally invoke an interpretivist project as an antidote to positivism (see, for example, Dworkin, "Law as Interpretation"). I am suggesting here that they have displaced positivism to the field of literary interpretation, and reimported it to the law via the claim that law is literature. For a related discussion of what Bourdieu calls "legalistic formalism" (equating social conventions with juridical rules) in ethnography, see Pierre Bourdieu, *Outline of a Theory of Practice*, trans. R. Nice (Cambridge: Cambridge University Press, 1977), 17; see also the related discussion in Pierre Bourdieu, "The Force of Law: Toward a Sociology of the Juridical Field," *Hastings Law Journal* 38 (1987): 814.

a collective consensus on substantive matters of norms, values, or interpretation is highly problematic in this regard, and I return to this issue below.

One need not accept the equation of language communities with normative communities to find a different sort of connection between domination and literary interpretation compelling. That is the one that Weisberg traces in his study of European fiction, that is, the link—more than a link: the identity—he finds between physical and textual forms of violence.[64] Weisberg's study of "procedural novels"— novels in which lawyers are prominent protagonists—focuses on the special textual facility of lawyers (both in speech and in writing) that, Weisberg claims, subverts the normal textuality of everyday life. Accordingly, lawyers—in fiction and, to some extent, in the European society Weisberg examines—escape from scrutiny and accountability. "In this way, they [lawyers] manage to gain influence and thus to expand their disguised rage outward until finally nothing of substance is permitted to survive."[65] In Weisberg's view, the lawyer's voice is the voice of *ressentiment*, of resentment, against the other; the disproportionate presence of lawyers cast in this role in Western literature between 1860 and 1960 reveals a profound social unease.[66] He pursues these developments to the point that he identifies as their culmination in the events now known as the Holocaust.

Weisberg's consideration of the connections between "narrative and real violence" precludes a categorical distinction between literature and the world.[67] Weisberg shows that events and representations not only cross from the page to the world and back again, each providing rehearsal space for what is practiced on the other stage, he also shows them to be the same stage. Indeed, reading cannot be separated categorically from the other practices that make up the world. The textual strategies by which people are represented as individuals or as groups cannot be understood apart from the ways in which those representations are wielded elsewhere, be they por-

---

64. Richard Weisberg, *The Failure of the Word: The Protagonist as Lawyer in Modern Fiction* (New Haven: Yale University Press, 1984); Weisberg, "Law in and as Literature: Self-generated Meaning in the 'Procedural Novel,'" in *The Comparative Perspective on Literature: Approaches to Theory and Practice*, ed. C. Koelb and S. Noakes (Ithaca: Cornell University Press, 1988), 224–32.
65. Weisberg, *Failure of the Word*, xiii.
66. Richard Weisberg, "Law in and as Literature," 226.
67. Weisberg, *Failure of the Word*, xiv.

trayals of gender, race, ethnicity, and so on. Precisely the same point might be made from the illustrative cases discussed previously, from the Ilongot and the Kaluli. The violence in their texts might at first seem exotic, but attending to the violence there soon reveals the links—historical, cultural, and accidental—between "them" and "us." The next section pursues such links from the point of view of an interpretive project that embraces them.

In what follows, I borrow Weisberg's identification of textual and physical forms of violence to respond to Cover's more-or-less implicit claims about the nature of ordinary reading. The response has two strands: first, I develop the idea that acknowledging the reality of textual violence is essential to an interpretivist approach to law. The second point is a corollary to the first. I propose that it is *not* solidary communities and common understandings among readers that substantiate interpretivist approaches to law (or anything else), but rather the differences among readers—the potential for incoherence and contradiction in texts and in life.

On these points, the ethnographic discussion in the first section is inconclusive. While the Ilongot and Kaluli examples can be read as demonstrating that violence does not, by definition, stand outside language and texts, that provisional conclusion begs the question of how violence is negotiated textually. In the following U.S. case, such negotiations are prominent. A comparative discussion drawing together the U.S. case and the earlier examples emerges later in the discussion.

Perry v. Louisiana

In 1985, Michael O. Perry was found guilty of murdering his parents and three other relatives by a Louisiana trial court.[68] Since then, he has lived in the expectation of his own execution in fulfillment of his sentence by the court. Mr. Perry is a schizophrenic, and, though he was found competent to stand trial, the state court ruled that he was not competent to be executed by virtue of his insanity. The trial court then ordered that he be "maintained on antipsychotic drugs, over his objection if necessary" so that the death sentence could be carried out. In October, 1990, Mr. Perry's appeal of that order reached the

---

68. My presentation of the case is based on accounts in *United States Law Week* and the *New York Times* (November 14, 1990).

United States Supreme Court. I quote the account of the case at
length from *Law Week*.

A case before the court this term will give the justices an
opportunity to add another restriction to the death penalty. Like
Ford [which prohibits a state from executing an insane prisoner],
the case centers on a mentally ill death row inmate. It presents
an issue, however, that the court did not have to face in *Ford:*
whether a mentally ill death row inmate may be made competent
enough to be executed by the non-consensual use of medication.
The case stems from Louisiana's attempt to execute a prisoner,
whose competency was clearly marginal at best, by forcibly
medicating him to the point that he became aware of his impend-
ing execution and the reason for it. . . .

The prisoner . . . suffers from schizoaffective disorder, a mental
illness that affects both mood and thought and is characterized
by, among other behavior, delusions and hallucinations. The illness is incurable, although its symptoms can be mitigated by
medication. The consensus of the doctors who testified at the
hearing held to determine the prisoner's competency to be executed was that the prisoner is competent when taking medication—
specifically, Haldol—but incompetent when the medication is
withheld.

The state argues that a sentence of death justifies restrictions
on a condemned inmate's rights that are necessary to effectuate
the death penalty. Thus, the state contends, the due process right
to refuse medication that the Supreme Court recognized in *Washington v. Harper*, . . . does not extend to death row inmates who
require medication to be competent for execution. But even
assuming the inmate has an interest in refusing such medication,
that interest is overridden, the state says, by its interest in carrying out the death penalty.

The inmate contends, however, that in ordering his forcible
medication, the state court considered only the state's interest in
carrying out the death sentence. It did not balance this interest
against the inmate's interest in avoiding the non-consensual
administration of psychotropic drugs. The order therefore failed
to accord the inmate the minimal protections guaranteed by the
Fourteenth Amendment. He also cites Louisiana laws that forbid

execution of the insane, require that insane inmates be treated, and define the conditions under which an inmate can be forcibly medicated, saying that these laws create expectations that are protected by the Fourteenth Amendment's Due Process Clause.

The crux of the inmate's argument, however, is that the Eighth Amendment and contemporary standards of human decency prohibit the use of forced medication to achieve the competency necessary to be executed. But the state stresses that because the antipsychotic medication is of benefit to the inmate, its nonconsensual administration to the inmate can't be considered cruel and unusual punishment. "In fact," the state's brief says, "because [the inmate] is incompetent to make his own treatment decisions, under the doctrine in *Estelle v. Gamble*, 429 U.S. 97 (1976), the State is *required* to treat [the inmate] with neuroleptic medication, with or without his consent, in order to relieve the suffering caused by his mental illness." The inmate, however, emphatically denies that the medication ordered for him by Louisiana courts is for treatment; it is a step toward his execution and part of his punishment, he claims.[69]

The Supreme Court did not rule in the case, but, on November 13, 1990, returned it to the Louisiana state courts. Mr. Perry cannot be executed until the constitutional question presented in *Perry v. Louisiana* is resolved.

There are many ways of reading this text, and many reasons to read it. One reason might be comparative. As in the Ilongot and Kaluli narratives of vengeance, this one centrally involves the construction of a corollary relationship between violence and order, surprising juxtapositions of killing and healing, and highly conventionalized forms of narrative. There are also more specific parallels: the specialists' confirmation of an individual's qualification for execution, the cultural distinctions between murder and execution, and so on. Comparisons of this sort would be worth pursuing. My purpose, though, is a different but related one, that is, to sketch an interpretive reading of *Perry v. Louisiana*—focusing on the question of whether interpretation prerequires common meanings and convergent understandings.

From the outset, the narrative makes explicit two points of view,

---

69. *United States Law Week* 59 (1990): 3175–76.

that of the appellant (Perry) and that of the state of Louisiana. Their respective positions are fundamentally opposed—even though the indirect discourse arguably minimizes their opposition by giving the narrative some of the form of ordinary conversation. The outcomes the litigants seek, the basic principles they invoke, and the logics with which they frame their arguments are obviously different. The question Cover presses us to ask is: Can an interpretivist read this text without minimizing or eliminating those differences and what is at stake in them?[70]

Let us begin where we left off with the Ilongot and Kaluli examples. Just as in those narratives, where violence was encoded in cultural concepts of time, place, and the overall representation of social order, here, too, we can productively consider basic issues of time, place, and self-representation as points of departure. This will be only the beginning of a reading of this case, but one that underscores its internal tensions and risks. A more complete reading would heighten those tensions, I believe.

The adversaries deploy antithetical concepts of time in defending their respective positions. Perry's appeal rests on the assumption that events that affect him are meaningful within the time frame of his own biography. The fact that the forced medical "treatment" will hasten his execution is at the heart of his case. That is the fact that he claims offends standards of human decency, which (he implies) maintain an opposition between healing and killing. The state, on the other hand, denies the relevance of this temporal framework. Perry is ill and must be treated; he is a criminal and must be punished. The link between these two imperatives—so literally vital to Perry— is of no consequence in the state's presentation. The state's interests are presented in terms of the relationship between the state and the criminal, the public interest in social control, and the requirement that the state guarantee the medical treatment of the ill. Though the execution is the state's goal, that goal is to be accomplished—if it is accomplished—as if it were a collateral incident in the course of Perry's medical treatment.

---

70. The depth of these tensions makes White's description of a legal hearing appear to be something of an understatement. "[A legal hearing means] testing one version of [law's] language against another, one way of telling a story and thinking about it against another, and . . . then . . . making a self-conscious choice between them" (White, *Justice as Translation*, 24).

It is against the background of Perry's insistence on the form of his biography as the form of his rights that the timeless quality of the state's self-representations comes sharply into focus. The state's case dismantles Perry's biography; Perry's lifetime is rhetorically extinguished in the moment that the state severs the normal connection between healing and the affirmation of life. This textual killing in the state's brief is not the same as Perry's biological death, but it is another kind of death, potentially related to it in very direct ways.[71]

Such juxtapositions of time and timelessness, and the extraordinary tensions of those juxtapositions, are familiar ones—not only in the law, and not only in literature, but from the general domains of public life in the West.[72] In the West, we are culturally sensitized to thinking of nations and public institutions as more-or-less fixed, and of a person's lifetime as ephemeral in relation to the longer, slower histories of nations and their causes. In this case, a whole array of concepts and terms are vexed with ambiguities that are rooted in that same temporal incongruity: individuality (counterposed as the self and as the inmate), life (counterposed as health and the competence to be executed), responsibility (counterposed as treatment and punishment), the state (counterposed as protector and executioner), rights (counterposed as protection against forced medical treatment and as requiring forced medical treatment), and so on. Where the violence of the Kaluli *gisaro* songs is in the irony of playing the familiar against the eventual, the visceral power of *Perry v. Louisiana* is in its refusal of irony—the text, like the case, literally contains these mutually exclusive meanings and possible outcomes. My main point for now is that the case is interpretable only to the extent that readers

---

71. For his discussion of criminal law, and particularly the distinction between punishment and torture, see James Boyd White, *Heracles' Bow: Essays on the Rhetoric and Poetics of Law* (Madison: University of Wisconsin Press, 1985), 192–214, esp. 201. For his "comparative anthology on death," which illuminates Western textual strategies for announcing and condoling death, see James Boyd White, *The Legal Imagination*, abridged ed. (Chicago: University of Chicago Press, 1985), 73–82. For anthropological discussions of the relationships among individuality, personhood, death, and social order, see Maurice Bloch and Jonathan Parry, eds. *Death and the Regeneration of Life* (Cambridge: Cambridge University Press, 1982); S. C. Humphreys and Helen King, eds. *Mortality and Immortality: The Anthropology and Archaeology of Death* (London: Academic Press, 1981); Richard Huntington and Peter Metcalf, *Celebrations of Death* (Cambridge: Cambridge University Press, 1979).

72. Carol J. Greenhouse, "Just in Time: Temporality and the Cultural Legitimation of Law," *Yale Law Journal* 98 (1989): 1631–51.

recognize these radical contradictions from their own experience and supply the irony themselves. Such understandings cannot emerge from the text alone, but are brought to the text in some interpretive process that confirms its expressions (and inversions) of everyday life.

The case also involves two places: the Supreme Court of the United States and the state of Louisiana. So long as the case moves between these two locations, Mr. Perry's execution will be deferred. The multiplication of readings of his case provisionally keeps him in life; no single reading has yet been definitive. The proliferation of interpretations, in law as in literature, underscores both the human "writtenness" of the text and the relative frailty of its living object. Any understanding of these companion mortalities is a cultural one— again, one that belongs neither to law or literature alone, but allows us to read both. And, again, any understanding would be flawed without some sense of the contests and indeterminacies that generate these new readings.

But Louisiana and Washington, D.C., are not just two places of the same kind. A case travels "up" to the Supreme Court, and "down" to the courts "below"—a familiar architectural or mountainous, or perhaps heavenly, reference? Whatever its referents and sources, the cultural relevance of this symbolic geography is in conveying the fact that aspects of Perry's personhood now depend on the hierarchy of readers who consider his case. The hierarchy of courts is not—except administratively—a convergent one; rather, the fact that courts are at different "levels" of the system allows multiple (even contradictory) interpretive regimes to exist simultaneously within the law. Accordingly, it is the hierarchy of courts that allows for the *textual* containment of radically different—even contradictory—logics and goals, such as in this case.[73]

These and other features of the text suggest that interpretation does not prerequire a solidary community of readers, though interpretation does require information and discipline. The narrative of *Perry v. Louisiana* gestures in mutually exclusive directions simultaneously. An interpretation that did not recognize the tensions in

---

73. See Cover, "Violence," 1623-25, on the relevance of judicial hierarchies in capital cases. He argues that the constitutionality of capital punishment is in the constant possibility of a stay, and that the judicial hierarchy both actualizes that principle and diffuses responsibility for judgment.

the adversaries' positions would be deeply flawed; so would one that presupposed that the conclusion of the case will fundamentally resolve them, except perhaps in Mr. Perry's personal case. This knowledge is not available in the text itself, but is introduced into the text, as it were, by an interpretive process. This being the case, interpretive communities are not readers for whom fundamental things go without saying, but for whom important cultural conflicts have to be made explicit.

Among other things, this case suggests the extent to which textual interpretation is itself a practice that absorbs and generates a certain amount of violence, as it probes the textual limits of the speakable. As interpretivism's critics note, violence made text can be claimed as a form of social order, granting that disorder can be a form of order. Disruption that cannot be made into text threatens order in an entirely different way. In response, I would stress that the limits of textuality are never fixed, but are negotiated within the text (and not only there) through successive readings; the interpretive process itself uncovers these negotiations by connecting their terms to those of everyday life.

In *Perry v. Louisiana*, for example, the adversaries vie to define the limits of the speakable: Perry places them at the connection between healing and killing, but the state—since Perry is convicted of murder—places them at a killing that goes unpunished.[74] Against Perry's claim that healing a man so that he can be put to death is to commit an act that is beyond words, the state does not defend that proposition as such, but finds words with which to express and defend alternative propositions that, combined, produce that result. Either way, Perry may not be executed until he is mentally capable

---

74. Bourdieu develops a distinction between the unspeakable and the unthinkable in his discussion of *doxa* as a universe of "competing possibles." In his view, orthodox discourse—"the official way of speaking and thinking the world"—involves a "radical censorship."

> [The] overt opposition between "right" opinion and "left" or "wrong" opinion, which delimits *the universe of possible discourse*, be it legitimate or illegitimate, euphemistic or blasphemous, masks in its turn the fundamental opposition between the universe of things that can be stated, and hence thought, and the universe of that which is taken for granted. (Bourdieu, *Outline*, 169–70; italics in original)

To this, I would add that these "universes" are not defined by settled or impermeable boundaries. It is precisely the textual intrusions of the unspeakable and the unthinkable into everyday discourse that are my concern in *Perry v. Louisiana*.

of visualizing himself as a prisoner on the verge of execution and expressing his understanding of that vision in narrative form. That narrative would qualify him to die. In effect, the law requires that he be able to textualize the violence about to be done to him and relate it to the violence he committed in a single narrative. His present inability to tell that story is a definitive sign of his illness in legal terms.

An interpreter of texts traces the shifting borders of the unspeakable; among other things, it is this that gives textual interpretation its ethical possibilities. Though critics legitimately question whether the interpretation of texts can expose the uses of violence that are built into the social order, I believe that an interpretive approach offers a comprehensive means of doing so—once textual violence is acknowledged as a form of violence and once the limits of textuality are acknowledged as an interpetive issue. The interpretation of symbols and texts is not a cosmetic for the world's violence, but its magnifying glass. The scenario of Perry being required to narrate his own death before he can be executed under the law reaches to the very heart of what is at stake in this debate.

Let us review the critical issues from the beginning of this essay. The first critical claim against the real-world relevance of interpretivism was that violence—"pain and death"—stands beyond language and texts. To this, Cover added a second claim, that literary texts are meaningful to the extent that their meanings are coherent and shared; since this sharedness is precluded by the law's violence, the techniques of literary interpretation are invalid in relation to the law.

In response to the first claim, the Kaluli and Ilongot narratives demonstrated the extent to which violence—physical violence—can be accommodated and celebrated in textual forms and can be considered a form of inscription in itself. In both ethnographic cases (in fact, in all three), the texts in question were ritualized narratives that played on the three-way corollary of violence, reciprocity, and interpretation. With regard to the second claim, the Kaluli and Ilongot narratives prepared us to consider the question of how more familiar texts contain (or fail to contain) incoherence, contradiction, and disruption, and how interpretation exposes these elements.

In *Perry v. Louisiana*, we reconsidered the nature of textual interpretation, particularly in relation to the cultural contexts in which specific texts are composed and read. The case illuminates the corollary relationship between textual and physical violence. It also suggests the extent to which textual interpretation presupposes conflict, not solidarity. Such tensions can be illuminated and transformed by an interpretive process that insists on an analytical distinction between a shared language and shared norms; a reading community is not necessarily a normative community.

One answer to prevailing doubts about the relevance and ethical status of interpretivism, then, might be along the following lines. If legal texts (spoken or written) function with more direct agency than other sorts of texts, it is not because legal language has some mystical power of instantaneous inscription in results, but because legal institutions are sustained, in part, by cultural practices that allow (even require) participants to control or deny the multiplicity of alternative meanings that are available in any text. All institutions face managment problems such as this—it is not a feature of the law alone.

Bourdieu considers the "relations of domination" to be relatively settled and impersonal in state societies with large-scale institutions, as compared with "societies which have no 'self-regulating market' . . . , no educational system, no juridical apparatus, and no state."[75] Some modification of this comparison would seem to be in order. Judging from *Perry v. Louisiana*, it would appear that, in state societies, too, "relations of domination can be set up and maintained only at the cost of strategies which must be endlessly renewed." Such contests take place in a wide variety of forms and contexts.[76] One task of interpretation is that of discovering those denials and strategies of renewal, and transgressing them, constantly reopening the question of how litigants, advocates, judges, wardens, and so forth frame meanings from among the possibilities that language, common sense, and their personal expertise make available. This sort of project has an ethical dimension that emerges from its defense of the premise that texts are meaningful in everyday terms.

Another line of response to critical doubts is suggested by the Ilongot and Kaluli, who worry about the capacity of their traditional

75. Bourdieu, *Outline*, 183.
76. See, for example, the discussion of courts and "popular justice" in Michel Foucault, *Power/Knowledge* (Brighton, Sussex: Harvester Press, 1980), 1–2; numerous additional examples from the ethnology of law can be found in the works cited n. 6, above.

textual forms to express the new forms of violence that they now experience.[77] To borrow an image from the Kaluli, whose *gisaro* poetically plays the seen against the unseen, any text or textual performance exists in some relationship to the possibility that things can happen that are beyond words. For this very reason, as *Perry v. Louisiana* shows, the question of where the limits of the text are is both a practical and an ethical one. That question cannot be settled in theory, but only provisionally in practice, by observation and interpretation.

If I cannot agree with critics' more categorical rejections of the technical and ethical relevance of interpretivists' engagements with the law, it is not because I do not share their anguish at what human beings are capable of doing to each other in the name of justice, nor the surreal distance between the tidiness of the page or television screen and the street or battlefield. The "field of pain and death" that Cover sees in the law would seem to be a spacious one that the law shares with other institutional domains and textual genres. Still, it is not law that delivers darkness, but some makers and users of law. It is not interpretivism or literary criticism that conceals the law's power, but habits of reading. It is not legal texts that defy interpretation, but particular uses of them. The textuality of the law may have its own forms and conventions, but its "writtenness," and the nature of reading, connect it to other texts and forms of life. It is

---

77. In general, see George Steiner, *Language and Silence* (New York: Penguin Books, 1967). Steiner evokes the limits of interpretation—silence—in a complex language of accountability.

One of the things I cannot grasp, though I have often written about them, trying to get them into some kind of bearable perspective, is the time relation. At a previous point in rational time, Professor Mehring [later dead at Treblinka] was sitting in his study, speaking to his children, reading books, passing his hand over a white tablecloth on Friday evening.... But in what sense? Precisely at the same hour in which Mehring ... was being done to death, the overwhelming plurality of human beings, two miles away on the Polish farms, five thousand miles away in New York, were sleeping or eating or going to a film or making love or worrying about the dentist. This is where my imagination balks. The two orders of simultaneous experience are so different, so irreconcilable to any common norm of human values, their coexistence is so hideous a paradox—Treblinka *is* both because some men have built it and almost all other men let it be—that I puzzle over time. Are there, as science fiction and Gnostic speculation imply, different species of time in the same world, "good times" and enveloping folds of inhuman time, in which men fall into the slow hands of living damnation? ... [At] Treblinka ... the painted clock [on the rail station platform] pointed to three. (192)

not culpability and innocence that distinguish the law's texts from texts of other kinds, but the public power and authority of their respective experts. Interpretation is a form of action. "Meaning" and "shared understandings" are not references to some comfortable or transcendant communion. Ethnography, literature, art—these are not routes of escape, but modes of critical engagement, especially in a violent world.

Time, Inequality, and Law's Violence

Douglas Hay

Describing the law as word may be to ignore, as Robert Cover pointed out in one of his last essays, the law as deed and the necessary bond between the two. His dominant image was the pyramid of carefully constructed state violence, at the apogee of which sits the judge. Judicial authority is transmitted down through the inferior layers of the administration of justice, the wardens, bailiffs, executioners, and others, and Cover appeared to celebrate, in some degree, the judge's command of violence. That the deed of the executioner waits on his word is a triumph, of a kind, of social organization: law's power and law's legitimacy both rely on that articulated hierarchy of violent domination, obedient to command. On it depends the curtailment of popular violence, the subordination of private revenge to the ordered and justified violence of the state; on it depends the rationality of that violence. But to ignore the violence is to ignore a central (the central?) fact about law, its distinctiveness as discursive practice.[1]

Cover's image of the pyramid was brilliantly apposite to his critique of accounts that reduce law to interpretive gambits between wordsmiths. The sentence of the judge is meaningless without the

---

1. Robert M. Cover, "Violence and the Word," *Yale Law Journal* 95 (1986): 1601. See also Cover's related article, "The Bonds of Constitutional Interpretation: Of the Word, the Deed, and the Role," *Georgia Law Review* 20 (1986): 815. I had the honor to know Bob Cover slightly during a year spent at Yale Law School in 1979–80, and, like all who knew him and read his work, I experienced a great sense of loss at his death. I am grateful to John Beattie, Harry Glasbeek, Reuben Hasson, and Michael Mandel, who made critical suggestions or provided contemporary comparisons. On the roots of U.S. preoccupation with the judicial control of death sentences, see n. 43, below.

wardens and the hangmen. Of course, we can, and increasingly some people do, choose to describe even executions as focal occasions of shared social understandings, understandings even shared by the man or woman in unimaginable pain.[2] To do so, however, is somehow a distancing rather than an understanding, a false equation. Cover, a man who had experienced imprisonment in the civil rights movement, found accounts of the law that reduce it to shared (or even contested) interpretive structures to be simply wrong. He explicitly protested against "grotesque" readings of the apparently consensual participation of defendants as signifying a shared understanding of the event. In the shadow of the prison, the accused (and even more the convict) is governed by the fear of pain, the context of massive, violent domination.[3] The relationship of executioner and capital convict, or torturer and victim, or judge and accused, while intimate, is highly unlikely to be one of shared discursive practice of any kind, let alone a solidary one. Law, and especially criminal law, seeks to prevent the victim of law from generating a public version of his or her life's argument, and law is usually sucessful. The public version is, almost always, law's word, and law's word is bounded by law's silences, a point to which I shall return.

The pyramid, then, is a compelling metaphor of hierarchical organization and also of the crushing weight of law. In other ways, however, it would be an inadequate image for exploring law's violence. As a description of the social significance of that violence it is teleological in its implication of a blueprint, formalist in its apparent assumption that the hierarchy of state violence has the same contours as the hierarchy of legal institutions, especially in the degree to which

2. Richard Andrews does so in an essay in a forthcoming collection he edits: the public agonies of the *question préalable* are cast as a redemptive mass, the invention of the humane Dr. Guillotine as the instrument that robs the condemned of dignity.

3. Cover "Violence," 1607. If I understand Carol J. Greenhouse ("Reading Violence," in this volume), she reads him to say that violence does not inform texts, and that reading a text is a sharing of common understandings. Certainly, the latter view appears to be that of some of those whom Cover criticizes, but I do not think it is his. And it is clear, as to the former, that violence shapes large tracts of any society's popular and elite cultures, and their constructions of meaning, including ours and those of the Ilongot and Kaluli. Cover's argument seems to me to make neither of the points Greenhouse finds in it. Cover emphatically agrees that readings of legal acts are arbitrary, multivocal, and the rest of it, but those of the legal professionals and judges are the public ones, and often appear to be the only ones. Also see n. 83, below.

it suggests that law always creates violence from above, knowingly and deliberately, when much evidence about policing shows courts ratifying, by silence, violence initiated below.[4] Above all, it is static, with perhaps unintended connotations of fixed stability. For historians, the principal questions must be how the violence of state law fluctuates over time, and why; how determinative of social relations it is in its manifold forms; and what relationship it bears, in origin and development, to other aspects of the state. From this perspective, the formalist pyramid dissolves into shifting images of fluctuating violence, a violence less predictably obedient to command. The picture is complicated when we add the ways in which civil law, as well as criminal, turns the judicial word into the violent deed.

The reasons for changes in law's violence, then, is one of my inquiries here: change over that midrange of duration that is, in practice, most historians' Time: centuries and decades, rather than millenia or years. In addition, all Cover's work testified to his passionate belief that the hierarchy of law had important congruences with other hierarchies of power. That is my second theme: how we explain, in time, the ways in which organizations of word-governed state violence have reflected and helped to construct specific social inequalities. The examples come mostly from eighteenth- and nineteenth-century England, with which I am most familiar, but the title of this lecture series seemed an invitation to speculate as well as to generalize, and I shall venture some U.S. comparisons.[5] The themes are punishment, social inequality, and silencing. Law in our tradition, not only in its administration but in its very categories, has often incorporated socially destructive force.

The Incidence of Punishment

Until recently, we have had little sense of how deep the penetration of law's violence has been over past centuries. Even the death penalty is difficult to track, for a variety of reasons: recording practices; the

---

4. But see Cover, "Violence," 1621 n. 48, 1624 n. 58.

5. These must be my excuses for the extent of references to my own work, published and unpublished, and for the errors I have no doubt made in interpreting the U.S. experience to a U.S. audience. I am grateful to Amherst College and the Mellon Foundation for the opportunity to do so, and to Austin Sarat for organizing the series.

interpretation of aggravated forms peculiar to some periods and some
societies (how much more punitive or significant is hanging followed
by hanging in chains or dissection, or is breaking on the wheel, than
a simple death on the gallows?);⁶ or even definitional problems (e.g.,
whether lynchings condoned by authority are to count as part of
law's violence also).⁷ If such problems surround accounts of the death
penalty, there are even greater ones when we consider the whole
range of premodern secondary punishments, from pillorying to whip-
ping to imprisoning. And we could argue that even more important
are the ways in which (both in the past and now) law's violence has
been enacted in the doctrines and legislation of civil law that sustained
authority, hierarchy, and inequality. The reluctance of ecclesiastical
courts in early nineteenth-century Britain to provide relief to abused
wives in the absence of physical violence (the judges counseled submission) is one instance.⁸ Another is the insistence of judges in all
the common law countries in the same period that the injured worker
should be almost always barred, under the doctrines of voluntary
assumption of risk, contributory negligence, and the fellow servant
rule, from suing the employer, and that the family of the dead worker
should be similarly barred from legal recompense.⁹ That economic
inequality was irrelevant in contracts of employment, that the worker
desperate to keep his job who agreed to dangerous conditions did so
voluntarily, that somehow the wage he had agreed to mystically
incorporated his assessment of the risks: the judges (and legal counsel
for the railway companies) held these truths to be self-evident, particularly in England. Such doctrines were also sustained by overt
penal sanctions to enforce employment contracts: breach by the
worker (as an individual, or joined with fellow workers in a strike)
resulted in more terms of imprisonment, in some English counties in

6. See D. Hay, "The Meanings of the Criminal Law in Quebec, 1764–1774," in
Crime and Criminal Justice in Europe and Canada, ed. L. A. Knafla (Waterloo, Ont.:
Wilfrid Laurier Press, 1981).

7. R. M. Brown, *Strain of Violence: Historical Studies of American Violence
and Vigilantism* (New York: Oxford University Press, 1975), chap. 7.

8. See A. J. Hammerton, "Victorian Marriage and the Law of Matrimonial
Cruelty," *Victorian Studies* 33, no. 2 (1990): 273–75; the author goes on to explain
the evolution of the law toward a companionate ideal.

9. See P. W. J. Bartrip and S. B. Burman, *The Wounded Soldiers of Industry:
Industrial Compensation Policy 1833–1897* (Oxford: Clarendon Press, 1983), 97–125;
"Comment: The Creation of a Common Law Rule: The Fellow Servant Rule, 1837–
1860," *University of Pennsylvania Law Review* 132 (1984): 579ff.

the early nineteenth century, than the courts inflicted for all ordinary larcenies.[10] We can never quantify the resultant human suffering imposed by the courts in these and other ways, except to say that it was immense.

Even when we return to the relative simplicities of capital punishment and can establish, with some degree of certainty, the numbers of men and women hanged or beheaded or burned, for felony or treason, by the state, we doubt any simple positive assertion that this is a measure of law's violence. For the meaning of such judicial violence to contemporaries is what we have the greatest difficulty reconstructing.

But let us be simple-minded about this, at least as a beginning. I want to construct some tentative arguments about long-term changes, and that can only be done by unapologetic oversimplification. Let us assume that a hanging in England in 1592 is the same thing as a hanging in 1792 or, indeed, an electrocution in the United States in 1992. Let us also assume that the average daily prison population over the last century or so is a similar measure of the coercive force of criminal law.[11]

The English figures appear to show a very high number of executions in the late sixteenth and early seventeenth centuries, perhaps 500 to 1,000 per year; numbers rose even higher in the 1620s, during a short-term crisis. Thereafter, there was a decline about the mid-1600s (or possibly a little later) to a remarkably stable average rate of about 100 per year throughout the country that endured throughout the eighteenth century, until the 1820s. Who was being executed did change: until then, about 75 percent of executions were for property offenses. Only in the 1830s did murderers come to dominate the scaffold, and only after 1830 did the total number executed decline to the very low level that characterized England until the abolition

---

10. D. Hay, "Masters and Servants, Justices and Judges: The Law of Master and Servant in England in the Eighteenth and Nineteenth Centuries" (paper presented to the Postgraduate Seminar on Law and Labour in the Commonwealth, Institute of Commonwealth Studies, University of London, 1988), 11.

11. The argument is partly about short-run change and very long-run trends. I have expressed doubt about the meaning of the latter, with respect to historical series of prosecutions for theft, but, in the present case, the differences in magnitude, the nature of trends within particular centuries, and the focus on the recorded incidence of punishment (rather than a postulated underlying process as in the case of theft) seem to me to justify the exercise. See D. Hay, "War, Dearth and Theft: the Record of the English Courts," *Past and Present* 95 (May, 1982): 123–24.

of capital punishment in the 1960s.[12] Throughout this period, there was, of course, a massive growth in population; the rate, therefore, declined even more markedly.

That decline in capital punishment for theft merged with the extension of transportation (in the late seventeenth and early eighteenth centuries) and finally the invention and rapid expansion of a network of prisons and penitentiaries a hundred years later, a revolution that is the basis for our most important forms of institutionalized legal violence to this day. The most rapid decline in capital punishment (between the 1820s and 1840s) was accompanied, in England, by the fastest increase in total prosecutions (and hence punishment): sevenfold to the 1840s, an increase in the per capita rate of four-and-a-half times.[13] We cannot (given the control/crime conundrum) say that crime necessarily increased; but we can say that, in the early nineteenth century, the noncapital range of law's violence in England undoubtedly was greatly magnified. Executions still took place for murder and arson and a few other offenses; transportation to Australia continued (although with declining numbers); meanwhile, custodial sentences rapidly increased in absolute number until the 1870s, amounting, in general terms, to a high plateau of per capita imprisonment for the whole period from the 1820s to the 1870s.[14] But the incomplete statistics for prosecutions suggest that, when all kinds of punishments are taken into account, the courts were most active in trying and sentencing offenders in the 1840s.[15] All the elements of law's violence that an organized police force can bring to bear informally was extended also: the numbers of policemen in English society increased dramatically, with the greatest increase in the decade before 1871.

What followed in England (as in many Western countries, although not the United States) was striking. Sometime between the 1840s and the 1860s a reversal took place: a long, secular decline in

---

12. D. Hay, "Capital Punishment in England, 1750–1832: A Quantitative Analysis" (paper presented to the American Society for Legal History, Toronto, October, 1986). I shall publish a detailed exposition of the sources and the figures.

13. V. A. C. Gatrell, "The Decline of Theft and Violence in Victorian and Edwardian England," in *Crime and the Law in Western Societies: Historical Essays,* ed. V. A. C. Gatrell, B. Lennon, and G. Parker (London: Europa, 1980), 239.

14. Gatrell, "Decline," appendix B; Malcolm Ramsay, "Two Centuries of Imprisonment," *Home Office Research Bulletin* 14 (1982): 45–47.

15. Gatrell, "Decline," 283, 303–4.

prosecution and then punishment that persisted until the early twentieth century. Prisons built in the 1840s and full in the 1850s and
1860s began to empty: the total prison population followed a largely
falling trend after 1880 until World War I.[16] Transportation ended by
midcentury, imprisonment terms gradually became shorter, and
imprisonment itself was increasingly replaced by fines.[17] Capital punishment had become increasingly attenuated, in numbers and in visible impact, falling to the very small numbers already noted, and,
after 1868, hidden behind prison walls, and then even further
obscured by increasing censorship of press accounts. Only in the first
decade of the twentieth century was there a slight reversal in this
trend of declining punishment: in 1906–10, prosecutions and imprisonment increased significantly, to the level of twenty years before.
It then dropped again, until World War II.[18]

I shall return to the later twentieth-century experience in a
moment, but first, how do we explain these changes over the long
term?

Inequality and Law's Violence

The points of high repression thus far identified are the early decades
of the seventeenth century; several peaks in the eighteenth century,
notably the 1780s and 1800–1801; the period after 1815 to the 1850s,
probably peaking in the 1840s; and the very beginning of the twentieth century. The most plausible explanations for them all revolve
around economic changes that provoked crime, and/or a fear of
crime, including vagrancy, theft, and public disorder. We can sum
up those economic changes as *increases in social inequality*. The
nature of those increases differed. In many instances, the evidence
suggests that those in the poorer half of the population were pushed
nearer to subsistence or below that level. In others, their stagnant
earnings stood in violent contrast to a great increase in income (and,
of course, wealth) higher in the social structure. We do not need to
pursue complicated definitions of absolute and relative deprivation
(and the sources for earlier centuries do not usually allow for such

---

16. Ramsay, "Two Centuries," 47.
17. Gatrell, "Decline," 303 and table B3.
18. Ramsay, "Two Centuries," 47; Gatrell, "Decline," 304.

sophistications) if we concede that both kinds of changes are the clearest indicators, to those who suffer them, that they have little power and run great risks in times of economic change.[19]

The quantitative evidence is often partly conjectural, but the pattern is persistent. The heavy use of capital punishment in Tudor and early Stuart England (say, 1500 to 1640) occurred during a period of rapid population growth and a decline in real wages, a conjunction that impoverished laborers and massively increased vagrancy of a kind that greatly alarmed the authorities. Only six capital statutes were enacted between 1327 and 1509, but thirty, among them those most used for the next two centuries, became law between 1509 and 1660. More important, great economic distress seems to be closely correlated with particular peaks in the violence of the gallows. The most notable, the large numbers of executions in the 1620s and early 1630s, are closely associated with food shortages, loss of access to land, the culmination of a decade of high food prices and trade depression, and the anger of the poor.[20] They are also associated with a great sense of insecurity on the part of the propertied and government. This conjunction of want and fear occurred at a period when there was an unusually large proportion of young men, those between 15 and 24 years old, in the population, the age cohort most associated with crime, particularly so in times of lack of work.[21]

The rest of the seventeenth century, when capital punishment for theft fell markedly (to the level that was to be maintained throughout the eighteenth century), was a time in which real wages markedly improved and population stagnated. In short, the demand for even

---

19. On recent work suggesting the importance of relative inequality, see n. 59, below.

20. Peter H. Lindert, "English Living Standards, Population Growth, and Wrigley-Schofield," *Explorations in Economic History* 20 (1983): 149; Leon Radzinowicz, *A History of English Criminal Law and its Administration from 1750* (London: Stevens and Sons, 1948), 1:4; J. S. Cockburn, *A History of English Assizes 1558–1714* (Cambridge: Cambridge University Press, 1972), 131; James Sharpe, *Crime in Seventeenth-Century England: A County Study* (Cambridge: Cambridge University Press, 1983), chap. 9, for high rates in Essex 1620–34; Sharpe, *Crime in Early Modern England 1550–1750* (New York: Longman, 1984), 63–65; Buchanan Sharp, *In Contempt of all Authority: Rural Artisans and Riot in the West of England, 1586–1660* (Berkeley: University of California Press, 1980), chaps. 2–4.

21. E. A. Wrigley and R. S. Schofield, *The Population History of England 1541–1871* (Cambridge, Mass.: Harvard University Press, 1981), 418.

unskilled labor was probably high.[22] Law's violence stabilized at the new, much lower average rate of about 100 executions per year, a rate that was to endure until shortly before the repeal of most of the capital statutes in the early nineteenth century. Throughout this period of low, relatively stable numbers, also a time of generally higher wages, there were short periods of dramatic increases in the number of hangings. All coincide with great or increasing inequality, either through increased unemployment or a great decrease in real wages. The most notable causes were large demobilizations at the conclusion of wars and extreme want in times of harvest dearth. Some crises were short term: the harvest failure of 1800–1801 caused the largest number of executions seen for over a century, but was isolated in its effects. On the other hand, the most prolonged period of high execution rates in the eighteenth century was one in which short-term suffering and anxieties merged with a longer crisis: the mid-1780s, when the temporary cessation of transportation due to the American revolution, and the loss of the colonies, heightened the sense of crisis in government about both its legitimacy and the administration of the law. Government and judicial policy was to impose the death penalty with utmost harshness.[23] Incidentally, the large numbers of hangings in Britain allowed the American revolutionaries to characterize capital punishment as pathological, a symptom of the inequality and tyranny caused by monarchy, aristocracy, and great wealth.[24]

For the nineteenth century, inconsistencies in the statistics, the growth of police forces, and the massive changes in economic structure arguably make interpretation more difficult than for either the eighteenth or twentieth centuries.[25] The best account we have of the

---

22. Lindert, "Living Standards," 149–50; Wrigley and Schofield, *Population History*, 408, 418.

23. See the sources in note 12, and D. Hay, "The Laws of God and the Laws of Man: Lord George Gordon and the Death Penalty," in a forthcoming collection edited by Robert Malcolmson and John Rule (London: Merlin Press).

24. Louis Masur, *Rites of Execution: Capital Punishment and the Transformation of American Culture, 1776–1865* (New York: Oxford University Press, 1989), chap. 3.

25. Economic historians have debated, for many generations, the effects of the demographic and structural changes of early industrialization in England, and in particular the effect on real wages. Such aggregates are very problematic for the study of crime levels, however, as the experience of the poorest, or rapid movements

nineteenth-century statistical picture concludes that the great increase in prosecution and punishment levels in the early nineteenth century was undoubtedly partly caused by increased policing and prosecution, but peaks in punishment primarily reflected economic conditions, notably the impact of depression, high food prices, and unemployment on the poorest.[26] We also know that as the cohort of young persons swelled (as had happened in the 1620s), the number of crimes coming before the courts between 1820 and 1840 increased, and real wages, particularly for the poorest, probably fell significantly. Income inequality also greatly increased, from its eighteenth-century levels up to 1851.[27]

Then came the striking Victorian decline in punishment, from the 1870s to the turn of the century. The standard of living in this period rose by 30 percent or more, as unions were able to resist wage reductions at a time of falling prices.[28] The decline in prosecution and punishment can be largely explained by a decline in theft; the cause seems likely to be a diffusion of economic benefits to the lowest levels of the working class and the smoothing out of cyclical economic movements (which had been violent in the first part of the century). In particular, price and unemployment cycles did not reinforce each other, as they had in the first half of the century when high food prices and loss of work had often coincided to produce great suffering among the poorest.[29] There was also undoubtedly an effect of the decline of the proportion of young men in the population from the very high levels of the 1820–40 period.[30]

---

of smaller groups into immiseration, can produce large changes in the level of prosecuted crime.

26. Gatrell, "Decline," 308ff. This knowledgeable and convincing analysis was based on a laborious reconstruction and recalculation from the voluminous, complex, and initially unenlightening official statistics.

27. Wrigley and Schofield, Population History, 216, 418; Lindert, "Living Standards," 145; N. F. R. Crafts, British Economic Growth during the Industrial Revolution (Oxford: Clarendon Press, 1985), 104–7.

28. Francois Bedarida, A Social History of England, 1851–1975 (London: Methuen, 1979), 135.

29. Gatrell, "Decline," 308ff.

30. Wrigley and Schofield, Population History, 418; Lindert, "Living Standards," 145. On the most tenuous evidence, one account attributes the Victorian decline to an increased sophistication at reintegrative shaming; see John Braithwaite, Crime, Shame and Reintegration (Cambridge: Cambridge University Press, 1989), 115ff. He offers no convincing explanation of why Victorian social institutions were more capable of doing this, or more likely to, than those of the early nineteenth century,

Finally, the rise in larceny figures (and in punishment) just before World War I reversed the decline of the later Victorian years. This was a period of strikes, social disorder, and conflict; it was also a period of hardship: between 1908 and 1914, inflation, depression, and falling real wages marked a sharp reversal of the later Victorian experience, a return to the earlier pattern of subsistence and employment crises that were particularly hard on the poor. Intensified policing, and an alarmed middle-class public, undoubtedly affected the figures on prosecutions and punishments; we should note, however, that their impact was somewhat moderated by sentencing reforms introduced by a reforming Liberal government that was also more committed to social welfare.[31]

It is evident that this summary of punishment levels and economic pressures over three centuries is impressionistic, based on imperfect statistics, and takes very little account of large structural changes between widely different periods. But it can be said that, within shorter runs of years and throughout the whole three centuries, our current knowledge suggests that the violence of the law, measured by prosecutions and punishments, was largely determined by the need to contain the effects, direct and indirect, of substantial social inequality, particularly changes in its incidence.

It is worth pausing at this point to note two things: a broad coincidence of state violence with interpersonal violence, and a contrast with the United States. Here, the argument is more speculative, suggesting that state violence is not simply a reaction to the need to contain disorder generated by social inequality, but that it generates, in turn, interpersonal violence on a wider scale.

A number of historians have remarked that scattered studies show a long-term decline in the homicide rate in England over the same period of time, 1600 to 1900. Although there is argument about how

---

nor makes any attempt to consider the kinds of economic explanations offered by Gatrell, in spite of the fact that Braithwaite's theory includes relative blockage of economic opportunity for the poor as an important explanatory factor. (He does note in passing the possible importance of demographic change [113].) The interacting effects of greater inequality—higher crime—stigmatization, and lesser inequality—lower crime—reintegration, provided for in his theory, probably better explain the late Victorian decline.

31. Gatrell, "Decline," 305, 313–14, and table A4. Divisions in middle-class opinion in this period may have been reflected in simultaneous Parliamentary reform and harsher enforcement of the law in many parts of the country.

much and even more argument about the reasons for it, it seems likely that the rate at which Englishmen and women killed each other fell to a fourth of what it had been. The sharpest decline took place at the beginning of the eighteenth century; the drop was delayed a little longer in London. The longest series of figures, for the county of Kent, shows a sudden halving of the rate at the beginning of the eighteenth century, and another halving beginning with the decade ending 1831. Thereafter, the pattern was the modern one: very low rates of homicide, at least in U.S. terms.[32]

A number of explanations have been offered. Virtually all end in references to increasing civility, aversion to cruelty, and self-restraint, manifested in everything from the decline of duelling to the founding of the Royal Society for the Prevention of Cruelty to Animals and the enactment of factory legislation. Causal sequences are unclear: as violence declined, upper-class and then all public opinion found violence less acceptable. The argument, which often appears circular in its formulation, can perhaps be interpreted as one of constant interaction. With respect to the violence of the law, it has been suggested that this shift in public opinion, apparently reinforced as actual levels of violence (including homicide) declined, eventually made possible the state's abandonment of most capital punishment.[33]

I want to suggest a different causal sequence. To the extent that we can rely on the statistics of both hangings and homicide, our two "best indicators" of law's violence and people's violence respectively, it appears that the two historic declines in the state's use of capital punishment in England *preceded* the two very similar drops in homicide rates, by perhaps a generation or two in each case.[34] This suggests the hypothesis that the violence of the state may be a powerful *determinant* of violence in a society. It is entirely congruent with the argument of the opponents of capital punishment in the

---

32. J. M. Beattie, *Crime and the Courts in England 1660-1800* (Princeton: Princeton University Press, 1986), 108, table 3.4; James Cockburn, "Patterns of Violence in English Society: Homicide in Kent 1560-1985," *Past and Present* 130 (February, 1991): 78, table 1. All authors stress the many problems with the figures, but agree that the change in orders of magnitude probably reflects a real change in violent behavior.

33. Beattie, *Crime*, 132–39.

34. Above, text at notes 12 and 32.

early nineteenth century in England, who thought that the agonies displayed at public executions destroyed the moral sentiments of those who witnessed them; indeed, it was in large measure this upper-class fear of brutalizing the mob that figured in debates for the ending, first, of capital punishment for theft, and second, public executions entirely.[35] If the argument has merit, we would expect, perhaps, to see the kind of delay between declines in state violence and societal violence of the kind I have identified: a generation or so.[36] The fact that England abandoned hangings for thefts in two decisive steps, followed by two similar, decisive shifts in homicide rates, after a significant delay, suggests the possibility that highly public, state-sanctioned death is a powerful reinforcement, at the very least, for resort to violence throughout a given society, with enduring effects perhaps analogous to the intergenerational violence that seems to resonate through families for a long time.[37]

Perhaps a comment on this suggestion is the very different pattern of prosecuted homicide in the United States, particularly in the nineteenth and twentieth centuries. The rate increased after the Civil War, and moved through several cycles of large-scale increases, particularly around the turn of the century and after World War II.[38] For most of the period, it was heavily concentrated in the southern states, where general levels of interpersonal violence and interracial violence

---

35. Randall McGowen, "The Image of Justice and Reform of the Criminal Law in Early Nineteenth-Century England," *Buffalo Law Review* 35 (1983): 89–125; David D. Cooper, *The Lesson of the Scaffold: The Public Execution Controversy in Victorian England* (London: Allen Lane, 1974); text at pp. 156–57.

36. Within the new, lower level of homicide from the 1830s, there was another sustained drop from the 1880s, about a generation after the end of public executions in 1868. See Cockburn, "Patterns," 78, table 1, for the figures.

37. This is presented as a hypothesis; to call it more requires closer consideration of many possibilities. The decline in the later seventeenth century of both social and state violence, for example, is probably also correlated with a general increase in the standard of living of the poorest in the late seventeenth and early eighteenth centuries. Other concurrent changes, perhaps including a Foucauldian substitution of discipline for spectacle (although this is far from established for the period of the earlier change), might also be involved. See also p. 157.

38. Ted Robert Gurr, "Historical Trends in Violent Crime: A Critical Review of the Evidence," *Crime and Justice: An Annual Review of Research* 3 (1981): 315ff. Gurr notes that the rate is much higher for African-Americans. However, given the other characteristics of southern criminal law, it seems certain that, in those states, black homicide rates were exaggerated and white homicide rates minimized by prosecutorial practice, and that both were high by northern standards.

were sometimes remarked on in horror by English visitors in the nineteenth century.[39] In the North, in such cities as overwhelmingly white Philadelphia, a decline in the nineteenth century in homicide rates rather resembles the English pattern.[40]

Meanwhile, in the South, African-Americans underwent a powerful education in the violence of the law, or what amounted to law for them. Lynching disappeared in England after the mid-eighteenth century, but was an endemic presence in the U.S. South from the end of slavery until the late 1920s. Lynchings in England in the early 1700s were mostly of suspected witches, they were rare, and they were repressed by the authorities, who, in the eighteenth century, prosecuted for murder, apparently with pressure for the condemned to renounce as superstition their belief in witchcraft.[41] Lynchings in the U.S. South, on the other hand, were massive public affairs, clearly openly tolerated by most public authorities in the states in which they were most common. To that extent, we can consider them a form of law's violence, exacerbated by torture and mutilation.[42] They constituted a massive reinforcement of racial oppression in the South between 1882 and 1929, with the ratio of black victims rising to 90 percent in the early twentieth century.[43] The rate of lynchings of African-Americans was almost exactly the rate of public executions in England in the eighteenth century.[44] A southern lynching usually

---

39. For European attitudes, see Ray Allen Billington, *Land of Savagery, Land of Promise: The European Image of the American Frontier in the Nineteenth Century* (New York: Norton, 1981), 267ff.; for their basis in fact, see Edward Ayers, *Vengeance and Justice: Crime and Punishment in the Nineteenth-Century American South* (New York: Oxford University Press, 1984), passim.

40. Roger Lane, "Urban Homicide in the Nineteenth Century: Some Lessons for the Twentieth," in James A. Inciardi and Charles E. Faupel, eds., *History and Crime: Implications for Criminal Justice Policy* (Beverly Hills: Sage, 1980), 92ff.

41. Witchcraft ceased to be an offense in England in 1736, and official prosecutions ended a generation earlier.

42. Arthur F. Raper, *The Tragedy of Lynching* (Chapel Hill: University of North Carolina Press, 1933); Donald L. Grant, *The Anti-Lynching Movement: 1883-1932* (San Francisco: R and E Research Associates, 1975), passim.

43. In the 1880s, about 40 percent; 1890s, about 70 percent; 1901–29, 90 percent. Total number of lynchings, 4,564, of which 3,285 were of African-Americans (United States Bureau of the Census, *Historical Statistics of the United States: Colonial Times to 1970* [Washington, D.C.: U.S. Government Printing Office, 1975, pt. 1, 422, ser. H 1168–70]).

44. The annual average in eighteenth-century England, of about 100 on an

meant extensive torture and mutilation of the victim before death, far exceeding the public violence that concluded some cases in eighteenth-century England.[45] If official public executions are added to lynchings,[46] presumably the level of law's violence in the early twentieth century in the U.S. South approaches that of England in the seventeenth century, before the great decline in official and societal violence began there.

To lump together lynching and legal execution may jar, because the curtailment of lynching has usually been seen as a triumph of control by the law.[47] But the distinction was irrelevant to those who suffered lynch law and to those who watched it: the local state could not protect black victims and, indeed, often connived in their murder. If we are looking for an explanation of historically high rates of murder in the South, the argument that public state violence is a powerful determinant of private violence, an argument that I have suggested may be relevant to England in preceding centuries, seems likely to be part of the U.S. explanation also. The effects also seem likely to have lasted longer through the generations in a society in which white racism continued to concentrate the experience of power-lessness and to employ less obvious forms of the violence that arose from the will to dominate that was so utterly clear in the social dynamics of lynching in the South.[48]

Englishmen, it should be added, dominated and colonized their "blacks" with the terror of the state too, to preserve the inferior status

---

average population of about 7 million, is 1.4/100,000, which is also the rate per 100,000 of the black population, based on lynchings 1889–1900, and the black population of the southern states in 1900 (*Historical Statistics*, pt. 1, 24–37, ser. A 195–209).

45. And in England, only after death, in the form of public dissection of murderers after 1752; for a variety of other offenses, including robbing the mails, "hanging in chains," that is suspending the corpse to rot in an iron framework, was also used.

46. The statistics in William J. Bowers, *Executions in America* (Lexington, Mass.: Lexington Books, 1973), 40 and appendix A, are not broken down by race for all the relevant jurisdictions for this period.

47. A distinctively American fact that must inform the comments of both Cover and Tushnet.

48. If higher rates of homicide committed by blacks are more than a statistical artifact of prosecution policies (see n. 37), the differential experience of lynch law may provide a large part of the explanation, on the assumption that the contribution to societal violence made by state violence is greatest on those groups who suffer it most; see also n. 51.

of a dominated labor force; and they evoked violence in response. But in the seventeenth to nineteenth centuries, they did so in such places as Ireland and the West Indies and India. Unlike the United States, the British state, in the nineteenth and twentieth centuries, never exposed a part of its own population to such massive, discriminating, and public official violence as occurred in the U.S. South.

Finally, we may ask why England so decisively curtailed capital punishment in the end. The movement to abolish capital punishment for theft in the early nineteenth century was motivated by a complex of concerns on the part of the Parliamentary elite: fear of corrupting a dangerous populace through exposure to state violence, fear of delegitimating the law in the eyes of the people, humanitarian instincts, political advantage. In a highly undemocratic society, the gradual extension of such opinions in a small parliamentary elite created a parliamentary opinion that was to endure; the declining, and very low, homicide rate in English society strengthened it and prevented the development of a strong popular demand for capital punishment. In all these respects, the United States differed: the power of a much more popular electorate, the cycles of growth in homicide rates in the nineteenth and twentieth centuries, and the racial dimension of both homicide and capital punishment all sustained a culture of law's violence, of social violence, that Mark Tushnet suggests cannot now be restrained by abolition. "A world without the death penalty is too far from our own for the law to bridge the gap."[49] He suggests that total legislative abolition in the United States would, were it possible, produce pathologies elsewhere in the administration of the law and the social order. The language is obscure and the analogies psychoanalytic, but the history of lynching surely must be inferred.

To summarize the argument to this point, the experiences of powerlessness and of powerfulness that we call inequality, particularly increases in its magnitude, have historically produced high levels of property crime. Those increases have been most marked when the proportion of young men in the society (or in its poorest subpopulation) has been large. The state, through much of the early modern period, resorted to highly visible staged demonstrations of law's vio-

---

49. Mark Tushnet, "Reflections on Capital Punishment: One Side of an Uncompleted Discussion," *Journal of Law and Religion* 7 (1989): 30, in an article commenting on Robert Cover's attitude toward the death penalty.

lence to deal with such property crime, the most dramatic of which was capital punishment. The level of that form of state violence seems closely related to levels of homicide, but when state violence declined, homicide levels did so also, after a generation or so. We infer that state violence may have been an important cause (or perhaps necessary condition) of levels of violence (as well as inequality) in the past. Law's violence (if we include lynching) continued for longer and at a higher rate in the United States than in England, and one of its effects was apparently to encourage private violence. Meanwhile, in England, punishment (in the form of imprisonment) continued to be highly correlated with changes in inequality, corresponding to cyclical changes in the economy, up to the early twentieth century. It must be reiterated that this is a sketch of an argument, based on admittedly contested and incomplete statistics and often ill-specified mechanisms. But over the long term, the recurrences of these patterns appear with striking regularity.

Does the argument from inequality, from powerlessness, obtain in the twentieth century? A number of studies provide evidence consistent with the longer historical record. From the 1920s to the present in England and Canada, correlations of punishment with the trade cycle are close.[50] The most recent study for England shows that economic changes that affect income, probably particularly among the poorer paid, are very highly correlated with property crime from 1950 to the present. That is, decline in the rate of growth of legitimate income produces an almost exactly equal increase in the growth rate of property crime and, hence, of punishment through imprisonment.[51] The most spectacular increase in punishment levels has been very recent, in both Britain and the United States. In the latter, the number of prisoners in state and federal institutions doubled in the 1980s.[52]

---

50. Hermann Mannheim, quoted in Gatrell, "Decline," 311; for Canada, see James Huzel, "The Incidence of Crime in Vancouver During the Great Depression," *B.C. Studies* 69/70 (1986): 211–48; Michael Mandel, "The Great Repression: Criminal Punishment in the Nineteen-Eighties," in *Criminal Justice: Sentencing Issues and Reforms*, ed. L. Samuelson and B. Schissel (Toronto: Garamond Press, 1990).

51. But a decrease in "personal" offenses, largely offenses against the person; see Simon Field, *Trends in Crime and their Interpretation: A Study of Recorded Crime in Post-War England and Wales*, Home Office Research Study 119 (London: HMSO, 1990). Moreover, Field points out, for this period it can be shown (through victim studies) that the official crime rates do indeed reflect very closely actual changes in crime. On the significance of relative inequality, see below.

52. *New York Times*, Nov. 26, 1989.

The total of those in custody tripled between 1972 and 1989.[53] And,
as Judge Patricia Wald has pointed out in her essay in this volume,
the adoption of a grid sentencing structure has had, and seems likely
to have, the effect of increasing the average harshness of sentences,
a policy in any case strongly supported by the administration and
by articulate public opinion.[54] The rate of imprisonment has now
reached 426.0 per 100,000. In England and Wales, the total prison
population exceeded the highest Victorian level in about 1960, but
the relevant statistic is again the per capita rate of imprisonment. In
1990, at 97.4 per 100,000, it is within striking distance of the early
Victorian peak of about 120 per 100,000.[55]

Is there any reason to believe that the long-run historical reason
for high punishment levels—social inequality and changes in it—is
a useful explanation now, as it was in earlier centuries, and earlier
decades this century? Poverty is notoriously contested as an absolute
measure; as relative inequality it can be specified with a high degree
of accuracy. We have evidence of greatly increasing inequality of
income. In England, the poorest 10 percent saw their real income
fall by almost 6 percent since 1979, while *average* incomes rose by
over 25 percent. The proportion below half-average income rose from
9 percent to 22 percent of the population.[56] In the United States, from
1973 to 1987, the income share of the richest 20 percent of families
reached 43.7 percent of all national income, while the income share
of the poorest 20 percent of families declined to 4.6 percent from
5.5 percent. From 1977 to 1989, income dropped for 40 percent while
the richest enjoyed an enormous increase.[57] In both countries, the
greatest increases in poverty have been among children and young
people, including the age cohorts most likely to be involved in crime.[58]
The impact of unemployment and low income, in both Britain and

53. *New York Times*, Oct. 13, 1989.

54. Wald, 81–83.

55. Ramsay, "Two Centuries," 47; *Guardian* (London), August 18–19, 1990 and
June 19, 1991. For Canada, see Mandel, "Great Repression," *passim*.

56. *Guardian* (London), July 27, 1990; July 16, 1992. See also Field.

57. *Economist*, November 10, 1990, 19–22; *New York Times*, May 12, 1989;
Reuters, March 6, 1992.

58. A recent congressional study suggests that one-fifth of U.S. children lived
in poverty over the past decade, up from fewer than 15 percent before 1979. That
compared with about 9 percent in Australia and Canada, 3 percent in West Germany,
fewer than 1 percent in Sweden (Reuters, May 11, 1991). In England, the percentage of
poor children more than doubled, to 25 percent (*Guardian* [London], July 16, 1992).

the United States, has fallen disproportionately on black communities that supply the disproportionately large part of the prison populations. In Canada, that has been the case with Canada's native peoples. The experience of powerlessness that comes from being at the bottom of a highly unequal distribution of income has been massive in such populations, even in periods when average incomes were rising.

In short, we have recently experienced the greatest increase in economic inequality in my lifetime (I was born in 1945), and also the greatest increase in punishment levels over the same period. Wider political support for even harsher punishment and for more prison building programs seems likely to make the 1990s even more striking in this respect. We are apparently leaving the high punishment levels of the 1930s behind. We soon may be approaching those of the 1620s.

Thus, law's violence, in the recent as in the more distant past, has coincided with the violence of social and economic inequality, real and perceived, purposive and contingent. The causal connections are undoubtedly multiple and reciprocal, ramifying in the complex social ties between social inequality and fear, resentment, anger, and despair that knit together real crime, perceived crime, and imagined crime into the resonating patterns of street violence and law's violence.[59] The complexity does not end there. For the ways in which the violence of law is experienced generates judgments about the significance of law in general for all those who experience it intimately and also for those for whom it is no more than a word. Such judg-

---

59. Some recent work on the relationship of health to income distribution since World War II is suggestive. It argues that relative inequality within a society is more destructive of health than the average wealth of the society as a whole: life expectancy is higher in Spain and Greece than in the United States, Luxembourg, or the former West Germany for this reason. A comparison of Japan and Britain appears to illustrate the process: as income distribution became more equal in Japan, life expectancy increased; as income came to be distributed more unequally in England, life expectancy decreased. In Britain, class differences in death rates have not been diminished by postwar prosperity; Japan, with the most egalitarian income distribution in the world, now has the highest life expectancy. Relatively small fluctuations in income distribution seem to have quite large effects on health, it is suggested, "partly through the damage which inequality does to human relations, partly through an effect on self-esteem of the difficulty of 'coping,' on stress and insecurity and on the quality of the social fabric more widely" (*Guardian* [London], June 12, 1991); Richard G. Wilkinson, "Income Distribution and Mortality: A 'Natural' Experiment," *Sociology of Health and Illness* 12 (1990): 391–412. On crime and punishment in Japan, see n. 63, below.

ments will be particularly problematic in times (such as ours) of great
inequality, high crime, and a highly punitive criminal law. At such
times there is a heightened importance not only of the physical coercion that follows on the word of law, but of law's evasions, trun-
cations, and misrepresentations of experience.

Inequality and Law's Silence

John Braithwaite has recently argued that a major problem with
Western criminal law is that it is excellent at stigmatizing and excluding the offender through the processes of prosecution, trial, and
imprisonment. (We have seen, indeed, that it is getting ever better
at it, if the growth in prison populations, the erosion of death penalty
protections, and greatly increased policing is any measure.) Braithwaite also argues that Western law is woefully deficient at reinte-
grating the offender into consensual, noncriminal relationships.
Indeed, through its emphasis on punishment, law's violence stig-
matizes so thoroughly that it creates crime: it encourages the growth
of criminal subcultures, of outlaws who have no incentive to find
their way back in.[60] If experience of law's violence, its stigma, is
crimogenic, and if inequality is also, we may expect a significant
proportion of the young male population in recent decades to have
experienced the sharp end of both the law and of economic inequality.
And, indeed, that is the case. In Britain, almost one-third of all
young men, mostly the poorest, now have serious criminal convictions.[61] In North America, I do not know of comparable studies, but
the figures for minority groups are suggestive. In the United States,
nearly one-fourth of African-American males in their twenties were
actually in jail, on parole, or on probation in 1990.[62] In terms of
Braithwaite's theory, such figures imply serious erosion, in a significant part of the population, of attachment to the values of the law,
because our system of criminal law so inadequately allows for for-
giveness and our distribution of income and opportunity is so for-
midably polarized.

---

60. Braithwaite, *Crime*, chaps. 7–10.
61. Home Office Statistical Bulletin, *Criminal Careers of Those Born in 1953, 1958, and 1963* (London: HMSO, 1985), table 1 and p. 13.
62. *Washington Post*, February 27, 1990; *Guardian* (London), February 28, 1990, reporting an interview with Marc Mauer of the Sentencing Project.

Braithwaite's analysis reminds us that our law deals not only in violence, but also in silence. The stories told by a society intent upon stigmatizing and excluding the offender are different than those told when the aim is reintegration and reconciliation.[63] Much of the power of the word was always partially based on its silencing of the dissentient voice of the lawbreaker, and of those who would criticize the violence of the law.[64] In the early modern state, this took many forms, but emblematic was the attempt to achieve a confession of the criminal on the scaffold, or, if one could not be obtained, the publication of an invented statement of contrition. That validation of law's violence was sought, more-or-less eagerly, by all regimes.[65] By the late eighteenth century, the possibility that contrition would not be forthcoming, that there would be too great a sympathy of onlookers and executed, brought significant change, and over the last two centuries we can see a progressive erosion of opportunities for the victim of law's violence to contest the word of the law. In 1782, at the execution of a gang of noted highwaymen (who behaved very well), the press reported with disapproval that one other young convict had shown "hardened insensibility." He had, in fact, calmly unbuttoned, "pissed most complacently," pulled his cap over his eyes, and died defiantly.[66] His act of theater was part of the extended exchange between crowd and condemned that accompanied the trip from Newgate (where the present Old Bailey is located) to Tyburn (near Marble Arch). By the nineteenth century, that theater had been ended. The first stage was the end of the procession to Tyburn the year after our hardened young convict made his statement; by the early nineteenth century, behavior on the scaffold outside Newgate was tightly controlled; in 1868, public hangings ended; finally, in the later nineteenth century, full press reports of executions were forbidden. In the shorter term, during particular periods of crisis such as the 1780s, the authorities prosecuted those who condemned the harshness of the law or of the judges as illegitimate. Lord George Gordon, who wrote of the injustice of execution for theft at the height of the

63. Compare the account of the behavior of Japanese policemen dealing with offenders in Braithwaite, *Crime*, 61–63.

64. As Cover emphasizes.

65. See n. 2, above.

66. D. Hay and R. Paley, eds., *Friends of the Chief Justice: The Osgoode Correspondence in the Archives of the Law Society of Upper Canada* (Toronto: Law Society of Upper Canada, 1990), 122.

hangings of the 1780s, was sentenced to what amounted to imprisonment for life.[67] A rash of seditious libel prosections in the early nineteenth century inhibited Bentham, among others, from publishing criticisms of the law, including capital punishment.

But there are limits to the extent to which one can legitimize a harsh law's violence by silencing testimonies against it.[68] Throughout these four centuries, state violence was often mediated or moderated or rendered partially unnecessary, by actions to render inequality less oppressive or less obviously glaring, to meet some of the demands of the poor or to try to appear to do so. Medieval, Tudor, and Stuart social policy and legislation was always attentive to the need to deal with popular unrest—riot, destruction of property, and especially attacks on the legitimacy of the regime—through the provision of foodstuffs and other acts of government that would relieve the suffering of the poor.[69] That policy was the root meaning of the word *police* until the late eighteenth century: the governance of populations, particularly cities, and the assurance of social peace, in large part through adequate provisioning when high market prices impoverished and starved the poor. A principal policy instrument was the mass of statutes designed to punish those middlemen who profited from the speculative resale or amassing of food: forestallers, regrators, and engrossers, and the early modern attitude of the common law to them was extremely hostile: "A Forestaller is called by my Lord *Coke, Pauperum Depressor & totius Communitatis & Patriae publicus inimicus* (a Depressor of the Poor, and a publick Enemy of the whole Community and to his Country), and therefore is punishable at Common Law." Acting on that assumption was a very large part of the response to the dearth and poverty of the early seventeenth century,

---

67. D. Hay, "The Laws of God and the Laws of Man."

68. In an important sense there was also a progressive silencing of the accused at trial. With the coming of counsel into the criminal trial from the later eighteenth century, and particularly in the nineteenth century, and the elaboration of rules of evidence (designed often to help the defendant), the experience of the accused was put into other words. The word of the court, and of the lawyers, became the word heard there. In that rare kind of prosecution in which the victim became, in important senses, the accused (the rape trial), social constructions of the "respectable woman" also silenced the complainant; see Anna Clark, *Women's Silence Men's Violence: Sexual Assault in England, 1770–1845* (London: Pandora, 1987).

69. Penry Williams, *The Tudor Regime* (Oxford: Oxford University Press, 1979), 185ff., esp. 191–94.

as at other such crises before and after.[70] Until the 1760s, that response was frequent, endorsed by the state at the highest level (through a royal proclamation) and sustained by episodic prosecutions of forestallers. Its logic was that the widespread disorder of riot, historically always prompted by great suffering among the poor, was a danger to the stability of the regime.

But by the time of Adam Smith a new silence began to grow at the heart of both private and public law in England: the excision of judicial rhetoric that attacked the rich profiteer, an abandonment of the policy of conciliation of the poor. The late eighteenth-century food riot crises marked an entirely new development: theories of free markets, by the 1770s, caused Parliament to repeal the statutes against forestallers and, in spite of judicial attempts (opposed by the government) to resurrect the doctrines in the interest of public order in the great dearth of 1800–1801, the old law was dead by 1815. So, too, was much of the Tudor and Stuart legislation that had come to protect skilled labor from competition, repealed by Parliament between 1800 and 1815 against great protest.

The project of political economy for establishing a wholly free market in foodstuffs in England (and other developments that had a similar effect on labor) required the obliteration of a set of widely held practices and expectations in the courts and in Parliament; it also necessitated a significant increment in the police powers of the state to take care of the ensuing protests, protests not only at the abrogation of what were seen to be elements of social justice, but also protests at the perceived (and I think real) increase in inequality that resulted. Once there was an ideological commitment by government to the unrestricted play of market forces and once troops and police could ensure that the state was, for perhaps the first time, not at risk from protest, law's violence increased to deal with the consequences.[71] The government had a strong hand from 1800, when Pitt built barracks in the disturbed manufacturing districts, until the end of the wars in 1815: large numbers of troops dealt with large numbers of rioters. Wartime provided a whole range of ancillary means of force to deal with popular discontent, including conscrip-

---

70. D. Hay, "The State and the Market: Lord Kenyon and Mr. Waddington," *Past and Present,* forthcoming.

71. Hay, "State and Market."

tion. In the 1820s, when it appeared that even the army might be becoming disaffected, the example of an experiment that the British government had been conducting in Ireland, something called a police force, was finally extended to England itself. And we have seen, in the evidence for crime rates of the early nineteenth century, the response of a poor population, exposed to strong cyclical movements in the economy, to their immediate problems of dearth. In short, the centuries-old state response to the demands of the poor—partial accommodation—was much less in evidence. Law became silent on issues of economic inequality. Under an ideological commitment to free markets on the part of both capital and government, Britain turned to an increased use of law's violence as its solution to the problems of inequality in the early nineteenth century. When unmediated market forces bear on the poor, it has been a common solution ever since.

What happens to the image of justice in the process? It is perhaps no coincidence that there was great concern with the legitimacy of law, and particularly with the legitimacy of both capital punishment in the first crisis of ideological commitment to free markets, the period from 1800 to the 1840s, again in the first decade of the twentieth century, and again in the 1980s. The repeal of the capital statutes and the formal extension of the right of counsel in felony trials in the 1830s was conceived by a highly undemocratic parliament of Whig statesmen to be the necessary guarantees of continued consent, by the majority of the population, to the exercise of law's violence. It was accompanied, as we have seen, by a massive expansion in policing and in the provision of prisons. The technology and organization of force was important in containment.[72]

Similar concerns arose in the years of strikes, class politics, and rising crime that, in England, preceded World War I. In this case, a radical Liberal government in fact moderated the force of imprisonment, exchanging some of the most overt forms of control for

---

72. There was considerable success of the new technologies of law's violence in the nineteenth century, as we have seen. It provided the background for a confident assertion of free-market principles in the courts themselves. Historians of contract doctrine date the apogee of freedom of contract in the courts (that is, the abandonment of the unlucky, whether an injured worker or incompetent capitalist), to the period between 1830 and 1870. That was also, as we have seen, the apogee of Victorian imprisonment.

welfare measures.[73] There was a willingness, dating from the 1870s, to meet some of the needs and demands of organized labor and also the poor, stimulated by the belated extension of the franchise in 1867 and 1884, in what had been the least democratic English-speaking government in the world. What had once been coerced from government by the threat of violence, was now to be coerced from government by the threat of violence and the use of the vote. A new set of choices arose about the image of justice in the modern state: the small beginnings of welfare Liberalism versus property-protecting Toryism.[74] In opposing the institution of slightly more generous provisions for the poor, Toryism again invoked English law, and in particular used the fact that it was silent on issues of economic inequality and vociferous on the rights of property. The Liberal government of 1906 to 1910 was accused of the most nefarious conspiracy against property, for providing free school meals, legislating for the unions, initiating the first, tiny, old age pensions provided by the state, and proposing to tax the wealthiest of the landed class. The violent political debates surrounding these issues, at the conception (I shall not say birth) of the welfare state, frequently invoked an image of justice, based on high law, to silence arguments from inequality. A classic instance was the vindication, in Parliament and the high court, of George Archer Shee, who was the son of a retired colonial civil servant and half-brother of a conservative member of Parliament, from the accusation of forging a five-shilling postal order while at naval cadet school.[75] His cause was taken up by Sir Edward Carson, a principal leader of the Tory party and a brilliant barrister, and was used to exemplify the "autocratic action of the state," a state whose collectivist and egalitarian impulses, however feeble, Carson despised and feared.[76]

No other boy kicked out of naval school got such treatment.

73. See David Garland, *Punishment and Welfare: A History of Penal Strategies* (Aldershot, Hants.: Gower, 1985).

74. The issue, as critics pointed out, was not really one of the market any longer: the competitive marketplace of the mid-nineteenth century no longer existed. See Patrick Atiyah, *The Rise and Fall of Freedom of Contract* (Oxford: Clarendon Press, 1979), pt. 3.

75. I have used the accounts in Ewen Montagu, *The Archer-Shee Case*, Celebrated Trials Series (Newton Abbot: David and Charles, 1974); Rodney M. Bennett, *The Archer-Shees Against the Admiralty: The Story behind* The Winslow Boy (London: Robert Hale, 1973).

76. Montagu, *Archer-Shee Case*, 40, 45.

Nor did the many thousands of other boys tried summarily and convicted in 1910 without the benefit of lawyers or juries in the criminal courts. The pretense, of course, was made that they did. Opening the lawsuit, Carson made just such a comparison with "street arabs," suggesting that they got far more justice than George Archer Shee, brother of an MP and son of an imperial administrator. Poor boys accused of theft, declaimed Carson, had full criminal trials before a trial jury, after a prior hearing before a grand jury, both under the supervision of a judge, with full rights of counsel and of appeal to the court of appeal.[77] This, of course, was nonsense. Most boys accused of petty thefts were convicted before magistrates, summarily, quickly, and with no jury, and had been for over fifty years; virtually none could entertain hopes of legal representation, let alone of launching an appeal. George Archer Shee enjoyed two hearings in the high court, an appeal to the court of appeal, and a debate of his case in Parliament, orchestrated by a leading politician who was also a leader at the bar. It was pure theater. The case had little to do with George's alleged innocence. It had everything to do with a party interest in protecting great property and in sustaining social inequality. The Liberal cabinet decided to settle, faced with clamor in both the Tory press and in Parliament. The Archer Shees received handsome conpensation (£4,000, although some members of Parliament thought they should get £20,000), costs, and the restoration of George's honor.

In short, political and class power gave a particular and powerful reading of the case, one that actually dominated English public opinion for a short while, even delaying Parliament's consideration of the naval estimates and the increasing German threat.[78] The Archer Shee case illustrates a point to which I shall return: the vulnerability of the instruments of the law, including the trial, to power. It also illustrates the fact that encomiums of high law are powerful means to silence the critics of low law, indeed, to deny (as Carson did in court, in his comparison with "street arabs") that such a thing as low law even existed.

It has always existed. In criminal law, it was, for many centuries,

---

77. For Carson's opening statement at trial, see Montagu, *Archer-Shee Case*, 45; Edward Marjoribanks, *Carson the Advocate* (New York: Macmillan, 1932), chap. 32.

78. The traditional reading is well summarized in Marjoribanks's authorized biography of Carson, written with his cooperation.

seen in the difference between state trials and the trials of ordinary felons. State trials for treason, for example, saw the explicit granting of the aid of counsel to defendants over a century before it was extended to those accused of felony—that is, "ordinary" serious crime. And the somewhat arbitrary and discretionary protections extended to defendants in felony trials were probably much less in evidence in the range of summary convictions before magistrates; certainly the high courts did little to supervise the magistracy.[79] But until the nineteenth century, jury trial largely prevailed in England, a trial that was increasingly dominated by exclusionary rules and the demands of counsel. The jury, like the jury trial, was constructed in the idiom of middle-class expectations and language, but it nonetheless had powerful resonances for working people too.[80] But jury trial was demolished in the nineteenth century as the prime venue for criminal cases, unprotected by a constitutional amendment as in the United States. From the 1820s, with a very significant expansion of police-wielded summary powers,[81] followed by massive extensions of summary powers of magistrates in 1847 and 1855, the jury trial was on its way to effective demise as the paradigmatic determinant of who should suffer the violence of the criminal law. By 1900, only one in ten of the most serious offenses were heard by juries; a far greater proportion of lesser ones virtually never were.

Yet the most loudly articulated account of law in England was that of high law, rare and expensive, not low law, its most common daily manifestation. This discontinuity is crucial to understanding the modes of legitimation by 1910 and in the twentieth century as a whole. High law is peculiarly insulated from direct acknowledgment of the fact of its own violence, its accommodations with socially destructive forces, and its contributions to them. Lawyers are paid well to articulate to each other severely edited versions of other people's lives; legal academics are most comfortable dissecting a lan-

---

79. D. Hay, Crown Side Cases in the Court of King's Bench (Stafford: Staffordshire Record Society, forthcoming), cases B.1ff.

80. See Donald Veall, The Popular Movement for Law Reform: 1640–1660 (Oxford: Clarendon Press, 1970); D. Hay, "The Class Composition of the Palladium of Liberty: Trial Jurors in the Eighteenth Century," in Twelve Good Men and True, ed. J. S. Cockburn and Thomas A. Green (Princeton: Princeton University Press, 1988), chap. 10.

81. E.g., the Vagrancy Act of 1824, largely used against young persons in the twentieth century.

guage of remarkable abstraction; judges prefer not to contemplate
the effects of their judicial utterances, even at the moment of sentencing, let alone at the moment of execution or through the years
of imprisonment.[82] Most overt manifestations of violence are confined
to low law: summary proceedings, including the formidable latitude
given to the use of violence in policing; the discipline of prisoners
and control of them on release; routine debt collection, releases signed
for compensation to workers. High law, on the other hand, is the law
of appellate courts, most law professors, and most opinion makers.
It celebrates jury trial, due process, and suit or defense by counsel. It
is the world of law that, to an overwhelming extent, is the one por-
trayed in printed and electronic storytelling, including journalism.

In a wider perspective, this is the received account of law endemic
in class- or status-divided societies, where the most privileged public
discourse is insistent that there should be one reading of law's texts,
including its rituals, as we have seen.[83] What is not so privileged is
silenced. In this dichotomy, the functional differentiation between
high law and low law has a particular significance. The celebration
of high justice as if low justice did not exist was to become the
characteristic mode of twentieth-century encomiums of the law and,
by extension, of the constitutional and political regime. It was done
in the press, in the music hall, in Parliament, at the bar, with constantly reiterated panegyrics on English justice—its fairness, its cer-
titude, its classlessness. Sir Edward Carson reiterated a commonplace
of received opinion, although a moment's reflection must have told
him it was a lie.[84]

---

82. The contrast is both explicit (the last example) and implicit in Cover's
argument, both in the fact that the judge, at the apogee of the pyramid of violence,
is remote from some of its most brutal manifestations, and in the tone of some of
Cover's references to the ambience of academic law.

83. I believe that this aspect of Cover's argument is one not addressed by Carol
Greenhouse in her use of ethnographic materials. She argues, persuasively, that a
humanist reading of law rejects precisely that claim of law: that there can be only
one right reading. (A claim judges themselves undermine in every dissent that they
write.) But on the wider issue of contested readings, the ethnographic evidence she
presents does not show that the Ilongot and Kaluli have specialized interpreters, of
high status and income, whose task is to generate *authoritative* texts, as we do.

84. The Archer-Shee case was resurrected again in 1946, as a play and a film.
The Winslow Boy, by Terence Rattigan, opened in London to critical and popular
acclaim in 1946. There were more than 700 performances of the play in London and
New York. It was based closely on *Archer Shee v. The King*, with some significant

The Archer Shee case illustrates one way in which those with the power to make texts can disseminate one version of a case, an instance of how law's violence disappears behind stories of law's justice, stories that benefit those with power rather than those who suffer law's violence. Such a privileging of one text must mean the partial or entire silencing of others. Of course, only those most disposed to believe the privileged text will be entirely convinced by it. The trial of George Archer Shee may have played to a largely middle-class audience, as did a generation later, the play and the film based on it. But it, like untold other cultural renderings of the meaning of law in our societies over the centuries, is nonetheless important in its implications for law's violence. It is a banal illustration of a general truth. The coercive impact of law is the important element for those who, in fact, are the most direct victims of its violence, the poor; the legitimation of the word is most compelling to those predisposed to believe it, who share in it and articulate it. But that legitimation is crucial, because it enables the coercion to take place. Without the acceptance of law by a large enough proportion of the population (how large, we must inquire), the coercion of the rest is rendered problematic. But for those who give their assent willingly, who see their values incorporated in the program of the law, its violence is legitimate, and they are prepared to further it, support it, even commit it in the name of law, and see in it their own ends.[85]

---

changes, largely in order to make out the Liberal government to be even more outrageous and autocratic than Carson claimed it was in 1910. Rattigan's own political purposes in refurbishing the case for the stage were identical to those of Carson. Rattigan and his wealthy friends were horrified by the defeat of Churchill's Tories in 1945. The Labour government looked serious about introducing socialist measures, from a free health system to free education to high taxation on income and inherited wealth. It was the hour for a tract on the times, and Rattigan's avowed purpose in writing the play was to defend English liberty—particularly, it seems, the liberty of those with a lot of property—from the program of the Labour party. The story of George (who quite possibly did forge the postal order, but who died an honorable death on the Western front in 1915) was thus used in 1946 in an attempt, once again, to discredit a reforming government, the first since 1910 seriously to challenge the inequalities of English society, by invoking the rhetoric of high law. See Michael Darlow and Gillian Hodson, *Terence Rattigan: The Man and His Work* (London: Quartet Books, 1979), chap. 7.

   85. D. Hay, "Prosecution and Power: Malice in the English Courts, 1750–1850," in *Policing and Prosecution in Britain, 1750–1850*, ed. D. Hay and F. Snyder (Oxford: Clarendon Press, 1989), 392–95. While preparing this essay, I found that Bob Cover makes much the same point: see Cover, "Violence," 1608, on interpretations stressing

And they will support more of its violence when they feel a threat to the benefits state violence confers upon them. At the same time, their celebrations of high law will silence or overshadow, as Archer Shee did in 1910, more realistic readings of the significance of law in the distribution of power.

For the speech enjoyed by the powerful is the obverse of the silencing of others. The Word is expensive. Sir Edward Carson had commanded the highest fees at the English bar ever since his destruction of Oscar Wilde; his biographer does not suggest that he appeared in courts of summary jurisdiction to defend poor boys. But then, Carson had to be persuaded of the justice of a case before he accepted his large fees: most "street arabs" accused of petty theft no doubt were guilty.

We can see why revolutionary movements for law reform always demand the abolition or curbing of the legal profession. For the Diggers and Levellers in the seventeenth century, lawyers were "insatiable cannibals whose carcases will never be full gorged with the spoils of the poor and innocent" without the complete monopoly that they demanded, a monopoly to deploy their "lying sophistry and quibbles." William Cole, the author of those words, recommended a local judiciary limited to a year's practice, with litigants obliged to present their own cases or have a friend speak for them.[86] There is an ancient and perennial popular criticism of lawyer's law; when it is loudly articulated (as in the interregnum) it is focused on some of those aspects of high law I have already mentioned. It revolts against two aspects of what the lawyers consider law's main virtues: the fact that it abstracts, generalizes, shears off many facts and interpretations from those situations it considers; and, second, that it is expressed in large measure in the idiom of the elite culture, and a specialized variant of it. To the critics, both those characteristics of high law have always instead been prime evidence for the fact that the law in practice is unfair in its process and in its purposes because it is remote, arcane, expensive, uncertain, and usually respectful of social class.

---

a community of shared values. "I do not wish to downplay the significance of . . . ideological functions of law. But the function of ideology is much more significant in justifying an order to those who principally benefit from it and who must defend it than it is in hiding the nature of the order from those who are its victims."

86. William Cole, quoted in Veall, *Popular Movement*, 103.

It is always in the hands of the lawyers, yet lawyer's law is usually withheld from the poor. In the eighteenth century, Lord Hardwicke rejected as unthinkable the notion that poor men condemned to death could ever appeal their convictions: all of them would want to do it. In 1947, Justice Frankfurter opposed claims of inadequate representation by counsel in the United States because they "would furnish opportunities hitherto uncontemplated for opening wide the prison doors of the land."[87] There was no general constitutional right to counsel in felony cases in the United States until 1964; today, the average payment for defense counsel in a capital case in the states carrying out most executions is $2,000 per case. For a lawyer, that is a derisory sum.[88]

In a market, there must be expensive justice and cheap justice, and, historically, this has, in large measure, translated into high justice and low justice. We become accustomed to accepting that justice is pretty good when low justice is being administered with some equity or compassion. But we do not demur at low justice because we know that it is impossible, in a market or in a class- or status-divided society, to give equal justice. If a visionary proposed that all persons accused of murder, including the Von Bulows of this world, be represented by the same counsel who defend the poor, picked at random from the same pool, we would conclude he or she did not know anything about "the administration of justice." Not all can have equal speech, not even in capital trials—perhaps even less there, as they are so expensive. The most important part of a successful collateral attack in a capital appeal is also the most expensive: the reconstruction of the life history of the convict, in sufficient detail that a jury can comprehend some of the human roots of a horrendous act. Few capital convicts are fortunate to have such counsel. Historical accounts of the lives of the poor are difficult to research and difficult to set forth adequately without prolixity. The courts do most of their work by reducing life histories to a few pointed questions. Law's violence is complemented by law's silence.

87. David L. Bazelon, "The Defective Assistance of Counsel," *University of Cincinnati Law Review* 42 (1973): 22 n. 63.
88. Anthony Paduano and Clive A. Stafford-Smith, "The Unconscionability of Sub-minimum Wages Paid Appointed Counsel in Capital Cases," *Rutgers Law Review* 43 (1991): 347; Charles L. Black, Jr., *Capital Punishment: The Inevitability of Caprice and Mistake*, 2d ed. (New York: Norton, 1981), chap. 10.

Conclusion

The social differentiation of law's violence, as well as its long historic role in sustaining social inequality, are thus sustained by both Violence and The Word; by coercion and by silence. The silence is always present, created by the market for law. The coercion changes with changes in the technology of policing and prosecution. Over most of the long period I have surveyed, the most notable fact of prosecution was its very low levels. Contemporaries, particularly in the age of transition (1750–1850), thought this justified harsh penalties. The important point today is that relatively few people in earlier ages came to suffer law's violence directly (or to invoke it). With the modern police that changed dramatically. The increasing prosecution levels in the first half of the nineteenth century can undoubtedly be attributed, in large measure, to policing, but it is only in the twentieth century, especially since World War II and most especially in the last decade or two, that the technology of policing and the constant increase in police resources has been most brought to bear on the criminal and the poor. It is highly unlikely that, at any time in the past of English-speaking societies, we have stigmatized such a large proportion of our populations.[89]

What does it mean for a society when the experience of law's violence, mainly directed against the poor, occurs at such high rates and at times of greatly increased inequality and sense of powerlessness among the poorest? The longer record suggests that the outcome is a sense of crisis and increased repression. I think that outcome is even more likely where the law's legitimacy is compromised by the fact that unequally distributed violence visibly extends beyond the criminal law. For lawyers are the visible agents of those institutions and persons who most benefit from material inequality.[90] But, as in the

89. See n. 61 and 62, above.

90. A visibly rapacious legal profession may stir great popular hatreds, but it can also have significant effects on the distribution of inequality, as well as enjoying its fruits. Braithwaite, (*Crime*, 129) comments that the problem of business forming crimogenic subcultures to resist regulatory enforcement seems to be much more widespread in the United States than in other Western industrial societies. He does not, I might add, take seriously the proposition that reducing economic inequalities might reduce other crime (in spite of citing the examples of European social democracies); he, instead, blames something called American "individualism." I wonder if *individualism* may be a polite word for a willingness to tolerate massive social inequality, and whether the greater "integrative" capacities of Japanese society may be related to its egalitarian distribution of income (see n. 59, above).

seventeenth or eighteenth or nineteenth centuries, law's violence has limits. The U.S. riots of the 1960s (with property damage of $160 billion and 263 persons killed) yielded some generous state provisions, including the first national, well-funded and somewhat effective program of proactive poverty law. That program has been largely destroyed. In the 1980s, the more common response to crime and disorder was more of law's violence.

In 1762, Adam Smith baldly observed to his students at the University of Glasgow, in language that could be frank because it was uttered within the private circle of the privileged,

> Laws and governments may be considered . . . as a combination of the rich to oppress the poor, and preserve to themselves an inequality of goods which would otherwise be soon destroyed by the attacks of the poor.[91]

He spoke in a society in which large, short-term shifts in inequality were common: both five years before and four years after his lecture, high food prices resulted in widespread riots and death sentences for rioters. It was a recurrent pattern, as we have seen, moderated by private charity and state intervention. But in the great dearth of 1800–1801, England's governors repudiated intervention in the market, the most serious riots of the century took place, and more men and women were hanged for property offenses than at any time since the seventeenth century. Troops battled with rioters, and soldiers were barracked throughout the manufacturing districts of England to repress the demands of the poor. In the ensuing decades, troops, conscription, the new police, and new penitentiaries were increasingly the means by which the discontent of the suffering poor was contained, at enormous social cost.

This is not a pattern from which our own societies are immune. If inequality continues to increase, law's violence, and the violence it generates in turn, must continue to increase also.

---

91. Adam Smith, *Lectures on Jurisprudence*, Glasgow ed., ed. R. L. Meek, D. D. Raphael, and P. G. Stein (Oxford: Clarendon Press, 1978), 208 (from the lectures of 1762–63). Smith's student (for our only texts of these lectures come from students' notes) added, ". . . who if not hindered by the government would soon reduce the others to an equality with themselves by open violence."

Private Violence as Moral Action: The Law as Inspiration and Example

Robert Weisberg

Violence and Meaning Making

In generating a "jurisprudence of violence," scholars tend to focus on the question of how law uses violence, and, in so doing, how law sustains its legitimacy by purporting to differentiate itself from violence.[1] Profs. Sarat and Kearns have posed a more specific question for those hoping to develop this jurisprudence—namely, how law, in its violence, impresses itself on its subjects, through moral imprimatur or pragmatic threat.[2] I hope not to dodge those issues—in fact, I hope to address them—in the somewhat oblique approach I would like to take to the question. Namely, I want to examine how the "nonlegal" violence we suffer in the world—the violence perpetrated by private individuals against each other—represents an act of law-making or law enforcement for the perpetrator, and how it often serves as the operative law of his or her culture.

The Anxiety over Law and Violence

Anglo-American law has traditionally suffered a serious identity crisis over its awkward relation to violence. Indeed, one of the major

Research for this essay was supported by the Stanford Legal Research Fund, made possible by a bequest from Ira S. Lillick and by gifts from other friends of the Stanford Law School.

1. See Karl Olivecrona, *Law As Fact* (London: Oxford University Press, 1939).

2. See Austin Sarat and Thomas R. Kearns, "A Journey Through Forgetting: Toward a Jurisprudence of Violence," in *The Fate of Law*, ed. Austin Sarat and Thomas R. Kearns (Ann Arbor: University of Michigan Press, 1991), 209–73.

themes in our jurisprudence has been the relationship between state-sanctioned physical force and what we normally call violence—presumably private, unjustified, gratuitous physical force. Our system assumes that the law is to hold a monopoly on violence, but this is a monopoly viewed as both necessary and discomfiting. It is necessary because it is viewed as the alternative to something worse—unrestrained private vengeance—and it is discomfiting because those who make and enforce the law would like to believe that, though they may be required to use force, force is somehow categorically distinguishable from violence. Violence is naturally imputed away to the other—to the image of a separate criminal class distinct from normal humanity.

Throughout our legal history, we observe the complex ways the law rationalizes itself out of this dilemma, while nevertheless at times punishing, permitting, accommodating, encouraging, or inspiring the very private violence it purports to suppress or replace. The first edition of *Law as Fact*, the great early legal realist work by Karl Olivecrona, is indeed a deft critique of the classic rationalizations of this problem. Olivecrona coolly refutes the traditional efforts to finesse the problem of the role of force in law, thus demanding that we face up to our anxiety honestly.

Olivecrona calls it a "fatal illusion" to think that violence is alien to the law just because it is contingent, in the background, just as it is false to distinguish law from the slightly less malign concept of force.[3] Any effort to distinguish the commands of law from the commonsense notion of forceful violence is a residue of hoary metaphysical illusions about law. Law, for this realist, is a social fact, not a Platonic cloud, and, as such, it includes violence. Nor can we distinguish law from force by holding that law is inherently independent of force and merely borrows the instrumentality of force as a means at hand to achieve certain goals[4] Rather, law is precisely a body of rules about force—rules that help shape ideas about right—and it is a use of force that must be monopolized by an organization.[5]

As Olivecrona probably would have predicted, the efforts of modern jurisprudence to finesse or deny the role of violence have not ceased. One major cause has been a new version of the debate

3. Olivecrona, *Law As Fact*, 126.
4. Olivecrona, *Law As Fact*, 133–34.
5. Olivecrona, *Law As Fact*, 169–72.

between those who say violence is essential to law and those who say it is irrelevant or tangential. Most notably, the liberal, postrealist tradition of H. L. A. Hart and Ronald Dworkin has tried to identify the legitimate source of forceful lawmaking in principles that are justifiable without reference to physical might. As Profs. Sarat and Kearns point out, Hart argued that legal rules are quintessentially normative. As means for their enforcement, legal rules rely mostly on respect for moral authority and only tangentially on threats of force.[6] While Hart somewhat evaded the problem of the forceful exercise of discretion in fuzzy areas where the rules require interpretation, his student, Dworkin, reassured us that there is always a body of meta-authorities—called principles—to which a judge can turn to derive the proper interpretation of ambiguous or vague rules.[7] Violence is irrelevant to law because discretion is not a matter of force or will. There are always sound, objective criteria of interpretation that determine correct law.

As Dworkin made virtually explicit, his view of principled reasoning has a highly aesthetic cast to it.[8] Since he nowhere relies on any immanently religious basis for natural law, his criteria for sound judgment from broad principles resemble aesthetic principles of organic coherence and elegant form. In that sense, one can trace a line from Hart-Dworkin jurisprudence to one of the newest forces in legal scholarship—the joint study of law and literature—and thereby see why we have returned quite viscerally to the problem of violence. As all who have been interested in a jurisprudence of violence know, interest in this idea has recently been sparked, somewhat indirectly, by the rise of law and literature scholarship.[9] Much of that scholarship has focused on law as a phenomenon of aesthetic expression, and, more specifically, on the writings and decisions of judges as acts of interpretation. Many writers have adopted the premise that law and literature are two parallel cultural phenomena: they are both attempts to shape reality through language, and both are concerned with

---

6. H. L. A. Hart, *The Concept of Law* (Oxford: Clarendon Press, 1961).

7. Ronald Dworkin, *Taking Rights Seriously* (Cambridge, Mass.: Harvard University Press, 1977).

8. Ronald Dworkin, "Law as Interpretation," *Texas Law Review* 60 (March, 1983): 527.

9. See, generally, Robert Weisberg, "The Law-Literature Enterprise," *Yale Journal of Law and the Humanities* 1 (December, 1988): 1.

matters of ambiguity, interpretation, abstraction, and humanistic judgment.

The highly aesthetic view of legal rhetoric and interpretation proffered by the law-and-literature movement caused one notable commentator, the late Robert Cover, to demand that attention be paid to the one unavoidable distinction between judges and purely intellectual and aesthetic practitioners of the arts of rhetoric and interpretation. Unlike their purely aesthetic counterparts, when judges engage in rhetoric and interpretation, they often make decisions that impose physical restraint or pain and violence on other people. They deprive people of life, liberty, property, and the pursuit of happiness.[10] Lawmakers may be rhetoricians and intellectual artists, but they are also the violent engineers of the state's policies. Cover's now famous rejoinder has been a crucial, if not always heeded, admonition in the world of law-and-literature scholarship: treating legal officers as moral artists tends to prettify the force and violence out of the law.

My goal here is to examine how, in the light of the implicit debate between Cover and the aesthetic interpretationists, our jurisprudence continues to worry over and explain away the role of violence in law. I will aim to do so from one particular perspective. Put simply, we observe a fearful symmetry in law, which I will call the violent self-help analogy. On the one hand, law commits violence in the disturbing sense that public authoritative force reminds us of the abrupt, gratuitous violence associated with private and legally unjustified individuals. On the other hand, we also observe that private individuals who, on commonsense observation, typify this form of gratuitous private violence are often subjectively, and even sometimes objectively, engaging in acts of lawmaking or law enforcement disturbingly analogous to public legal authority. The violent self-help analogy exacerbates the challenge that the more general or abstract issue of legal violence poses for theorists and apologists of law. I hope to trace some recent observations of this vestige of self-help legal violence in our culture and to see how it inspires some interesting new versions of some old rationalizations, rationalizations ranging from the political to the moral to the sociological to the economic.

---

10. Robert Cover, "The Bonds of Constitutional Interpretation: Of the Word, the Deed, and the Role," *Georgia Law Review* 20 (Summer, 1986): 815; see also Robin West, "Adjudication is Not Interpretation: Some Reservations About the Law-As-Literature Movement," *Tennessee Law Review* 54 (Winter, 1987): 203.

Self-Help Violence as Law

Let me now be more specific about how and why violent criminals can be seen not as violating the law, but as upholding it. I will begin with the most common notion of "self-help." At one level, we can try to dismiss this entire phenomenon by saying that violent action taken by one individual against another for the purpose of upholding what the perpetrator believes to be some sort of law or rule is precisely the "self-help" remedy that the rule of law *forbids*.[11] But even if this proposition is true for our legal culture, it is most assuredly not true for others distant in either time or space. The simple fact is that, for much of recorded history, this (apparently) anomalous form of law enforcement—self-help—has been a dominant and legitimate mode of law enforcement. The work of Donald Black illustrates that it takes no extreme cultural relativist to recognize that what is murder in some societies is legal self-help in others.[12] The presumption that killings or other attacks are "legal" remedies for what are often non-violent wrongs may be so strong that the notion of "illegal" violence itself may almost be anomalous in some societies. Violence is presumed to be legal revenge, often for earlier crimes invisible to all but the wronged. On the other hand, of course, in most societies, there

---

11. I mean this in the sense of a heavy presumption against self-help remedies, with such rare exceptions as the right of peaceful self-help repossession for secured creditors in the law of debt collection.

12. As Donald Black has ably demonstrated, in Mayan civilization, for example, the assumption of the legitimacy of self-help violence as a method of redressing wrongs is so powerful that, when a person is ambushed, the overwhelming legal presumption is that the victim was, in fact, being punished for a harm he had caused. In short, premeditated violence is *presumed* to occur most often in legitimate form. The normal "homicide" is presumptively legal revenge. (As we will see later, what is at least partly a legal phenomenon in Mayan civilization may operate as a psychological phenomenon in all civilizations—most notably our own.) The Mayan "presumption" is apparently equally operative in some equatorial African societies and among the Eskimos of the Arctic. Of course, neither the original wrong nor the remedial act need be homicide. The wrong may be adultery or insult or nuisance, and the remedy may be almost any violent attack or taking. In Venezuela and Brazil, women may be legally beaten by husbands for petty offenses. Property seized as debt collection or destroyed as revenge may be a house or an animal. And where women are property, rape may be retaliatory theft. In fourteenth-century England, a widow might be gang raped in revenge for the conduct of her late husband. See Donald Black, "Crime as Social Control," in *Toward a General Theory of Social Control*, ed D. Black (Orlando: Academic Press, 1984) 2:1–5.

is plenty of visible illegal violence that is recognized as such, but even in these societies, the legitimacy of self-help revenge may make an illegal homicide self-canceling, since the crime will carry its own punishment, will invoke its own legal remedy (a reciprocal, law-enforcing homicide). Law in such societies is transparent. In an almost Hammurabian sense, one only need look to the wrong itself to see the punishment or remedy. Thus, here again, there is no clear distinction, as our system purports to have, between private violence and law.[13]

Self-Help Law Enforcement as Social Fact

Moreover, lest we see these facts merely as interesting anthropological atavisms, if we look below the formalities of the law to the most fundamental sociology of crime in the United States, we see a kind of practical continuity between ours and the less familiar regimes described by Black. Much privately inflicted violence in our society may be logically remedial in some factually grounded or morally coherent sense, wholly aside from whether it is legally authorized. Thus, Black notes, without regard to the legalities of the matter, how many acts of violence in our society are, indeed, efforts at law enforcement.[14] Perhaps the majority of intentional killings in the United States are committed by people against victims who are not strangers to them, and a great portion of those nonstranger killers act on the perception that they are redressing a grievance against the person killed. Moreover, a surprisingly high number of the killings or non-fatal shootings between strangers are defensive or preventive acts by crime victims. Whether or not their actions are later ratified as legal, these shooters pose a far greater threat to robbers and burglars than do the police.[15] Indeed, only a small fraction of the homicides in the United States fit the model of the predatory crime that most people (wrongly) view as the modal form of dangerous violence.[16]

---

13. Then, as Black points out, there is the opposite of statelessness—Stalinist societies where it is so easy to get the state to do the dirty work of avenging one's enemies that the public/private distinction breaks down from the other direction (Black, "Crime," 18–19, n. 21).

14. Black, "Crime," 5–12.

15. Gary Kleck, "Policy Lessons from Recent Gun Control Research," *Law and Contemporary Problems* 49 (Winter, 1986): 35, 43–44.

16. Black, "Crime," 6–7.

Homicide is often the natural response to insult or to jealousy. It also may be a response to such matters as the failure to pay a debt, conflict over child custody, the complaint that the person against whom revenge is sought has turned one's relative to drugs, and so on. If this is true of homicide, it is obviously, quantitatively, even more true of the vast number of nonhomicidal assaults—the most common acts of violence in the world. Obviously, definitional games may occur in courts prosecuting these crimes. Who is the victim? Who is the punisher? In assaultive quarrels, the state may impose the names victim and offender where the very dispute was over who was who in these terms.[17]

In fact, though, as Black points out, such self-help crime is not limited to assaults or homicides.[18] There are plenty of other violent, or at least aggressive and potentially violent, acts that can carry out this remedial purpose. There are plenty of moralistic, remedial burglaries and robberies, particularly as forms of aggressive collection of debts that are perceived to be legitimately compensable. Moreover, one of the most common types of remedial crime is vandalism. Some random vandalism is juvenile revenge against the conduct of specific adults. Apparently random violence against the police or storekeepers may be a marking of collective liability. However used we may be to the fact, noted previously, that most killings are of nonstrangers, many may be startled to learn that, for example, in one New York study, one-third of a sample of burglaries appeared to be acts of private revenge against known victims.[19]

To focus for the moment on an aggressive but usually nonviolent crime, one of the dominant forms of theft in the United States—and probably the fastest growing—is larceny by employees against their employers, often grounded in a perception of economic or other mistreatment for which the theft is appropriate recompense.[20] Indeed, it has been suggested that one reason this phenomenon is such a surprise is that many victims of such remedial crimes are themselves never made aware of the true motive for the crime. In that sense, remedial crime has been described as a "secret form of self-control,"

---

17. Black, "Crime," 12.
18. Black, "Crime," 9.
19. Black, "Crime," 8–9.
20. Donald Cressey and Edwin Sutherland, *Criminology* (Philadelphia: Lippincott, 1978), 25.

whether as a means of scaring private individuals, however indirectly, into restraining their own aggressive actions for fear that someone out there will exact revenge, or, in cases such as employee theft, as a form of radical income redistribution.[21]

Thus, only in theory at best has the modern state achieved a monopoly over violence as law enforcement. Much violence is committed by people thoroughly persuaded that they are enforcing legitimate legal or moral norms. Many killers willingly turn themselves in to authorities, having felt they had no choice, and still feeling no shame.[22] This form of violence is obviously less deterrable than the coolly rapacious crime most citizens think is the dominant kind. Indeed, it may be the very absence of public faith in the ability of the police to deter or stop criminals that inspires citizens to engage in self-help remedies. As a result, in some corners of society, the major deterrent to crime may indeed be the threat of private remedial action. In some neighborhoods, Black points out, when you steal from the poor, you gamble with your life.[23] Such well-regulated illegal markets as numbers games depend on efficient deterrent threats; very young or very old people who travel through certain neighborhoods transporting money for numbers games, though apparently the easiest targets for robberies, may indeed be the safest property holders, since it is well known that the punishment for attacking them will be swift and violent, with little due process. Ironically, the efforts of the state to superimpose its own deterrent power over the self-help scheme may not work: Black points out that the incidence of rape among the Gisii of Kenya rose dramatically after the British imposed their formal laws against rape to replace feudal revenge.[24] Doubtless the British thought that the public deterrent scheme had major benefits in reducing general social chaos and perhaps even more effectively distinguishing the innocent from the guilty, but whether the public scheme netted out as more socially beneficial is unclear.

Crime as Self-Help Legislation, Dissent, and
"Community Empowerment"

Another traditional form of self-help force or violence has been private remedial action against illegitimate laws, especially where the

---

21. Black, "Social Control," 9–10.
22. Jack Katz, *Seductions of Crime* (New York: Basic Books, 1989), 25.
23. Black, "Crime," 15.
24. Black, "Crime," 15.

perceived illegitimacy of state law has precisely been its own perverse use of violence. The subversive carnival tradition in European culture, with its imagistic transgressions of propriety, also involves legal transgression—"transgression giving itself a law."[25] In the English tradition, the Robin Hood myth is that of law and legal imagery being manipulated by the outlaw, either to execute law or to protest law, and public protest tinged with collective, celebratory violence remains a persistent trope in that regard; in this tradition, carnival-esque subversion often involves a form of private law enforcement, since the targets were often adulterers.[26]

Law in the United States obviously manifests a continuity with the tradition of self-help violence associated with attacks on legal regimes that lack legitimacy. Our history is obviously full of noble examples, from the Boston Tea Party to antiwar protests, of cere-monial actions that, while violating positive law, purport to invoke higher law. From the perspective of one myth of this self-help tra-dition, self-help action of this sort can be benign, because the tech-nically illegal conduct is not only relatively nonviolent, but, as in

---

25. Stallybrass's study of the charivari-type carnival procession in medieval Europe amply demonstrates its literary and structuralist attacks on official standards—its fracturing of discourse, its inversion of hierarchy, its degradation of the sacred, but this morphology has its roots in remedial action for wrongs, with its image of Robin Hood celebrating his triumph over the sheriff. See Peter Stallybrass, "'Drunk with the Cup of Liberty': Robin Hood, the Carnivalesque and the Rhetoric of Violence in Early Modern England," in *The Violence of Representation*, ed. Nancy Armstrong and Leonard Tennenhouse (London: Routledge, 1989), 45. In this medieval mythology, the forest was to be a utopia of perfect liberty for masterless, indeed homeless, men, so that Robin Hood took "legal" action against efforts to enclose and divide it. He challenged the sheriff's punishment of free deerslayers in the forest who were allegedly taking deer that "belonged" to property owners. To protest the law, Robin would become the law, disguising himself as the sheriff's agent and then hanging the sheriff.

Indeed, the charivari was sometimes seen as a legitimate form of church penance, upheld by manor courts as a quasi-legal means of correcting domestic crimes. An incontinent widow might lose her rights to free bench (part of her husband's land) unless she rode backwards on a black ram to manor court reciting a ludicrous ballad. The concept of law was complexly entangled with gender. Paradoxically, when women were brought before the official law of the state, as when women enclosure rioters were brought before Star Chamber, the state accused these women of being outlaws in the sense of having violated the law, while the popular defense of these women was either that they were truly outlaws—too inherently lawless to have to obey the rule of law—or that women were only subject to the private "outlaw law" of the charivari (Stallybrass, "Drunk," 45–76).

Thus, the charivaris, at different times in history, either reinforced common morality or represented a kind of constitutional action against common morality.

26. Stallybrass, "Drunk," 49–50.

the case of Dr. King's actions in the South, takes as its very premise
the Gandhian principle of nonviolence in the name of a claim under
a higher natural or constitutional law.

It would be gratuitous here to offer even a brief summary of the
U.S. tradition of civil disobedience as self-help. Instead, I want to
offer one admittedly perverse footnote to that noble history. The
notion of private violence intended as an instrument of law may find
better underscoring in examples of riotlike, carnivalesque conduct
that is obviously malevolent, not noble, and that thereby better illustrates the evocatively powerful role of the law-enforcing motive
as an inspiration to criminal violence. When the Southern anti-
integration protesters met the forces of the federal government in
Arkansas,[27] they thought they were acting in the name of law. When
white men forced a black man to his death on a highway in Howard
Beach, Queens, or where others killed a black youth in Bensonhurst,[28]
some may have been acting subjectively according to a moral or legal
norm. According to the twisted moral and legal culture of the killers
in these cases, the black victims had transgressed. In the minds of
many local whites, the blacks had wrongly entered a white enclave,
violating property rights and cultural integrity.

To the extent that the local whites recognized the blacks' wrongful
entry as merely naive, the whites nevertheless viewed their violent
remedy as almost obligatory, since a sacred territorial line had been
crossed.[29] Thus, some neighborhood defenders of the Bensonhurst
killers, though incapable of identifying any actual wrong or provocative act by the victim, Yussef Hawkins, nevertheless insisted,
often in a studied tone of tragic realism rather than ranting condemnation, that this was an inevitable outcome when a black person
went where he did not belong. The killers in these cases are the
children of a generation of urban whites who did not succeed as the
middle-class dream might have led them to think they would—they
did not make it out to the suburbs. Thus, they created enclave suburbs
out of old urban neighborhoods, but instead of escaping the urban
minority populations, they felt encircled by them, and their children,

---

27. Cooper v. Aaron, 358 U.S. 1 (1958).
28. See Patricia J. Williams, *The Alchemy of Race and Rights* (Cambridge,
Mass.: Harvard University Press, 1991), 58–72; William Glaberson, "Bensonhurst:
A Weakened Murder Case Opens Today," *New York Times*, April 16, 1990.
29. Williams, *Alchemy*, 58–59, 69.

however subliminally, learned the message that violence against the outsider is a legitimate remedy against any further threat to their culture's residual integrity.

The phenomenon of carnival, ritual violence thus reflects the tension between orthodoxy and heterodoxy; culturally, it is or seeks to be a licensed form of misrule. In a stable culture, it is a form of "colonized conflict, a ritual contestation organized from above and separated off in time and space from the quotidian."[30] In an unstable culture, it is a threat to law, and a particularly ominous one because it is experienced and often expressed as a threat in the name of law. The very danger of the malevolent versions of this tradition is that it may be experienced by those who practice it as having continuity with the nobler origins of the tradition. Nothing so inspires group violence against outsiders or perceived transgressors as the sense that the group is carrying out a legal, lawmaking, or law-preserving mission. And the very need for unity in a haphazardly organized group often finds the pretense of law a particularly useful theme for inducing a sense of coherence and meaning in its conduct. Armed with the belief that it is acting in the name of law, a group of rioters feels like a state itself, a body politic. Indeed, the psychology of private legal violence helps explain an important paradox in criminology. Criminologists have questioned the common assumption that a youth's criminal propensity may derive from his or her indoctrination in and loyalty to group or gang values, when the gist of criminal conduct seems to be anomic individual narcissism.[31] The explanation may lie in the special appeal of law-enforcing or law-establishing criminal conduct.

Self-Help Law Enforcement as Existential Achievement

A still subtler category of violence feeling like law, the category where there is no question of any legal recognition of excuse or justification, is where the legal element is "purely" psychological and analogic. The remarkable recent work of sociologist Jack Katz has illuminated this phenomenon. As Katz reminds us, the modal killing in our legal

---

30. Stallybrass, "Drunk," 69.
31. James Q. Wilson and Richard Herrnstein, *Crime and Human Nature* (New York: Basic Books, 1985), 294.

culture is between nonstrangers; as a matter of psychological interpretation, it is often a form of moral revenge, an impassioned attempt
to perform a sacrifice to embody one form or another of the Good.[32]
Such an impulse to serve a high moral principle may be a major
explanation of homicidal rage. Katz implicitly performs a "violent"
reversal of our purely legal notions of affirmative defense. In our
positive law, an intentional killing is presumptively a murder; only
an express exception to the rule can justify, excuse, or mitigate it.
Katz argues, however, that if we are to understand the moral and
psychological dynamics of crime, we must look at things in an opposite manner. That is, we must view the typical homicide as presumptively *feeling*, in the mind of the killer, as if it is a legitimately
justified act of law enforcement.

The victim sacrificed to such a moral principle can be as apparently inoffensive as a crying infant. For the parent who strangles the
child, the killing feels like a justified form of discipline. The parent
defines the child's crying as willfully defiant. Katz's theory is even
more obvious in spousal killings, where the killer, usually male, may
act to assert his sexual rights, to punish an insult to his honor, or
to preserve a certain orderly image of the relationship. Many spousal
killings also occur, however, over disputes concerning the proper
handling of domestic business, such as a dispute over the proper
priority (by legal or moral standards) among a couple's financial
obligations—that is, over the principle of how one affirms to the
world that one is a debtor of integrity. Many killings occur over
slight insults, such as disputes over parking places or proper respect
or civility in a bar or over a pool table,[33] but it is important, Katz
argues, to see that such trivial matters are viewed psychologically
not only as assertions of legitimate property rights, but as affirmations
of the general principle of property ownership and civil order. Ironically, though this form of killing is greater among the poorer classes,
it might be seen as a defense of bourgeois values—marital order,
property rights, or responsible debt.[34]

---

32. Katz, *Seductions*, 12–51.

33. Significantly, the modal time for these killings is during the casual hours
of Saturday night or Sunday morning, when the expected release from the workaday
humiliations of job and schedule produces a sense of entitlement to peace and respect,
an entitlement so viscerally assumed that its violation produces violent rage (Katz,
Seductions, 21–22, 46).

34. Katz, *Seductions*, 17–18, 45.

In describing the psychological stages of these killings, Katz notes that, though intentional, they are not premeditated in the sense of including a plan for escape. The killer engages in a mixture of resignation and justification. In one sense, he stays at the scene because he views his act as one of legitimate law enforcement, merely to be reported when the police arrive. On the other hand, to the extent that the killer recognizes that his claim of justification will not be legally recognized, he simply awaits his fate, because, given the demands of the moral norms to which he was responding, he views himself as having had no choice—he was commanded by the situation to affirm the good and the orderly.[35] (In this sense, the sane killer is like the psychotic killer who believes his act is justified because it is obligatory.) As with much of the self-help violence in other cultures described by Black, this killer feels innocent of any willful violence because his own law was "transparent"; he was merely the medium for the natural, automatic retribution that certain evil acts merit.

The process includes an initial sense of humiliation, then a turning to rage. Just as Foucault's premodern executioners would mark the body of the condemned to honor the Good they violated,[36] so the killer must honor the willfullness of the offense that he or she is avenging by marking the body of the offender with violence. For Foucault, the old purpose of torture was to construct the truth of the crime, to demark the nature and gravity of the offense, as where men beat their wives to give them black eyes that will serve as a "purdah"—a veil of shame.[37] So it is for the self-help killer; the violent marking is a form of cursing, of pronouncing sentence, an act of community service. The killer curses to show that he is willing to be tainted by the touch of the profane, thereby to sacrifice his own purity to purge the public of evil. In the killer's view, he was left no choice—the offender virtually asked for it. Indeed, the anecdotal reports of some of these killings suggest that sometimes the deceased had, indeed, dared the killer to act, and the killer then felt obliged to preserve his personal honor and the overall Good, to reestablish status, power, and order.[38]

35. Katz, *Seductions*, 25.
36. Michel Foucault, *Discipline and Punish*, trans. Alan Sheridan (New York: Vintage Books, 1979), 34.
37. Foucault, *Discipline*, 34.
38. Or the criminal sometimes is egged on by bystanders who point out moralistic necessity (Katz, *Seductions*, 20).

Now one might argue that this notion of the modal killer is simply irrelevant to the other large category of killings—the category that most people—wrongly—fear they are most likely to be victims of: so-called senseless killings of total strangers. But Katz's theory of righteous slaughter extends to these as well.[39] Many "senseless" killers think they, too, are engaged in righteous slaughter—they kill "Nietzscheanly." They punish people under a private norm of strict liability, to replicate the "unjust" world in which they have personally suffered. That world is Lear's, where we are to the gods as flies to wanton boys, and the killer is then the replication of or agent of these gods. To kill "unnecessarily" is to replicate the order or disorder of the moral universe. It is an "obligatory" ritual, one the killer has no choice but to perform, in which he expresses his awe before the sacred perverse principle he assumes rules the world. In some of these killings, such as the notorious slaying of the Clutter family in Truman Capote's *In Cold Blood*, the victims believe their deaths would be senseless, and would give up any valuables in exchange for their lives; they cannot imagine the value of their deaths to the killers.[40] This is, of course, the helpless reaction of misunderstanding mortals before the sacred. That is why the killers, who do understand the sacred, perform the homicidal ritual with almost priestly care.[41]

Many of the killers are robbers, but the most vexing killings are those utterly unnecessary to the accomplishment of the robbery, or those where it is otherwise clear that eliminating a witness was no part of the motive for the killing. The killing is designed to establish moral dominance, not to effect a larceny. And, as with nonstranger killers, here the killer acts with the fatalistic sense that his action is demanded and foretold and destined, and that he accomplishes it proves that it was ordered by law. Of course, this category overlaps considerably with the others. So that if one sees Bernhard Goetz as wounding senselessly because he shot the last boy as the latter lay utterly helpless and harmless,[42] then Goetz's defense is that this was only an "apparently senseless" shooting—not that it was practically necessary to save his own life, but that it was in defense of a higher moral order he wanted to restore to the subways.

---

39. Katz, *Seductions*, 274–309.
40. Katz, *Seductions*, 277–78.
41. Katz, *Seductions*, 289.
42. See People v. Goetz, 197 N.E.2d 41 (1986).

Thus, it is precisely, if ironically, in the case of the apparently senseless killing that we most frighteningly see the power of the state, as lawmaker and law preserver, to embolden people to violence. It is precisely in some of the most chaotic, misguided, self-destructive, "meaningless" souls that we see a passion for some self-redeeming meaning and coherence that finds fulfillment in a self-image as law-maker and law preserver. These are the postmodernist killers for whom law, twisted from its role as a social device to enhance public order, is an aesthetic and existential dramatic instrument to achieve private order.

Finessing the Violent Self-Help Analogy: A Variety of Approaches

These instances of the analogy between private violent action and legally authorized force offer a peculiar version of the broader theme of law's relationship to violence. We might, therefore, see how they, like the broader issue, invoke a variety of moral, intellectual, and legal devices of denial, rationalization, and accommodation. In this part of the essay, I want to examine these devices, with the admission that, in some cases, I am imagining or constructing various responses to the violent self-help analogy that are only implicit or immanent in more general legal perspectives.

No Meaningful Relationship

The simplest approach is to suggest that the parallel is an imagistic accident or contrivance of no legal, moral, or political significance at all. From a political perspective, the moral hegemony of the state in defining right and wrong conduct may be so coherently inarguable that the purported imitation of the state by a private avenger is simply illegitimate because it is not performed by the state under authorized conditions. Yet this denial of any significance to the violent self-help analogy has a psychological component as well. The law-enforcing mentality of the private avenger might be seen not as a moral lie or false legal position, but simply as a moral delusion in a world where positive law is simply assumed to be legitimate. That is, private law enforcement is a sort of paranoid syndrome, and we dismiss away the parallel as a psychological aberration.

One version of this view is exemplified by Stephen Morse in his implicit insistence on a coherent moral principle that distinguishes good acts from bad in far more cases than we normally accept. In arguing against the broad use of any diminished capacity formula, he insists that it is not very difficult to obey the law—that there is a coherent set of moral principles derived from parental, religious, educational, and cultural training, that most people are adequately trained in this way, and that the differences among offenders are morally insignificant compared to their similarities.[43] For example, in condemning one new proposed affirmative defense in spousal abuse cases, Morse insists that the fuzzy thinking that confuses an ill-founded justification with an ill-founded excuse weakens the moral legitimacy of the law of homicide and denies the consensus of moral principle on which law rests.[44]

This overall treatment of the parallel between public law and private self-help violence rests on a broader moral perspective exemplified by Michael Moore. For Moore, one need not resort to natural law metaphysics to derive a body of consensual moral principles distinguishing legal rules from private, vengeful goals. A "realist" theory of moral meaning discovers that moral words have a "semantic depth" akin to those possessed by "natural kind" words. In a manner recalling Dworkin, they present "the best theory we are able to articulate about what sort of quality pain or justice really is."[45] If one applies to moral knowledge the standards of meaning, ontology, and justification thought adequate in contemporary philosophy for non-moral knowledge, the former does not suffer at all in terms of the objectivity of its epistemology.[46]

Of course, the best critique of this "denial maneuver" is a reference to those approaches, examined subsequently, that insist that

---

43. Stephen Morse, "Undiminished Confusion in Diminished Capacity," *Journal of Criminal Law and Criminology* 75 (Spring, 1984): 30–32. For example, Morse would wholly abolish the provocation-manslaughter doctrine.

44. Stephen Morse, "The Misbegotten Marriage of Soft Psychology and Bad Law: Psychological Self-Defense as a Justification for Homicide," *Law and Human Behavior* 14 (December, 1990): 595. For a harsh critique of the implicit moral relativism of the use of expert testimony in battered wife cases, see Mira Mihajlovich, "Does Plight Make Right: The Battered Woman Syndrome Expert Testimony and the Law of Self-Defense," *Indiana Law Journal* 62 (Fall, 1987): 1252–82.

45. Michael Moore, "Moral Reality," *Wisconsin Law Review* (November, 1982): 1152–53.

46. Moore, "Moral Reality," 1152–53.

a linear distinction between true public law and illusory (that is, illegitimate or insane) private law misses salient consequences of the violent self-help analogy.

The Sociological Approach

The perspective on self-help violence that is most associated with the very name "self-help" is precisely the sociological perspective exemplified by Donald Black, and this perspective offers its own unique intellectual finesse of the issue of how law and violence can be so intimately related. Essentially, this perspective would cure us of our surprise at this relationship by telling us that there is nothing so special about law in the first place that should cause us to expect it to transcend violence. Law is a species of social control. It does not categorically differ from other forms of social control by virtue of some special moral or political legitimacy. Rather, it differs from other forms—including private self-help—according to more relative and mundane criteria, among which Black notes the criteria of form, style, and quantity.[47]

Similarly, John Griffiths, attacking the taxonomic theory that treats law as a distinct form of social control, argues that there is a relative criterion of social control we can call "legalness" which is essentially the degree of complexity of delegation of social control to third parties to disputes.[48] Legalness is just one dimension of variation in the degree of division of social control labor.[49] So one does not speak of social control as legal or nonlegal, but rather as more or less legal, and any categorical reliance on the concept of legality is essentially a folk concept that a culture may use to distinguish its control system from another.[50]

The sociological approach is obviously vital to the study of the relationship between law and violence because it is the tool best

47. Donald Black, "Social Control as a Dependent Variable," in *Toward a General Theory of Social Control*, ed. D. Black (Orlando: Academic Press, 1984), 1: 1–29. Social control, for Black, can be identified by form (between principals or with third parties) and by style (penal, compensatory, therapeutic, and conciliatory). It ranges from the formal to the informal, from violent self-help to formal punishment.

48. John Griffiths, "The Division of Labor in Social Control," in *Toward a General Theory of Social Control*, 2:37.

49. Griffiths, "Division of Labor," 38.

50. Griffiths, "Division of Labor," 38.

designed to produce the impressive data about the prevalence of the
law-enforcing motive for much criminal behavior. Whether such sociologists like Black exaggerate the frequency of this motive in the
conduct of U.S. killers, robbers, burglars, and thieves is an empirical
question that cannot be tackled here, except to note that, unless we
include in the data some of the more exotic existential delusions
captured by Jack Katz, Black's category of self-help does not seem
to capture the general run of purely acquisitive narcissistic impulse
crimes. But the subtler problem with the sociological approach lies
in its opposition to the earlier approach that denies any meaning in
the private violence legal analogy. Where the former perhaps too
readily assumes the moral hegemony or political legitimacy of law,
the latter somewhat too casually denies it, viewing law as simply an
alternative instrument to contain deviance where deviance has no
independent moral significance. A purely sociological approach risks
paying too little heed to the special moral charisma of law among
other forms of social control. It therefore fails to appreciate the peculiar political, moral, and psychological attraction that the lawmaking
or law-enforcing justification holds for private illegal actors. A criminal may well be emboldened to aggressive action precisely by the
delusion that he or she is the mere amanuensis of a higher power,
that he or she is the instrument of a higher social control.

The Inference of Moral Significance

Another approach, or set of approaches, assumes that there may well
be some important moral and jurisprudential significance to the
observed analogy between public and private acts of legal enforcement. The simplest version of this approach is what we might call
the chastened view. This somewhat sentimental perspective straightforwardly deduces that if we start with a baseline of violence as
bad—as a rupture to the human body or soul that destroys the
possibility of meaningful life—then the violent self-help analogy
should lead us to embarrassment and discomfort about our legal
system. Law can either commit violence the way private inflictors
do, or it can manifest its complicity by simultaneously tolerating
private violence and hypocritically invoking jurisdictional barriers
to interference in certain private domains.[51] Once so chastened, we

51. Martha Minow, "Words and the Door to the Land of Change: Law, Language, and Family Violence," *Vanderbilt Law Review* 43 (November 1990): 1665.

essentially face two choices. First, we can accommodate the violent self-help analogy out of a Hobbesian belief that the difference is solely due to the need to have collective organized violence in order to prevent greater and more gratuitous private violence. Second, we can sustain a tragic or ironic vision of law as an engine of the gratuitous violence of the mighty, a vision that might at least induce us to remain vigilant about the most awful excesses.

A somewhat richer version of this approach might be constructed from Robert Cover's original argument about the inherent violence of law. For Cover, law is "originally" violent in that it derives from a revolutionary act of constitution making that is essentially agonistic.[52] Legal interpretation takes place on a battlefield, and the judicial act is inherently "jurispathic"—it kills competing normative traditions. Thus, legal interpretation, and the resulting execution of legal rules, can never be "free." It is "bonded" to deeds and to jurisdictional roles as part of schemes of domination. Hence, for Cover, the analogy between public law and private self-help violence would be a form of allocation of power within the scheme of domination. In the "ecology of roles," some violent deeds will be allocated to individuals who think they are acting out the terms of the original constitution. Due process is an instrumentality that must regularly do the deed it is authorized to do. Just as in Rome a man has no natural right to possess anything—he merely has the right to acquire and then to use force to defend his acquisition[53]—so it is in law generally, and even private lawmakers or law enforcers, like picketers or right-to-life groups, must be able to impose violence to affirm their constitutional vision.[54] Thus, for Cover, the violent self-help analogy would be of great heuristic value in borrowing from the jurispathic image of the Darwinian fight among violent private parties to remind us of the Darwinian sources of constitutions and laws.

On the other hand, the law and literature scholarship, to which Cover was responding in his biting reminder about legal violence,

---

52. Kenneth Burke, quoted in Cover, "Constitutional Interpretation," 816.

53. A. W. Lintott, *Violence in Republican Rome* (Oxford: Clarendon Press, 1968), 30.

54. See Walter Benjamin, *Reflections*, trans. Edmund Jephcott (New York: Schocken Books, 1978), 277–301. For Benjamin, peace is actually a euphemism for the violent settling of new law after a war. Law is the great rationalizer of violence. In the absence of the threat of violence there cannot be a true legal contract, and without that threat the institutions of law decay.

can be read as offering a counterresponse to the violent self-help
analogy. As exemplified by one of its major practitioners, James B.
White, the law and literature movement implies a more affirmative
version of the analogy between public and private lawmaking and
law enforcement. From White, we can derive the view that if violent
activity, whether public or private, is seen as simply one subspecies
of the larger genus of human activity designed to create and identify
meaning in the world, then the violence issue is safely subsumed in
a somewhat larger one.

For White, law, like literature, is a "constitutive rhetoric" that
enriches the phenomenological forms of our culture.

> Law is in a full sense a language, for it is a way of reading and
> writing and speaking and, in doing these things, it is a way of
> maintaining a culture, largely a culture of argument, which has
> a character of its own. . . . [R]eading literature (like reading law)
> is not merely a process of observing and receiving, but an activity
> of the mind and imagination, a process that requires constant
> judgment and creation. Like law, literature is inherently com-
> munal: one learns to read a particular text in part from other
> readers, and one helps others to read it. . . . This is an interpre-
> tative culture rather like the culture of argument established by
> lawyers.[55]

The essence of social and individual life is the construction of meaning, and the principles of coherence, complexity, and integrity that
the moral and political life can draw from aesthetic standards can
be applied to and found in law.[56]

Now White himself has somewhat addressed Professor Cover's
concerns, at least by applying his general notion of law as constitutive
rhetoric to the troublesome case of the criminal law.[57] White's vision
of criminal law, as of all law, is that it is a collective expression of
moral meaning, a collective exercise in constitutive rhetoric. Specifically, it is a form of blaming, and, in assigning blame, we reaffirm

---

55. James B. White, *Heracles' Bow* (Madison: University of Wisconsin Press,
1985), 78.

56. James B. White, "Intellectual Integration," *Northwestern University Law
Review* 82 (Fall, 1987): 1, 18.

57. White, *Heracles' Bow*, 194–203.

our moral values. The key to White's understanding of the criminal law is the perceived symbiosis between the individual and collective. In White's view, the conflict between defendant and state is a conflict between two different claims of meaning for the defendant's conduct in the world. The collective act of blaming by the state must be appropriately empathetic to the moral claims of the defendant, but, at some point, the empathy must stop. Empathy, or acquiescence in the moral claims of others, becomes, in the real world, a zero-sum or finite-sum game, and some defendants must lose for the good of the victim, the society, or the state.[58]

But, for White, in a proper criminal justice system, the defendant, though he loses, will accept his punishment because he has been afforded the appropriate degree of empathy—the appropriately patient audience for his claims. That is what due process is all about. And the rhetorical structure of criminal justice is such that as the defendant—even if unsuccessfully—engages in his own legal talk, he will learn to speak in recognition of competing rhetorics; he will understand that through his conduct and his claims he is composing *his* world, not *the* world, and that he will achieve ethical enlightenment in regard to others' claims of significance. "In doing this, the community claims and performs a meaning for its own action or inaction; it defines and maintains a character of its own."[59]

The most obvious problem with White's view of criminal law is his questionable maneuvering between the collective and the individual. The "community" asks the individual to accept, at least theoretically, the practical constraints on his own power to have his composed world accepted. White views these two cultural compositions as two competing individualist aesthetics, but individualist aesthetics is a rather transparent mask for the political power that lies wholly on one side of the competition. White's real interest is in the phenomenology of the solitary, leisurely, luxuriating mind, and his benign vision of the state is a projection of that mind. In short, he does not acknowledge that the collective meaning making is also what is known as ideology. The raw power of the state is not just an adjunct to, but causes a qualitative change in, the nature of its moral endeavors. In all White's talk of "community," he underestimates the valence of the state as a social engineer.

58. White, *Heracles' Bow*, 206.
59. White, *Heracles' Bow*, 209.

The problem, of course, is that though there is, indeed, a lot of truth in his view of a symbiosis or parallelism between the individual and collective moral claims that may simultaneously actuate criminal conduct and state punishment, it is not the benign relationship he imagines. White's view of the purpose of criminal law is consistent with certain types of quasi-retributivism, particularly Durkheim's notion of collective denunciation as a means of solidifying the moral bonds of the virtuous by condemning or expelling the sinners. And the grimmer side of criminal violence is not entirely inconsistent with White's somewhat Panglossian view. As the many instances of the violent self-help analogy demonstrate, much crime is indeed an act of meaning making, of moral claiming. In fact, much crime, rather than offering a moral counterclaim to society's vision of the good, is a directly parallel and purportedly supplementary form of moral claiming and, indeed, law enforcement.

As Katz shows, some of the most apparently irrational and pathological criminals view themselves sincerely—if unjustifiably—as executors of the moral law and preservers of the social order, as ordained assigners of collective blame and prophets of collective meaning. Thus, rather than view law as punishing or deterring criminals, while finessing the issue of whether we must use violence to accomplish these goals, we might view law as inspiring and emboldening these criminals. The construction of criminal conduct offered by such sociologists as Black or Katz perversely confirms White's view that criminals are indeed meaning artists—that they are moral aestheticians who proffer their crimes as legitimate and even morally obligatory acts of expression and construction. The irony is that Katz's killers do not really offer a counteraesthetic to the collective act of blaming; rather, they actually purport to be carrying out the collectively sanctioned act of blaming. They think they are serving and indeed imitating the law in their violent marking of meaning, and, in that sense, they demonstrate how brutal the act of meaning making is.

Instrumental and Economic Approaches

Another large set of approaches to the public law–private violence parallel eschews the metaphysical and moral implications of the issue and accepts as social fact that private self-help vengeance is perceived sincerely—whether or not reasonably—as a legitimate form of law-making or law enforcement. This approach, however, sees a variety of risks of social disorganization resulting from the parallel and seeks to suppress or properly channel the private side of the analogy to achieve the best economy of moral impulse. Two somewhat "global" versions of this approach and one more conventional doctrinal version deserve mention.

The Victorian Reform Movement and Legal Violence

The first instance of an "economic" approach is a particularly striking example of a modern law reform effort consciously concerned with the violent law analogy. This is the early Victorian English reform movement that sought to distinguish violent from nonviolent offenses and to lower the punishment, or remove the violent punishment, for the latter.[60]

As background, consider that in Anglo-American jurisprudence, one of the oldest maneuvers for rationalizing legal violence treats the state not so much as, in the Hobbesian sense, an instrument for suppressing private violence, but rather as an entity legitimated by its violence; any violence in state action is attributed to God's righteousness. The state acts violently out of obligation, not out of will; it is the servant of a higher call for revenge and order. Earlier English rulers had been unembarrassed by violent punishment for nonviolent offenders—most notably thieves. Such punishments as hanging, branding, and drawing and quartering were appropriate for all felons.[61] In particular, hanging was meant not just as punishment, but as an eloquent statement of divine law. In Michel Foucault's image of old-style punishment, the broken body of the condemned represented the restored order of the body politic,[62] and the prisoner became a human sacrifice to restore the fear of God.

---

60. McGowen, "Punishing Violence, Sentencing Crime," in *The Violence of Representation*, ed. Nancy Armstrong and Leonard Tennenhouse (London: Routledge, 1989), 140.

61. But see Douglas Hay, "Property, Authority and the Criminal Law," in *Albion's Fatal Tree: Crime and Society in Eighteenth-Century England*, by D. Hay, P. Linebaugh, J. Rule, E. P. Thompson, and C. Winslow (New York: Pantheon, 1975), 17–63 (on selective, "legitimating" use of death penalty).

62. Foucault, *Discipline*, 47–48.

The Victorian reformers offered the perfectly sensible instrumental argument that if the criminal law punished nonviolent offenses as harshly as it punished violent ones, it was removing any disincentive to violent crime, or, assuming that violence was an efficient means of stealing or raping, it was providing a relatively positive incentive to use violence.[63] At the same time, the reformers felt sympathy for victims of state violence, the criminals who were not themselves violent. This was essentially a moral argument, but the reformers had an instrumental goal as well, since they feared the hardening of the hearts of the populace, the suppression of the sympathetic impulse that might be the most civilizing of forces. In making this combined moral and instrumental argument, the reformers were identifying—to a postmodernist, "inventing"—a notion of the populace as nonviolent. This was true in two senses. First, it assumed a useful distinction between violent and nonviolent criminals. Second, it assumed the existence of a noncriminal populace that could condemn crime by categorically distinguishing itself and distance itself from an alien breed of human—the violent criminal.[64]

Thus, the motive of the reformers in rewriting the criminal law was not just to reform the law but to redefine the very concept of civilization and image of state. The assault on the gratuitous use of the gallows proclaimed the dignity of human life while underscoring its vulnerability to violent assaults from the alien breed of humanity. By defining crime as the most irrationally violent form of conduct and so clearly distinguishing it from what normal humans do, the reformers aimed to discourage self-help as infeasible and increase the dependence of the citizens on a beneficent state. The state became more beneficent because it was defined in terms of the normal human community from which violent criminals were exorcised, and which would receive physical protection from the limited but efficient use of state violence. The paradox is that while the state was taking on a greater role, its role was to become, in some ways, less visible. If violent punishment was only imposed on those violent offenders whose acts were proportionate, in the retributive sense, to the punishment they would suffer, the "law" was not so much a willful form of regulation as a more efficient version of the transparently correl-

63. McGowen, "Punishing Violence," 141.
64. McGowen, "Punishing Violence," 152–53.

ative, self-punishing notion of crime and punishment Black describes in supposedly less-developed legal cultures.

The opponents of reform warned that such a change would undermine the role of the state as the visible, willful enforcer of order. They wanted criminal punishment to be active and visible, not transparent, because only through the ritual theater of punishment could order be sustained.[65] Still, the reformers wanted to circumscribe this narrow sphere called violence and distinguish both the state and the populace from it. Their Whiggish view of the moral evolution of humanity was that violence was an atavism of the primal. Thus, the gallows were a sad reminder to reformers of the primal residue—it unsettled their self-identification with the civilized and made them fearful that foreigners seeing gallows (and also all the condemned criminals) would think of the British as barbarians.

To the reformers, violence was bad for the state that inflicted it in the same way that it was horrible to its victims: it destroyed all sensibility and mind; it attacked the social affections that created civilization. At the same time, the reformers were economizing violence by suggesting that its only legitimate goal was to protect human life or physical safety, not private property. They viewed the old legal regime that punished property thieves with death as dividing society along class lines, whereas if the punishment for theft were reduced, the poor would feel united with the rich because the most visible punishments—death for homicide—would be the common denominator of legal protection for them. Moreover, to ensure that the poor could experience this bond with the rich, the spectacle of widespread public execution had to be removed—since the poor uneducated were the ones most likely to be inspired by this spectacle to revert to primal behavior. Thus, the point of legislative reform was to calibrate punishment according to the degree of violence in the offense. The law would finally become "transparent"—or, to change the metaphor, merely "reflective"—it would simply correlate with the degree of violence in crime.[66] The new violence was to be more calibrated and efficient, appealing to conscience as well as terror, creating not so much a practical horror of punishment as a moral horror of crime.

---

65. More mundanely, the opponents probably felt that, in the absence of a viable police force, the prospect of great *severity* of punishment was necessary to counterbalance the perceived *uncertainty* of punishment.

66. McGowen, "Punishing Violence," 151.

The very restraint in legal violence was part of the message. This was a way of marking the criminal as being outside society.

If this tradition of proportional punishment was intended to deter self-help violence, it does not seem very well advised in its design. First, of course, when the state tries to limit serious punishment to the most violent crimes, it takes an empirical gamble—that the populace will agree with its calibrations. If the populace does not—if, in fact, it views the state as having been too lenient toward certain types of criminals—then the gamble may fail and self-help justice may remain potent. (The problem, of course, is exacerbated where the procedural side of the law, the defendant's due process rights, obstructs the state from exacting even the reduced substantive justice it seeks.) Second, the state is taking a sort of psychological gamble. It assumes that if it alters its image from that of a willful, invasive law imposer and violent punisher to that of the mere medium of retribution, the transparent correlator of crime and punishment, it will cease to inspire or embolden individuals to inflict violent revenge themselves. This psychological gamble may fail, because potential private self-helpers may actually find that the state's "transparency" rationalization is every bit as inspirational as the cruder model of the willful violent punisher. As Jack Katz's work and as much of the literature on insanity and crime suggest, many violent criminals give way to their most murderous impulses precisely by recharacterizing their willful actions as the mere reflexes or obligations of one commanded or required to restore order and root out evil. Indeed, the state's role modeling lies precisely in the rationalization, not the violence itself.

The Example of the Death Penalty in the United States

The Victorian reformist approach to the violent law analogy, then, was to call for a carefully calibrated machine of state violence that could be justified as not only proportional to, but, in a sense, caused by, the crimes themselves. The result was to be a decrease in private self-help violence. The goal was a rational monopoly of state violence. In that regard, another rationalization for the monopoly is the familiar one that if violent self-help cannot be discouraged in the moral or psychological sense imagined by the Victorian reformers, it must be rendered wholly unnecessary and redundant by appropriate violent action by the state. This view of the monopoly principle is summed up by Justice Potter Stewart in the landmark death penalty decision, *Gregg v. Georgia*,[67] which described and ratified the legitimate version of capital punishment that is now the law of the land. In rejecting the argument that the death penalty was categorically unconstitutional because it served no legitimate social purpose, Justice Stewart says,

> The instinct for retribution is part of the nature of man, and channeling that instinct in the administration of criminal justice serves an important purpose in promoting the stability of a society governed by law. When people begin to believe that organized society is unwilling or unable to impose upon criminal offenders the punishment they "deserve," then there are sown the seeds of anarchy self-help, vigilante justice, and lynch law.[68]

Significantly, Justice Stewart assumes that self-help against murderers is the natural lot of society, and that the state must intervene to kill—presumably more selectively and more rationally—to prevent the more random or widespread killing by private avengers. This is a version of Stephen's famous analogy of law and violence to the relationship of the marriage bed to wanton lust,[69] though it is important to note that the image of lawless society here is a bit inapt. What legal state violence replaces is not random, Hobbesian, self-interested rapacity, but the very *lawlike* phenomenon of retributive violence for perceived wrongs.[70]

A few obvious problems with Justice Stewart's monopoly idea come to mind. First, like the Victorian law reform project, it takes an empirical gamble that the populace will feel that its perceived need for redress against wrongs has been satisfactorily addressed by the state. But substantive and procedural limitations on the death

---

67. Gregg v. Georgia, 408 U.S. 238 (1972).

68. *Gregg*, 308 (Stewart, J., plurality opinion).

69. See James Fitzjames Stephen, *A History of the Criminal Laws of England* (1883), 81–82.

70. See Sarat and Kearns, "Journey." For a discussion of how Weber and Foucault treat the zero-sum game of social vengeance, including the state's selective delegation to private parties, see Jonathan Rieder, "The Social Organization of Vengeance," in *Toward a General Theory of Social Control*, ed. D. Black (Orlando: Academic Press, 1984), 131.

penalty and other serious punishments may render that a losing gamble. Second, there remains the danger, for which there is indeed some anecdotal evidence, that the state's message will be received the wrong way. Instead of feeling that their justified complaints against others have been adequately redressed by the state, people with homicidal impulses against wrongdoers may feel more inspired by the volitional act of the state to carry out violent vengeance themselves.

If violence feels like law, one might assume that, other things being equal, violent revengers might prefer to defer to the law to do their revenge for them. Hence, one empirical observation is that self-help is more common when wronged people feel they cannot rely on the state to help them. This is trivially true in cases where government will not act at all—as in gambling and drug contracts where violence may be a method of debt collection—and is more seriously true in ghetto life, where self-help may be a cry for help from the police.

Yet the evidence that murders tend to increase after executions suggests that quite the opposite may be true.[71] Namely, many wronged people, as a practical matter, have no reason to defer to the state in matters of revenge, but, because the very inspiration for their violence is that violence gives them the moral satisfaction of law enforcement, the state, in executing a killer, actually serves as an inspirational role model for private avengers. It may therefore seem quixotic for the state, relying on Justice Stewart's assumptions, to think that its monopoly on violence can be successful. But, indeed, for a variety of complex reasons, the modern U.S. legal system hedges its bets anyway, because, though Justice Stewart's view might seem to support an absolute monopoly over fatal violence in the case of capital punishment, as a general matter the modern state takes on only a qualified form of monopoly. The law seeks stasis, so it tries to accommodate the impulse toward self-help legal violence by encouraging or tolerating the optimal amount and form of it, or it discourages "excess" violence by rendering private violence superfluous. If the goal of the monopoly of violence is to cure violence, it is not necessarily optimal to have a complete monopoly, and the modern state is deeply ambivalent about how to divide up the market shares.

Thus, though reinstituting capital punishment for, among other reasons, the one cited in *Gregg v. Georgia*, the state has economized

---

71. William J. Bowers, *Legal Homicide: Death as Punishment in America, 1864–1982* (Boston: Northeastern University Press, 1984), 271–302.

at least on this most severe punishment by essentially limiting it to retribution for the most severe category of crimes—first-degree murder.[72] But beyond its self-limitation on appropriate justifications for capital punishment, U.S. law, viewed as a social and cultural as well as legal entity, authorizes numerous self-help crimes and, indeed, tolerates them profligately. With respect to some types of crimes, a shockingly low number of incidents are prosecuted. Moreover, as with some cases of domestic violence, so with nonstranger crimes generally, the attitude of the police may be that self-help is permissible so long as it is properly targeted—that is, so long as it does not have wider, disruptive effects on "innocent people." Thus, the common view of the alternative between law and private violence, or the association of self-help violence and statelessness, is a very superficial one. Put differently, the principle enunciated in *Gregg* should be viewed as one of optimal complementarity, not complete substitution. In fact, the mutual associations between public and private violent revenge are complex and symbiotic.

Legal Defenses as Doctrinal Adjustments

Following on this notion of optimal complementarity, we can turn to the formal doctrinal machinery by which U.S. law qualifies its supposed key principle—the forbidding of self-help violence. The most important area of legal doctrine here is the panoply of justification and excuse defenses, the so-called affirmative defenses.[73] Without getting excessively technical, their common denominator is basically this: they are arguments and facts that a defendant can invoke after the state has successfully proved that he or she has committed the elements of an offense with the appropriate mental state. That is, they are to be distinguished from such claims as alibi or mistake of fact, which are essentially refutations of the state's proof that the elements of the crime exist. Therefore, in a sense, they are the arguments a person can make in favor of his or her "right" to commit a "crime"—very often a violent one.

The key affirmative defenses are necessity, duress, defensive force,

---

72. See Coker v. Georgia, 433 U.S. 584 (1977).

73. See, generally, Paul Robinson, *Criminal Law Defenses* (St. Paul: West Publishing, 1984); Joshua Dressler, *Understanding Criminal Law* (New York: Matthew Bender, 1988).

and insanity. Though the specific doctrinal criteria of all of them are complex and important, perhaps the most relevant question about them is general and conceptual: how to distinguish those affirmative defenses that are "justifications" from those that are excuses. To set the distinction in general, we can look at the one very uncontroversial application of the distinction: insanity is always and only an excuse, not a justification.[74] That is, if we assume a person has, say, committed an intentional homicide with the required exhibition of mental state—intent—we may nevertheless find, depending on the complexities of the applicable insanity formula, that he was so disordered by a mental disease that he ought not be held blameworthy, but, in so saying, we are not finding any social utility in his homicidal action. We wish he had restrained himself or been restrained, but we cannot blame him—with criminal punishment—for the outcome.

In contrast, self-defense is often (not always) viewed as a justification, not an excuse.[75] Assume an innocent citizen is accosted by a mugger. The mugger is about to stab the citizen with a knife, but the citizen, grabbing a (legally possessed) gun, shoots the mugger to death. Arguably in this case, unlike the insanity case, the reason we will not punish the citizen is that we approve his action as socially useful—we want to save his life. Of course, we may prefer to save both lives (at least until the mugger can get due process), but if we are denied that option, we find it better for society that the citizen live than the mugger.

Various general principles support justification. We say that some "justified crimes" serve the larger public benefit—for example, where a policeman kills a fleeing felon; we view the decedent as having acted so wrongly as to forfeit his or her moral right to safety and legal protection; we see the defendant as protecting a private interest that is recognized as a social entitlement or a private interest that it is in the public interest to enhance. In contrast, excuse doctrine assumes that, under certain sorts of circumstances, certain conduct

---

74. Except to note that many maniacs think they are avenging higher principles or paranoically ridding the world of evil. Insanity is simply useful as the excuse pole to help us test, for example, whether duress is an excuse or justification.

75. True self-defense includes cases where the killer mistakenly, but rationally, infers that the other person is about to attack him or her violently. "Imperfect" self-defense, which is punished as manslaughter, occurs when the actor wrongly and unreasonably—but sincerely—believes he or she faces imminent harm. The latter is an excuse defense, as may well be the former.

is not deterrable and therefore should not be punished, that the person is not blameworthy if overcome by a force acting on his emotions, or that an excused act casts no aspersions on the defendant's moral character.[76] Of course, we can also characterize the self-defense claim as an excuse. That is, we may refuse to find it at all socially useful that the mugger die without due process, but we can say that, for objectively grounded reasons, the citizen felt terrified for his or her life, and though the mugger was killed intentionally, the citizen acted in a distraught frame of mind that we cannot find blameworthy.

Now a common objection to putting this question at all is that it is both abstract and unnecessary, simply because little turns on it. Whether we call the defense an excuse or a justification, the result is the same—acquittal of the citizen.[77] Prof. Kent Greenawalt has raised this objection in an especially subtle way.[78] Greenawalt gives the example of the rule of retreat for dwellings. Where a legislature decrees that a person acting in self-defense need not retreat from aggression if she is in her own dwelling, it may have two different reasons. It may view the refusal to retreat as a positive good, affirming the sacredness of dwellings, or it may view it as merely a morally tolerable (if socially counterproductive) alternative. A third view is that refusal is wrong, but irresistible to most retreaters and not worth trying to sanction. Both proponents of justification doctrine and proponents of excuse doctrine believe that the self-defender here should be acquitted, but if they had to resolve the grounds they might never establish the rule. Conversely, if the doctrinal conflict were resolved, some powerful voice would feel silenced.[79]

Prof. Joshua Dressler disagrees.[80] He argues, as do many feminist critics,[81] that requiring legislators and juries to work out these difficult distinctions does have important consequences. As a legal matter, it

---

76. Dressler, *Understanding Criminal Law,* 179–86.

77. What effects do the classifications produce? The law might treat the refusal as justified where there is no safe escape but merely excused if there is a safe escape. A verdict of acquittal would not reveal the true grounds.

78. Kent Greenawalt, "The Perplexing Borders of Justification and Excuse," *Columbia Law Review* 84 (December, 1984): 1897.

79. Greenawalt, "Borders," 1905–7.

80. Dressler, *Understanding Criminal Law,* 188–90.

81. Phyllis Crocker notes that ideological consequences with regard to gender follow from the distinction; see Crocker, "The Meaning of Equality for Battered Women Who Kill in Self-Defense," *Harvard Women's Law Journal* 8 (Spring, 1985): 121, 130–31.

might affect procedural issues such as retroactivity,[82] the burden of proof, the liability of accomplices, or the right of third persons to stop one of the parties. But the real issue is one of moral guidance to society—whether law, beyond pragmatically deciding which individuals merit punishment, is supposed to be a moral instrument demarking the boundary between right and wrong violence.

Thus, the often-decried failure of U.S. law to draw a fully coherent distinction between justification and excuse reveals its ambivalence about this more fundamental set of issues concerning when private justice is tolerable and laudable. In developing a jurisprudence of violence, it may be important to tell when the state is *approving* violence because violent law enforcement power is of definable social utility, and when the state is merely *tolerating* violence because it acknowledges that its own law enforcement powers cannot satisfy the self-help legal impulses of individuals. Our system may keep the line blurry precisely to retain flexibility in asserting the general principle of the state monopoly on violence, while subliminally sending signals to private avengers that a certain amount of socially useful (or inevitable) self-help violence will go overlooked.

The ambivalence of our system over when to rely on justification rather than excuse doctrine—or over whether to ask the question at all—produces some of the most interesting questions in specific applications of affirmative defense doctrines, including questions of private citizens' rights to attack fleeing felons, battered wife self-defense cases, and, with reference to the notorious Goetz case, the purported "battered citizen" self-defense claim. With respect to fleeing felons, the Supreme Court recently took on the issue of the right of the police to use fatal violence against dangerous but non-death-threatening felons,[83] but the parallel right of private citizens remains unclear.[84] This issue is especially interesting, since, by definition, it raises the problem of when a citizen can act precisely analogously to an agent of the state. The battered wife cases, which have caused us to reassess our overly abstracted notions of when a "reasonable person" feels threatened by "imminent" harm, have so well illuminated the special perspective of the battered wife as to blur any easy distinctions

---

82. One can rely on a justification later repealed, but not on an excuse, since no one can claim to rely on the notice provided by an excuse.

83. Tennessee v. Garner, 471 U.S. 1 (1985).

84. See People v. Couch, 439 N.W.2d 354 (Mich. App. 1989).

between the subjective and objective, which is to say between the excusable and the justifiable.[85]

The Goetz case raises some of the very same issues as the battered wife cases, though in a context that, to many people, seems so crudely different that it forces us once again to consider how our abstract treatment of excuse or justification helps us finesse our deep ambivalence about self-help violence. To some, Goetz was a hero; to others he was pathetically crazy; to others still, he was a racist criminal. The Goetz case is at the very border of our ambivalence, because his claim was tested as one of conventional self-defense,[86] but the subjective quality of it—and probably the reason for his acquittal of attempted murder—is that he saw himself as acting on behalf of law for the greater good of the innocent citizens of New York City.

"Necessity" doctrine also raises interesting instances of the larger problem. Though most of the modern cases in the area, even where they involve breaches of the peace, are not violent in the intuitive sense, they bear on the symbolic issue of law and violence. Some may view necessity as an excuse—the subjective belief in the necessity of order-restoring or sin-punishing action may exculpate the person from blameworthiness. That view, however, is rare, especially since, universally, some sort of objective grounding for that defense is necessary. The more interesting cases, the modern political ones involving nuclear or abortion protestors,[87] raise the paradoxical question of how a person can be legally justified in taking action that is known to be against the law—indeed, precisely action taken as a protest against the law. Is a government in a state of hopeless self-contradiction if it finds justification here? Or is this apparent condition of self-contradiction in fact a pragmatic maneuver for the state to hedge its bets, again, on its monopoly over both law and violence? Or is the state simply required to give individual jurors the chance to subvert and nullify the law to let off steam? The issue arises interestingly in the nuclear cases, where the issue is often whether the violent action bears on a political or economic question that the legislature has not fully addressed.[88] Is violence then a method of legislation or lobbying, as well as law enforcement?

---

85. E.g., State v. Leidholm, 334 N.W.2d 811 (1983).
86. See People v. Goetz, 197 N.E.2d 41 (1986).
87. See Dressler, *Understanding Criminal Law*, 151–53.
88. State v. Warshow, 410 A.2d 1000 (1980).

A further expression of our rationalizing efforts to place optimal limits on the state's monopoly over violence and law enforcement is the provocation-manslaughter doctrine. It is an instance of ambivalence precisely because provocation cases are avowedly compromises and, often, admittedly awkward ones. A successful provocation claim, unlike an affirmative defense, does not cancel, but only mitigates, liability; it turns murder into manslaughter.[89] Historically, provocation can be seen as a partial excuse. It views the provoked person as crazed by passion; though he kills intentionally, he is not as culpable as a more cool-headed killer. Yet the classically rigorous laws delimiting the types of legally adequate provocation raise the subjective/objective distinction again.

The old rules might be viewed as partly justificatory. If the victim had done something identifiably wrong—assaulted the defendant or his relative or engaged in adultery with his spouse—the law accommodated the law-enforcing impulse experienced by the defendant. Indeed, the partial mitigation doctrine coexisted with another version—the full honor defense—as well as the informal acquittal doctrine based on the behavior of juries.[90] Many manslaughter cases have involved righteous but clear-headed indignation, not crazed passion. Though the laws often required proof that the killer had seen the act personally, thus apparently relying on deterministic assumptions about what would cause an excusing state of mind, they might also be viewed as due process or evidence rules that serve as premises for the legal revenge volitionally exacted by the killer. Put another way, the awkward compromise might have been viewed as a subtle distribution of deterrent power. By signaling that a provoked killer might be at least partly excused, the law also signals assaulters and adulterers that they ought to be deterred from their provocative conduct because the law would not apply the full deterrent sanction against their killers.

In recent years, inspired by the Model Penal Code, many states have greatly expanded the category of adequate provocation. Instead of enumerating specific categories of provocative conduct, they permit

---

89. E.g., Model Penal Code §210.3. To be perfectly technical, the provocation is not a defense at all, but a rebuttal to an element of the "malice aforethought" that the state must bear the burden of proving in order to convict of murder.

90. Laurie Taylor, "Provoked Reason in Men and Women," *UCLA Law Review* 33 (Spring, 1986): 1679.

the partial excuse where the killer was placed in heat of passion by some—or any—reasonable cause.[91] As a subjective matter, this may appear to be a psychological correction of the earlier rules—a wider variety of things might "reasonably" provoke people than was imagined by the common law. But the concept of reason here has always been a paradox. Reasonable people do not kill, except in certain situations where we wholly justify or excuse their killing because it is, indeed, a reasonable thing to do. The partial reasonable excuse is a bizarre enigma, one we resolve by saying that the reasonable person would have *felt* homicidal, but that *this* person was excessively unreasonable because he or she *acted on* the impulse.[92] But we might also view this new, more flexible provocation doctrine as expanding the range of situations in which violence can feel like law—in any case of slight or insult or humiliation. Whether this expansion is a sign of moral progress or of greater psychological sophistication is unclear. It may be a concession not so much to human frailty as to the increasing recognition that law cannot satisfy people's need for law. In any event, it demonstrates the law's concession to limits on its monopoly over violent law enforcement. Judges, legislators, juries, and academics tirelessly rearrange the doctrines of mitigation and defense, uncertain how to achieve the optimal allocation of market shares in violent legal redress.

Conclusion

The analogy between public legal authority and private remedial violence seems fraught with legal and moral salience, yet it remains an elusive, if tempting, subject. My goal here has not been to derive any unitary significance from the analogy, but rather to show how it is or can be as vexing a challenge to jurisprudence as is the more general issue of the link between law and violence. Certainly the majority of predatory crimes are too simply acquisitive and selfish to fall within the reach of the analogy, and a criminal's claim that he or she was serving as a proxy for the law may often be a lie, a

---

91. A notorious example is People v. Berry, 18 Cal.3d (1976), where the killer-husband introduced expert psychiatric evidence that his wife's suicidal impulses led her to engage in sexual taunting of the defendant that, in turn, caused his homicidal response.

92. Model Penal Code, commentary to §210.3.

delusion, or a nice literary construction served up after the fact. However, Robert Cover's admonition that we recall the inherently violent nature of law suggests that, for a great many criminals suffering a stressful or threatening relationship to friends, relatives, neighbors, employers, or, in some more abstract way, "society," the attractiveness of self-perceived legal justification as a motive or inspiration to crime may be powerful. I am, therefore, inclined to side with those who sense a discomfiting moral lesson in the analogy. Though the law and literature movement has treated the act of meaning making as a bit too precious and sentimental, it seems right in viewing human endeavor as largely concerned with constructing moral order for humans to live in. Crime is largely a form of purposive endeavor, and the vocabulary, ideology, symbols, and sentiments of public lawmaking and law enforcement are alluring and useful tools.

Making Peace with Violence: Robert Cover on Law and Legal Theory

Austin Sarat and Thomas R. Kearns

"Violence," Walter Benjamin argues, "violence crowned by fate, is the origin of law. . . ."[1] Violence is a perverse utopia of action without form and instinct without deliberation[2] from which all law—natural or positive—is the fall.[3] Absent the threat, prospect, or possibility of disorder and aggression in the worlds that all of us inhabit, law, as we know it, would be unnecessary.[4] And what is law, after all,

We are grateful for the helpful comments of Lawrence Douglas.

Portions of this essay appear in revised form in *Narrative, Violence, and the Law: Essays of Robert Cover*, edited by Martha Minow, Michael Ryan, and Austin Sarat (Ann Arbor: University of Michigan Press, 1992).

1. Walter Benjamin, "Critique of Violence," in *Reflections*, trans. Edmund Jepchott (New York: Harcourt, Brace, Jovanovich, 1978), 286. For an important commentary on Benjamin and the search for the origin of law, see Jacques Derrida, "Force of Law: The 'Mystical Foundation of Authority,'" *Cardozo Law Review* 11 (1990): 919.

2. See Nietzsche, *The Birth of Tragedy and The Genealogy of Morals*, trans. Francis Golffing (Garden City, N.Y.: Doubleday, 1956); see also Benjamin, "Critique," 277.

3. As Friedrich Nietzsche puts it,
   I take bad conscience to be a deep-seated malady to which man succumbed under the pressure of the most profound transformation he ever underwent— the one that made him once and for all a sociable and pacific creature. Just as happened in the case of those sea creatures who were forced to become land animals in order to survive, these semi-animals, happily adapted to the wilderness, to war, to free roaming, and adventure, were forced to change their nature. (Nietzsche, *Birth of Tragedy*, 217)
   Benjamin also suggests that, while natural law regards violence as a product of nature, positive law sees violence as a product of history (Benjamin, "Critique," 278).

4. See Thomas Hobbes, *Leviathan*, ed. C. B. MacPherson (New York: Penguin

but a partially realized promise to overcome disorder and aggression,[5] tame and domesticate force, and subject action and instinct to reason and will?[6]

Violence stands before the law, unruly; it defies the law to protect us from its cruelest consequences.[7] It demands that law respond in kind, and requires law to traffic in its own brand of force and coercion.[8] It is thus that point of departure from which complete departure is impossible.[9] It is the task of law and of much legal theory to insist, nonetheless, on the difference between the force that law uses and the unruly force beyond its borders.[10] Legal theorists name the superiority of the former by calling it legitimate.[11] In that naming is the

Books, 1986). As Mark Taylor argues, "Force is comprehended in law. Since the structure of force is isomorphic with the structure of law, each perfectly mirrors the other" (Taylor "Desire of Law/Law of Desire," *Cardozo Law Review* 11 [1990]: 1270).

    5. Laws, Paul De Man argues,

    are future-oriented and prospective; their illocutionary mode is that of the *promise*. On the other hand, every promise assumes a date at which the promise is made and without which it would have no validity; laws are promissory notes in which the present of the promise is always a past with regard to its realization. (Paul de Man, *Allegories of Reading: Figural Language in Rousseau, Nietzsche, Rilke and Proust* [New Haven: Yale University Press, 1979], 273)

    6. In the well-known case of *United States v. Holmes*, this promise is described in the following terms: "The law of nature forms part of the municipal law; and in a proper case . . . , homicide is justifiable, not because the municipal law is subverted by the law of nature, but because no rule of the municipal law makes homicide in such cases criminal" (26 *Fed. Cas.* 360 [C.E.D. Pa. 1842], reprinted in Joseph Goldstein, Alan Dershowitz, and Richard Schwartz, *Criminal Law: Theory and Process* [New York: Free Press, 1974], 1028). Yet the promise is at best partially realized because law itself is a disordering force in social relations. See Peter Fitzpatrick, "Violence and Legal Subjection" (University of Kent, 1991, Photocopy).

    7. For a fuller description of how the image of a defiant, unruly violence works in legal theory, see Austin Sarat and Thomas R. Kearns, "A Journey Through Forgetting: Toward a Jurisprudence of Violence," in *The Fate of Law*, ed. Austin Sarat and Thomas R. Kearns (Ann Arbor: University of Michigan Press, 1991).

    8. Taylor, "Desire of Law," 272; Fitzpatrick, "Legal Subjection," 2.

    9. As Derrida puts it, "If the origin of law is a violent positioning, the latter manifests itself in the purest fashion when violence is absolute, that is to say when it touches on the right to life and death" (Derrida, "Force of Law," 1005).

    10. See Sarat and Kearns, "Journey." Robert Paul Wolff contends that, in the eyes of law and legal theory, "murder is an act of violence, but capital punishment by a *legitimate state* is not; theft or extortion is violent, but the collection of taxes by a *legitimate state* is not" (Robert Paul Wolff, "Violence and the Law," in *The Rule of Law*, ed. Robert Paul Wolff [New York: Simon and Schuster, 1971], 59).

    11. See H. H. Gerth and C. Wright Mills, eds. and trans., *From Max Weber: Essays in Sociology* (New York: Oxford University Press, 1946), 78; also see Wolff, "Violence"; Edgar Friedenberg, "The Side Effects of the Legal Process," in *The Rule*

idea that violence can be cleansed, if not purified, by its contact with law.[12]

Yet the violence that calls law into being and becomes part of its arsenal makes law, or at least the achievement of particular kinds of law, impossible. It both provokes the hope of law and defeats the hope that law can be other-than-violence.[13] Violence, indispensable as it is to the generation of law, casts a persistent shadow and requires us to ask how, if at all, the force of law differs from the force it is called into being to regulate as well as whether law can accommodate and control violence without becoming a captive of its own violent instincts. While the threat of force provides a constant justification of and apology for law, it is also a constant reminder of what all law really is. ". . . [I]n this very violence," Benjamin writes, "something rotten in law is revealed"[14]

All too often, and all too much, legal theory has asserted and attended to the alleged legitimacy of law's violence without paying heed to the "rottenness" that violence reveals and to the price that it exacts from law.[15] In this essay we attend, in particular, to that

---

of Law, ed. Robert Paul Wolff (New York: Simon and Schuster, 1971), 43; Bernhard Waldenfels, "Limits of Legitimation and the Question of Violence," in *Justice, Law, and Violence,* ed. James Brady and Newton Garver (Philadelphia: Temple University Press, 1991). For an interesting examination of the way law legitimates itself, see Samuel Weber, "In the Name of the Law," *Cardozo Law Review* 11 (1990): 1515.

12. Karl Olivecrona calls for an explicit recognition that the violence of law is neither transformed nor purified. As he argues, in most writing about law,

actual violence is . . . kept very much in the background. . . . Such a state of things is apt to create the belief that violence is alien to law, or of secondary importance. That is, however, a fatal illusion. . . . [Law's] real character is largely obscured and this is done by metaphysical ideas and expressions. It is not bluntly said, e.g., that the function of the courts is to determine the use of force. Instead their function is said to be the "administration of justice" or the ascertaining of "rights" and "duties." (Karl Olivecrona, *Law As Fact* [Copenhagen: Einer Munksgaard, 1939], 125)

13. As Sarat and Kearns argue,

Force is disdainful of reason; it pushes it aside; it takes over completely. Reason and force have no way to share control of human agency. Where the two meet in battle only one can win, and given the levels of force, pain, and violence at law's disposal, law, wherever it wants, is assured of victory. It appears, then, that law's violence does not sit well—indeed it wars with—the conception of human agency that is built into, and held out to us by, a jurisprudence of rules." (Sarat and Kearns, "Journey," 269)

14. Benjamin, "Critique," 286. In this phrase, Derrida contends, Benjamin meant to suggest that "law is a violence contrary to nature" (Derrida, "Force of Law," 1005).

15. A good example of this tendency in legal theory is provided by Ronald

price; we ask what difference violence makes to, and in, law, and whether law can ever make peace with violence. Can law do homicidal deeds[16] without itself being "jurispathic"?[17] What possibilities for law are precluded by its continuing reliance on force and coercion? Against those who believe that law can tame and conquer violence, we attend to the ways law is conquered by violence. We do so by examining the work of Robert Cover.[18]

We focus on Cover because he was both a visionary legal thinker who saw law as a bridge between the world-of-the-present and the world-of-our-imaginings,[19] and someone who nonetheless provided the most compelling contemporary account of the relationship between law and violence. In Cover, we find both a critic of and an apologist for law's violence; we find an insistence that law be different from, and more than, violence; and that law lead human society toward toleration, respect, and community, combined with a reluctant embrace of legal force. In Cover, we find a self-proclaimed anarchist, "with anarchy understood to mean the absence of rulers not the absence of law,"[20] nonetheless seeking to identify the conditions for the *effective,* but domesticated, organization and deployment of law's violence.[21]

Cover was hopeful about law even in the shadow of violence. We are much less hopeful. He sought to acknowledge law's violence

---

Dworkin, who treats the occasion of law's violence as that which requires an examination of the adequacy of the "principles" that justify it. See Dworkin, *Taking Rights Seriously* (Cambridge, Mass.: Harvard University Press, 1977), 15.

16. The most striking and important example of such homicidal deeds is the death penalty. As Benjamin puts it, "In the exercise of violence over life and death more than in any other legal act, law reaffirms itself" (Benjamin, "Critique," 286).

17. This phrase is used by Robert Cover to describe the tendency to kill or destroy legal meaning. See Cover, "Nomos and Narrative," *Harvard Law Review* 97 (1983): 4, 40.

18. We focus on three articles in particular, "Nomos and Narrative," "Violence and the Word" (*Yale Law Journal* 95 [1986]: 1601), and "The Bonds of Constitutional Interpretation: Of the Word, the Deed, and the Role" (*Georgia Law Review* 20 [1986]: 815).

19. For a discussion of Cover's vision, see Ronald Garet, "Meaning and Ending," *Yale Law Journal* 96 (1987): 1801.

20. Robert Cover, "Folktales of Justice: Tales of Jurisdiction," *Capital University Law Review* 14 (1985): 179, 181.

21. Mark Tushnet explains this by saying, "I doubt that Cover was a romantic anarchist who believed that the practice of individual violence would disappear in a well-ordered anarchy" (Mark Tushnet, "Reflections on Capital Punishment: One Side of an Uncompleted Discussion," *Journal of Law and Religion* 7 [1989]: 25).

and temper or domesticate it in a reconstruction of the premises of law's relationship to society. We, however, fear that the violence of law stands in the way of such a reconstruction. To use his own language, he believed that law could be homicidal without being "jurispathic." We do not share his belief. While we admire Cover for taking the violence of law seriously and for facing up to the way that violence is both an indispensable feature of law and, at the same time, deeply antagonistic to it, we do not think that he saw fully the difficulties of accommodating violence and law.[22]

How could this self-proclaimed "anarchist" and visionary legal thinker nonetheless embrace and defend the violence of law?[23] How could Cover so clearly understand the dangers of organizing and deploying violence and not recoil from the danger that such violence would destroy any normative vision that opposed it? How could he make peace with law's violence? These are the questions we seek to answer about Cover, and, through Cover, about the violence of law itself.

The Emergence of "Law's Violence": A Conceptual Revision

Despite the obvious importance of the relationship of law and violence, it is a subject about which little is written and little is known.[24] Though there are several famous explorations of the coercive and punitive dimensions of law,[25] contemporary jurisprudence, at least until Cover, largely avoided the subject.[26] Cover, in essence, rein-

---

22. We worry that he did not see the way in which an acceptance of the violence of law imprisons legal theory and limits the legal imagination. Describing tensions and limitations in Cover's thought about law and violence is one way of getting a handle on the tensions and limitations that plague law whenever it, as inevitably it must, traffics in violence.

23. For a similar question asked about Cover in the context of capital punishment, see Tushnet, "Reflections."

24. There are, of course, notable exceptions. See Gerth and Mills, *From Max Weber*; Hans Kelsen, *General Theory of Law and the State*, trans. Anders Wedberg (New York: Russell and Russell, 1945); Noberto Bobbio, "Law and Force," *Monist* 48 (1965): 321; also see James Brady and Newton Garver, eds., *Justice, Law, and Violence* (Philadelphia: Temple University Press, 1991).

25. For a useful overview and summary of this work, see Jack Gibbs, *Crime, Punishment, and Deterrence* (New York: Elsevier, 1975).

26. Contemporary scholars treat the violence of law as too obvious to merit

vented the subject of violence and its relationship to law; indeed, it may seem odd, but we think it is not too much of an exaggeration, to claim that, before Cover's writings on law's violence, the topic was in danger of being lost to contemporary legal theory.[27] By this we mean more than just that, prior to his work, contemporary writers had largely lost their taste for the subject. Though it is true that law's violence was receiving little attention in legal theory, this was hardly the result of mere inadvertence or neglect. Rather, it was a consequence of a purposive effort to free thought about law from its fixation on law-as-force, to kill once and for all the distracting ghost of Leviathan. Meaning and normativity, not physics and force, were, before Cover's intervention, fast becoming the centerpieces of law talk.[28] Violence, where it was noted at all, was treated as marginal or vestigial.[29] In this setting, it was no easy matter to celebrate the death of Hobbes's beast and yet resurrect for renewed study the continuing and unavoidable reality of law's violence. But such was part of Cover's accomplishment.

Cover, though he did not believe that law was force and only force, insisted that law's violence was neither vestigial nor marginal. He claimed that all "legal interpretive acts signal and occasion the imposition of violence upon others: A judge articulates her understanding of a text, and as a result, somebody loses his freedom, his property, his children, even his life."[30] This is certainly not news to

---

sustained attention and choose instead to emphasize the ideological, interpretive, meaning-affirming qualities of law. While no one pretends that law does not coerce and punish, many push such facts to the margin or claim that the violence in and around law is vestigial and incidental to our understanding of what law is. For one explanation of this development, see Robert Gordon, "New Developments in Legal Theory," in *The Politics of Law*, 2d ed., ed. David Kairys (New York: Pantheon, 1990).

27. Since Cover wrote "Violence and the Word," there has been a revival of interest in the subject of violence and its connection to law. See, for example, Derrida, "Force of Law."

28. This is not to suggest that his intervention derailed, or was intended to derail, this development. For recent examples of the emphasis on meaning and normativity, see James Boyd White, *Justice As Translation* (Chicago: University of Chicago Press, 1990); Robert Post, ed., *Law and the Order of Culture* (Berkeley: University of California Press, 1991).

29. This is a point amply illustrated by Michel Foucault; see *Discipline and Punish*, trans. Alan Sheridan (New York: Vintage Books, 1979).

30. See Cover, "Violence," 1601.

even the most casual observer of the legal system. As Karl Olivecrona put it almost fifty years before Cover,

> According to an old and well-known line of thought law and force are regarded as opposite things. Force as such is put in opposition to law. In view of the extensive use of force, under the name of law, in the state organization, the contrast is, however, obviously false. Law as applied in real life includes a certain kind of force. It is organized, regulated force used against criminals, debtors and others according to patterns laid down by lawgivers.[31]

Indeed, by Cover's own account, to observe that "neither legal interpretation nor the violence it occasions may be properly understood apart from one another," is merely to state the "obvious."[32] Yet he wrote about violence, about the violence in and around law, and its inseparable connection to interpretation as a reminder of what he knew would seem obvious once stated;[33] he wrote to bring to mind what he feared would be too easily forgotten in the rush to assimilate law into humanistic scholarship,[34]

---

31. See Olivecrona, *Law As Fact*, 126, 134.

32. Cover, "Violence," 1601.

33. "In law to be an interpreter is to be a force, an actor who creates effects even though or in the face of violence" (Cover, "Constitutional Interpretation," 833). See also Drucilla Cornell, "From the Lighthouse: The Promise of Redemption and the Possibility of Legal Interpretation," *Cardozo Law Review* 11 (1990): 1687.

34. Though Cover lent his own considerable intellectual energy to the project of opening legal scholarship to humanistic impulses and to the materials of humanistic disciplines—history, literature, philosophy, and religion—he believed that law would neither sit comfortably with those materials nor be easily reconciled with those impulses. While he was eager to explore similarities between law and the humanities, as well as the interpretive dimensions of legal activity and the community-building, meaning-making aspects of law, he worried that an exclusive focus on those things would produce a distorted view. This view would, even if unintentionally, encourage or tolerate the violence of law or, worse yet, make it possible for us to live easily, complacently, with that violence.

Cover candidly acknowledged that exploration of differences, tensions, and discomforts in the relationship between law and the humanities might, given the nature of his own earlier work, seem "surprising, even contradictory" (Cover, "Constitutional Interpretation," 815). Yet it is perhaps characteristic of his love of the plural, the diverse, and the contested that he would take issue with scholars who sought to identify an essential "unity" between the meaning-making, interpretive

namely, what he called "the organized social practice of violence."[35]

When Cover contemplated that practice, he confronted a fault line that gave law a shape and character not replicable in any interpretive activity that did not make its mark on bodies.[36] When Cover contemplated violence, he understood the fancy way in which interpretation, because it is never entirely innocent nor entirely harmless, does violence;[37] he understood and acknowledged how contests over meaning always carry the possibility, and the danger, that one will prevail and extinguish all others. But the violence in which he displayed his most sustained and engaged interest (and the violence in which we are interested in this essay) was the brute physical force available to, and used by, the state against those who disobey or defy its authority.[38]

Such force is translated routinely, though not without studied and careful organization, the marshaling of strong justifications, and recognizable roles and structures, into pain, blood, and death, words that Cover himself used as if they were synonyms for violence. "In

activities of law, and the work of the humanities. And it is in this effort to deny the unity of law and the humanities where Cover's interest in violence found its location and its home.

35. See Cover, "Violence," 1602 n. 2.

36. Cover's exploration of differences between law and other interpretive enterprises, and the nature of his disagreement with others in the effort to promote interdisciplinary legal scholarship, are perhaps best glimpsed in a long footnote to "Violence and the Word" (1601–2 n. 2). In that footnote, Cover observes that "there has been a recent explosion of legal scholarship placing interpretation at the crux of law," acknowledges the rhetorical, interpretive, meaning-making quality of law, and, in this way, allies himself with Ronald Dworkin (see Dworkin, "Law as Interpretation," *Texas Law Review* 60 [1982]: 527), James Boyd White, and other humanist scholars of law. At the same time, however, he notes, with some alarm, that "the violent side of law and its connection to interpretation and rhetoric is systematically ignored or underplayed" in humanist scholarship (Cover, "Violence," 1602 n. 2). Because of law's inexorable tie to violence, because of the painful consequences of all legal activity, because its interpretations and meanings are inscribed on bodies, law, Cover claimed, could never be just another domain of meaning making and interpretation.

37. On the violence of interpretation, see Harold Bloom, *The Anxiety of Influence: A Theory of Poetry* (New York: Oxford University Press, 1973).

38. This is not to suggest that Cover denied the interpretive violence of the legal act. As he put it, "My point . . . is not that judges do not do the kind of figurative violence to literary parents that poets do, but that they carry out—in addition—a far more literal form of violence through their interpretations that poets do not share" (Cover, "Violence," 1609 n. 20).

this," Cover insisted, judges and others who wield the power of the
state "are different from poets, from critics, from artists."[39] Showing
impatience with those who insist that there is a strong resemblance
between the violence done by judges and the interpretive violence
done by poets, critics, and artists, Cover warned that ". . . it will not
do to get precious—to insist on the violence of strong poetry, and
strong poets. Even the violence of weak judges is utterly real—in
need of no interpretation, no critic to reveal it—an immediate, pal-
pable reality. Take a short trip to your local prison and see."[40] The
violence to which Cover draws attention in this passage is a violence
in need of no mediating representation; it is transparent and it speaks
for itself. Such violence renders all representation both unnecessary
and inadequate.[41] It is a violence that can be seen and felt directly,
a violence quite unlike the "psychoanalytic violence of literature
or the metaphorical characterization of literary critics and
philosophers."[42]

Cover was not much interested in splitting epistemological hairs
when it came to the conversation about violence. He appealed to
something more immediate, more authentic, than a debate about the
relationship between violence and its representation. Go "see" is what
he said. In that simple, innocent admonition he identified what was,
for him, beyond question, a central experience with and knowledge
about law, an experience and a knowledge instantiated in police and
their weapons, jailers and their prisons. He warned legal scholars of
the ". . . danger in forgetting the limits which are intrinsic to . . . legal
interpretation, in exaggerating the extent to which any interpretation
rendered as part of the act of state violence can ever constitute a
common and coherent meaning."[43] He wanted them to open their
eyes and see what he, Cover, believed could only be ignored in a
perilous act of willful blindness.

For Cover, the continuing tragedy of law is the way violence
"distorts" meaning. Meaning in the shadow of a violent reality can
never be pure. But to make this stick as a statement about legal

---

39. Cover, "Constitutional Interpretation," 818.
40. Cover, "Constitutional Interpretation," 818.
41. On the inadequacies of representation in the realms of pain and violence,
see Elaine Scarry, The Body in Pain (New York: Oxford University Press, 1985),
3–11.
42. Cover, "Constitutional Interpretation," 818–19.
43. Cover, "Violence," 1628.

practice, Cover was committed to the search for pure or undistorted meaning.

> [F]rom the mundane flow of our real commonalities, we may purport to distill some purer essence of unity, to create in our imaginations a *nomos* completely transparent—built from crystals completely pure. In this transparent *nomos*, that which must be done, the meaning of that which must be done, and the sources of common commitment to the doing of it stand bare, in need of no explication, no interpretation—obvious at once and to all. As long as it stands revealed, this dazzling clarity of legal meaning can harbor no mere interpretation.[44]

In the face of such a commitment, one might ask Cover to identify some, any, realm in which meaning is, or can be, pure.[45] Because even poets and critics exist within communities and conventions that "leave traces" on their interpretive activity, the search for pure meaning is a search in vain; our focus must be not on the fact of distortion that violence introduces, but the *way* violence distorts when compared to other distorting factors. This is a question that Cover's work raises but does not address.[46]

Cover's interest in the violence of law was, however, not just the product of an arid academic debate. It emerged as a somewhat surprising expression of his utopian imaginings as well as his own deep doubts and anxieties. His writing about law's violence displays a profound engagement with the possibilities of law itself.[47] He wrote

---

44. Cover, "Nomos," 14.

45. As Richard Sherwin claims,

I submit that *every* meaning contains within it the contingency and deceit of social structure. Put differently, within the realm of human history and understanding, a decontextualized (or ahistorical) utterance is unthinkable. On this view, then, the deceit (or "made-up" aspect) of meaning and its conceit (*viz.*, the denial of partiality) are present in discourse even when interpretation falls short of coercive (or imperial) enactment. (Sherwin, "Law, Violence and Illiberal Belief," *Georgetown Law Journal* 78 [1990]: 1808)

46. This criticism of Cover was suggested to us by Lawrence Douglas.

47. Thus it is not surprising that he asked his readers to see the world of law from the perspective of those deeply attached to normative visions quite at variance with law's own; he asked us to see the world of law from the perspective of the resister and the civil disobedient, and he wrote movingly, eloquently, and even admiringly of the miracle of martyrs, of those who hold to a normative vision, an

as if by insistence and repetition he could help his readers know and feel the possibilities for human social life that are all too often erased by law's violent impositions. But he also wrote about law's violence as a way of noting and taking seriously the unreconstructed everyday reality of despair and pain to which the law responds and contributes.[48]

Cover achieved a crucial conceptual breakthrough, penetrating a venerable intellectual deposit that nearly succeeded in completely concealing law's violence as violence. According to this accretion, when violence is made part of law, it is transformed by being made orderly and predictable. It becomes something other than violence, something perhaps more properly called "legitimate force."[49] This transformation, this remarkable alchemy—while now commonly

imagining of other worlds, in the face of world-destroying, world-shattering pain (Cover, "Violence," 1604). What is somewhat more surprising is that he also asked us to see the world of law from the perspective of the ordinary criminal defendant and the death row inmate for whom questions of justification, meaning, and interpretive authority fade from view (1608).

His intent in so doing was not to equate the ordinary criminal or the death row inmate with the resister or the martyr. As he put it in talking about those sentenced, "If I have exhibited some sense of sympathy for the victims of this violence [the violence of criminal sentencing] it is misleading. Very often the balance of terror in this regard is just as I would want it" (1608). Or, as he put it elsewhere in talking about capital punishment, "I am not an abolitionist. If the death penalty is constitutional, and it is, . . . there must be deaths. Ours is not a Platonic Constitution. We do not adjudicate the nature of pure forms of the death penalty that can never be realized materially" (Cover, "Constitutional Interpretation," 831). In the request that we see the world of law as the criminal and the condemned see it, Cover takes us back to his concern about the interpretive turn in legal scholarship, for in humanist scholarship on law we are much more likely to be drawn to the articulate voice of those engaged with legal texts than to the inarticulate, almost inaudible voice of those subject to law's violence. See McCleskey v. Kemp, 107 S.Ct. 1756, 1794 (1987) (Justice Brennan dissenting).

48. See Cover, "Violence." In Elaine Scarry (Body in Pain), Cover found someone who courageously wrote about the knowledge and experience of pain even as she acknowledged the limits of our ability to know and experience someone else's pain. It was a courage that he himself emulated as he tried to communicate about the hurts done and pain experienced in the most mundane as well as in the most dramatic of legal acts. He wrote about violence and pain as someone who was fully aware of the limits of his own ability to communicate. But he wrote about violence and pain nonetheless, and, in so doing, expressed his own deep faith in the human capacity to bridge worlds, to move from the world of experience to the world of possibility, from the present to the future.

49. See Wolff, "Violence." Jan Narveson, "Force, Violence, and Law," in Justice, Law, and Violence, ed. James Brady and Newton Garver (Philadelphia: Temple University Press, 1991).

viewed as a questionable consequence of equally questionable views in legal and moral theory—threatened to become imperviously protected as a definitional truism, as if it were true by meaning alone that law's force is never the same as violence.[50] In this view, while explosions, storms, and persons can be violent, law, no matter how great, vicious, or wanton its use of force, cannot, *by definition*, be violent.[51]

Of course, law's force remains in full view—no semantic gerrymandering can make it vanish too—so whether legal coercion is called "force" or "violence" hardly matters, or so it might seem. Yet it is, then, an achievement of considerable importance that Cover was able to rescue the phrase "legal violence" from the status of near-oxymoron and almost single-handedly reverse received assumptions regarding law and its own violence. However, his success in reviving the subject of law's violence did not come solely from engaging in what must have struck some of his readers as a vaguely churlish (if not perverse) abuse of language.

But this abuse of language obviously mattered to Cover; why did he so pointedly and repeatedly write, not of law's legitimate force, but its violence? We think it was to call attention to, and challenge, the easy and apparently widespread assumption that there is something automatically (or prima facie) legitimating about law's force, that law's force is normatively different, that it is entitled to at least a presumption of warrantability. Contrary to any such presumption, Cover believed that law's violence is deeply anomalous. In Cover's view, then, there is no "natural" reason to regard law's violence as different, as being entitled to a favorable presumption regarding its legitimacy. On the contrary, there are much stronger reasons to be ill at ease with law's violence, to regard it as an inharmonious feature of law, one that unavoidably wars with law's constructive purposes and its contributions to social and cultural meanings.

"[B]etween the idea and reality of common meaning," Cover wrote, "falls the shadow of the violence of the law, itself."[52] This one sentence reveals, with great simplicity and directness, Cover's awareness of the world altering reality of law's violence, a reality so disturbing that its mere "shadow" stands as a barrier between present

---

50. Bobbio, "Law and Force."
51. See Wolff, "Violence," 59.
52. Cover, "Violence," 1629.

experience and the realization of an "idea." Yet Cover accepted and defended, rather than denounced, the violence of law,[53] and he attempted to reconcile that violence with law itself.

Thus, to read Cover on violence is to be pulled in different directions. In his work, one finds a mournful story of inescapable violence set against utopian possibility and an appeal to scholars to enter the shadows and explore law's violent underside.[54] One also finds an acknowledgment that the violence of law is, despite its tragic character, an aspect of law that can and should be tolerated. Cover refused to give in to the violence that he believed was an inevitable part of law. He refused to recognize, as we believe he and we inevitably must recognize, the way violence distorts law and limits the possibilities and prospects of law itself. To understand why he did so and how he did so, we first take up his thoughts about the nature of law and its place in social life, and then we consider what he wrote about the need and justification for an apparatus of force that claims the name law.

Law in a Normative Universe

Cover's confrontation with and description of law's violence is part of a larger project in which he advanced a distinctive conception of law while exploring classic themes in political and legal theory—meaning and power, freedom and order, community and state.[55] Cover's political and legal theory begins with the proposition that

> We inhabit a nomos—a normative world. We constantly create and maintain a world of right and wrong, of lawful and unlawful, of valid and void. . . . [N]omos is as much a part of "our world"

---

53. Sherwin, "Illiberal Belief," 1797.

54. This is an invitation that others are taking up. See, for example, Derrida, "Force of Law."

55. In that exploration, he both departs from, and remains tied to, the premises of liberal political thought. His departure from liberalism is seen in his emphasis on community over individualism and his insistence on the priority of values over interests. His ties to liberalism are seen in his use of the polarities of freedom and order to describe the tensions of human social life and in his reluctant apology for, and endorsement of, the violence of state law. For an interesting point of comparison, see Judith Shklar, "The Liberalism of Fear," in *Liberalism and the Moral Life*, ed. Nancy Rosenblum (Cambridge, Mass.: Harvard University Press, 1990).

as is the physical universe of mass, energy, and momentum. Indeed, our apprehension of the structure of the normative world is no less fundamental than our apprehension of the structure of the physical world.[56]

This image of normativity as the basic condition of human social life stands in stark contrast to the liberal image of society without law as a relentless war of all-against-all.[57] For Cover, the world outside law is an already constituted social world of communities and associations, each articulating a distinct vision of the good and encouraging commitment to that vision, rather than isolated or alienated individuals.[58] It is a world of vision and commitment, of shared values and shared aspirations rather than opposed interests; it is a nomos. The task of law is to participate in that nomos, and to support the generation of normative vision and the life of commitment; the task of law is to tolerate, respect, and encourage normative diversity even when that diversity generates opposition to the rules and prescriptions of law itself. The danger of law is that, faced with such diversity, it will insist on the superiority of its rules and prescriptions and, in so doing, that it will circumscribe the nomos.

For Cover, law is more than the rules and prescriptions enacted by state institutions.[59] State law should itself embody and articulate a normative vision. This is the particular strength of a constitutional legal order like that of the United States since, in Cover's view, our constitution is a statement of values rather than a body of rules.[60] Law, properly understood, contributes to the articulation of present ways of being as well as the identification of future possibilities. It arises neither in contract, in the arm's-length relations of persons

---

56. Cover, "Nomos," 4, 5.

57. See Hobbes, *Leviathan*, 184–85. As Shklar argues, "Of fear it can be said without qualification that it is as universal as it is physiological. . . . To be alive is to be afraid. . . . The fear we fear is of pain inflicted by others to kill and maim us" (Shklar, "Liberalism of Fear," 29).

58. See also Michael Sandel, *Liberalism and the Limits of Justice* (Cambridge, Mass.: Harvard University Press, 1982).

59. He worried lest students of law "identify the normative world with the professional paraphernalia of social control," and he contended that "the formal institutions of law . . . are . . . a small part of the normative universe that ought to claim our attention" (Cover, "Nomos," 4; see also Garet, "Meaning and Ending").

60. See Robert Post, "Theories of Constitutional Interpretation," in *Law and the Order of Culture*, ed. Robert Post (Berkeley: University of California Press, 1991).

seeking to forge common ends, as liberals would have it,[61] nor in the commands of governments, rulers, or sovereigns.[62]

Law, Cover claimed, links nomos with narrative.[63] As Cover put it, ". . . law and narrative are inseparably related."[64] Associated with every prescription is an insistence that it be located in a discourse, that it be supplied with "history and destiny, beginning and end, explanation and purpose."[65] Law, then, "includes not only a corpus juris, but also a language and a mythos—narratives in which the corpus is located," and narratives that "establish paradigms for behavior" and describe "a repertoire of moves—a lexicon of normative action."[66] The narratives in which law is embedded include, too, images, ideals, and counterfactuals about what is not the case but what might or should be; "a nomos is a present world constituted by a system of tension betwen reality and vision."[67]

Cover believed that, insofar as the health of the nomos is concerned, there need be "no state."[68] State law provides, for Cover, but one among many sources of meaning, a source that cannot, simply by virtue of its connection to the state, claim that its normative vision

61. For a discussion of the place of contract in liberal thought, see Vicente Medina, *Social Contract Theories: Political Obligation or Anarchy* (Savage, Md.: Rowman and Littlefield, 1990); also see Michael Lessnoff, *Social Contract* (Atlantic Highlands, N.J.: Humanities Press, 1986).

62. See John Austin, *The Province of Jurisprudence Determined*, reprinted as "Law as the Sovereign's Commands," in *The Nature of Law: Readings in Legal Philosophy*, ed. M. P. Golding (New York: Random House, 1966).

63. The "imposition of a normative force" upon a real or imagined state of affairs is, Cover contends, the act of creating narrative. All "genres of narrative—history, fiction, tragedy, comedy" (and not just the law)—are accounts of states of affairs that have been subjected to various "normative force fields." All of them, including law, are "models" of a socially constructed world that has been screened, shaped, and transformed by some relatively stable set of normative commitments and aspirations. In sum, "the codes that relate our normative system to our social constructions of reality and to our visions of what the world might be are narrative" (Cover, "Nomos," 10). For other discussions of the nature and possibilities of narrative, see Robert Scholes and Robert Kellogg, *The Nature of Narrative* (London: Oxford University Press, 1966); D. A. Miller, *Narrative and its Discontents: Problems of Closure in the Traditional Novel* (Princeton: Princeton University Press, 1981).

64. Cover, "Nomos," 5. This point is now widely recognized; see "Symposium on Legal Storytelling," *University of Michigan Law Review* 87 (1989): 2073-2496.

65. Cover, "Nomos," 5.

66. Cover, "Nomos," 9.

67. Cover, "Nomos," 9.

68. Cover, "Nomos," 11. Here again one hears echoes of Cover's anarchism; see Cover, "Folktales," 181.

is correct or superior to visions articulated in other places.[69] It provides just one among many visions of the good, one among many bridges between the world as it is and the alternative realities that comprise the human image of the future.[70] Thus, when a judge interprets the law of the state and gives it meaning as against interpretations and meanings identified in communities beyond the state, what makes the meaning provided by the judge work in the world is something other than its hermeneutic superiority, since that status cannot be guaranteed in advance, and is, in Cover's view, not regularly achieved.

If we are to accept and defer to the interpretations of judges, the reasons for so doing must be found elsewhere. In this search for other reasons, Cover held up a high standard for measuring the impact of state law even as he began to anticipate tensions between the state and other sources of law. "A great legal civilization is marked by the richness of the nomos in which it is located and which it helps to constitute."[71]

But a great legal civilization is made rich, as we have already seen, by the diversity of the visions and commitments it contains. And, in every nomos, "it is the multiplicity of laws, the fecundity of the jurisgenerative principle, that creates the problem to which the court and the state are the solution."[72] For Cover, it is not too little order, but too much order, not too thin a moral world, but too thick a moral world, that, in his view, creates the problematic of state and law. Nevertheless, the problematic of the state and its laws begins, as it does in liberal political thought, with the specter of conflict. In such a world, Cover believed that state law should play a modest, restrained, "system-maintaining" role.[73] It should be tolerant and respectful of alternative normative systems rather than trying to make

---

69. Describing the position of the Mennonite Church in Bob Jones University, Cover argued that "within the domain of constitutional meaning, the understanding of the Mennonites assumes a status equal (or superior) to that accorded to the understanding of the Justices of the Supreme Court. In this realm of meaning . . . the Mennonite community creates law as fully as does the judge" (Cover, "Nomos," 28).

70. Here, Cover displays his sympathy for a radical legal pluralism. See Sally Merry, "Legal Pluralism," Law and Society Review 22 (1988): 869; see also John Griffiths, "What Is Legal Pluralism?" Journal of Legal Pluralism 24 (1986): 1.

71. Cover, "Nomos," 6.

72. Cover, "Nomos," 40. For a very different perspective on the same problem, see Martin Shapiro, Courts (Chicago: University of Chicago Press, 1981).

73. Cover, "Nomos," 12.

them bend lest they be destroyed by the ferocious force that the state routinely deploys.[74]

In such a world, law, and more precisely state law, is, according to Cover, always pulled in two directions, and, as a result, there is "an essential tension in law."[75] On the one hand, state law participates in the generation of normative meaning; on the other, state law plays in the domain of social control and uses violence to enforce just one (namely its own) conception of order.[76] Meaning-making, meaning-generating normative activity in plural communities and associations sits uneasily and complicates the task of maintaining order. Thus, as Cover put it, "there is a radical dichotomy between the social organization of law as power and the organization of law as meaning. . . . The uncontrolled character of meaning exercises a desta-bilizing influence upon power."[77] Where the law resorts to power, it seeks to limit meaning, but meaning is always greater than power can accommodate.

This formulation is quite typical of Cover's work in many ways. Meaning is, by definition, uncontrolled; power, left to itself, is stable. Thus, meaning and power, or interpretation and violence, exist sep-arately, as forces in tension, working on and against each other. Meaning, because it is uncontrolled, is the domain of freedom; "the social organization of law as power" is the domain of order. The basic problem of society, politics, and law remains—despite Cover's effort to distance himself from this formulation—the problem as defined by liberalism,[78] the problem of freedom and order, restated and redescribed no doubt, but reinscribed nonetheless.[79]

The internal coherence of systems of meaning and the order already within freedom, as well as the fragility of power and the possibilities of freedom already within the domain of order, seem to escape Cover's gaze just as they escape the gaze of liberalism. For

---

74. Cover, "Nomos," 53.

75. Cover, "Violence," 1602 n. 2.

76. This is not to say that violence is only the province of the state. Cover seems to grant that *some* imposition, *some* force, is always a feature of law. Even the largely paideic Massachusetts Bay Colony sought to maintain its "holistic integ-rity" by forcefully *excluding* such heretics as Roger Williams and Ann Hutchinson.

77. Cover, "Nomos," 18.

78. For a rich exploration of the tensions between Cover's work and liberalism, see Sherwin, "Illiberal Belief."

79. See Roberto Unger, *Knowledge and Politics* (New York: Free Press, 1975).

Cover, only the realm of meaning and interpretation is fluid; it, and only it, is, or can be, the realm of the plural, the possible, the imagined, the free. Yet we know, following Foucault,[80] that hierarchies of power proliferate in all meaning-generating activities.[81] Moreover, despite Cover's own efforts to interpret and give meaning to the domain of legal violence, power and violence seem, in his account, to exist outside meaning and interpretation. Thus, the social, political, and legal world can only be a world in tension, moving now toward one pole and then toward another, a world where meaning is always a threat to power and where power is always the death of meaning.

Judges, it turns out, play a central role in the achievement of Cover's vision of a diverse, normatively rich culture and a restrained state, and they are crucial in his understanding of the place of violence in law. They sit at the fault line between meaning, the interpretive possibilities of the legal text (freedom), and power, the capacity to take one meaning and, through force, make it *the* meaning (order). Yet, in all their actions, they "are people of violence."[82]

There are two linked senses in which Cover thought of judges as people of violence. The first involves the literal deployment of force that is available to judges as state officials.[83] Judges are people of violence because they are able to bring physical force to bear in making their interpretive acts work in the world.[84] In a second sense, however, judges become people of violence when they repress and reduce the rich normativity of the social world.

80. See Michel Foucault, *Power/Knowledge,* ed. Colin Gordon (New York: Pantheon Books, 1972), chap. 6.

81. This point was suggested to us by Lawrence Douglas.

82. Cover, "Nomos," 53.

83. This kind of violence is more fully explored by Cover in "Violence."

84. Violence, coordinated and controlled in and by the interpretive acts of judges, appears, in Cover's exploration of the internal perspective, as an achievement of considerable social importance. Awareness of the need to coordinate and control violence, in turn, presses on and shapes the interpretive activities of judges who sit atop what Cover called "a pyramid of violence" (Cover, "Violence," 1609). Interpretation is transformed and made different by the presence of violence for, as Cover so vividly put it, "Legal interpretation takes place in a field of pain and death" (1601). Or, as if that were not enough to make the point, "legal interpretation occurs on a battlefield—it is part of a battle—which entails the instruments both of war and of poetry. Indeed constitutional law is ... more fundamentally connected to the war than it is to the poetry" (Cover, "Constitutional Interpretation," 817). But law's violence is not just an issue of interpretation; it is, in addition, a question of social organization, of the implementation of judicial decisions, of the translation of words into violent deeds.

Because of the violence they command, judges characteristically do not create law, but kill it. Theirs is a jurispathic office. Confronting the luxuriant growth of a hundred legal traditions, they assert that *this one* is law and destroy or try to destroy all the rest.[85]

Cover called upon judges, and the law they represent, to be less "jurispathic," to be less insistent on singularity or hierarchy among normative visions; he called on them to stop circumscribing the nomos, and to "invite new worlds."[86]

Seen from the outside, from the perspective of the nomos and from the perspective of worlds yet to be, the violence of state law is a strong impediment and an important barrier. That force is, in Cover's account, destructive, and unnecessarily so, of the world-affirming, world-building normative activities and commitments of communities and associations outside the state. It is, in addition, incompatible with narrativity, with the evolving network of beliefs, practices, and understandings that constitute or make possible a nomos. It puts an end to interpretation and meaning construction; it cuts off conversation. It does not elicit and evolve; it concludes. Violence puts an end to the hermeneutic impulses that generate narrative.[87]

Law's violence is, as a result, a continuous threat to law's principal involvement in the production and maintenance of meaning in diverse normative communities. State law especially, because of its peacemaking and boundary-keeping roles, threatens to become imperial in character; its prescriptions purport to be general and universal, requiring or forbidding what must or must not be done if there is to be law at all. It is easy for statist judges to become so intent on order, so insistent that only one law, the state's own, shall prevail, that the efforts and commitments of other rich sources of meaning,

---

85. Cover, "Nomos," 53. "By exercising its superior brute force," Cover argued, "the agency of state law shuts down the creative hermeneutic of principle that is spread throughout our communities" (44). In this passage, Sanford Levinson argues that Cover is writing about a "'merely' metaphorical" violence (Sanford Levinson, "Conversing About Justice," *Yale Law Journal* 100 [1991]: 1865).

86. Cover "Nomos," 68.

87. As Cover put it, "the coercive dimension of law is itself destructive of the possibility of interpretation" (Cover, "Nomos," 48).

other normative enclaves, are needlessly limited or destroyed. Here, law's violence threatens law itself by being immoderate in its regulation of the sources of law.[88]

Law's violence signals, at some level and to some degree, a normative insufficiency, an inability of the controlling narratives to control. Or it may signal the inability to generate and maintain a unified nomos in a world of competing nomoi. In either case, the employment of force to retain control immediately raises questions about the normative basis, the justification, for that force. For if the use of force is required because of an indeterminacy or erosion in normative understandings, it would appear that those understandings are insufficient to ground and justify violence.

Legal force is perhaps most transparently problematic when it is used against opposing normative orders, since it is clear that taking refuge in what Cover calls "the self-referential supremacy of each system" contributes nothing to resolving the normative issue at hand. Far from being a genuine justification, an appeal to such supremacy is only an artless refusal to engage the justificatory question. The "hermeneutic of jurisdiction" simply insists on order above all else.[89]

---

88. Sometimes law's violence damages the source of law not from imperial motives but from excessive deference to the claims of state bureaucracy. In so doing, law condones the violence of administration. While Cover calls for modesty and restraint with regard to the normative communities outside the state, with regard to the state bureaucracy, Cover allows himself to imagine the judge as resister already inscribed in the sanctuaries of power, as a privileged rescuer of meaning and freedom from the forces of violence and order. In this imagining, he works through what seems like a rather familiar argument about the rule of law in which the office of judge is set apart from the rest of the state's administrative apparatus (see John Norton Moore, "The Rule of Law: An Overview" [University of Virginia, 1990, photocopy]), and he reminds us of Lord Coke's resistance to King James, Taney's resistance to Lincoln, and the resistance of judges in Ghana to the perpetrators of a military coup in the late 1970s. He urges judges to commit themselves to a "jurisgenerative process that does not defer to the violence of administration" (Cover, "Nomos," 59) as the only way to temper law's all too close association with violence.

89. It is in the confrontation of the judge with the deep normative commitments of resisters, civil disobedients, and members of communities so committed to their way of life that they are willing to suffer for their beliefs that the violence of law is put to its severest tests. Faced with such tests, and stripped of the illusion that their interpretations are superior, judges usually resort, Cover argued, to systemic rationales for their deployment of violence, to what he called the "principles of jurisdiction" (Cover, "Nomos," 55). Those principles provide "apologies for the state itself and for its violence" (54). In his view, however, they overvalue power and order, and under-

It does nothing to establish normative superiority. But, lacking this quality, it is difficult to see how law's violence is to be justified to those against whom it is used. It appears, then, that, in Cover's account of law, force used against competing normative orders is inescapably questionable and, in a certain sense, lawless.

Too often, too routinely, judges defer to that violence; too often, too routinely, judges aggressively assert the supremacy of state law. In either posture, Cover believed that jurispathic state law is needlessly destructive of the nomos it is required to regulate. Such excess constitutes a serious danger to the world of meaning. Despite the "radical instability" of the paideic world, "warring sects" are the wellsprings of normative commitment; they make life normatively significant. To destroy or limit them is to threaten the principal sources of articulated value, commitment, and aspiration. Law threatens to kill off what its very existence presupposes—a world that is normatively rich, normatively diverse, and normatively inventive. That violence stands in the way of tolerance, if not respect. Given Cover's commitment to tolerance, respect, and plurality, one expects a rejection of violence, and a vision of law without force or coercion.

In Cover's exploration of the relationship between law and other normative orders, one does indeed find dark moments of sadness, of concern, and of critique. Yet Cover cannot imagine law without violence. On the contrary, Cover insists that "the jurisgenerative principle by which legal meaning proliferates in all communities never exists in isolation from violence."[90] And the shadow of that violence

---

value meaning and freedom (Cover, "Folktales," 180–81).

The principles of jurisdiction are premised on a profound fear of differences and the problems that accommodating differences create. As a result, those principles promote closure and justify intolerance toward normative visions seemingly at odds with the commitments embodied in state law. Jurisdiction is a way of avoiding normative engagement; it allows judges to separate themselves from the violence they authorize and to avoid measuring the strength of their commitment to violence against the persuasiveness of their understandings of law. In this, Cover believed that judges are different from, and often inferior to, resisters whose interpretive commitments cannot be abstracted and are, in Cover's view, measured in and through their willingness to suffer and die for their beliefs.

90. Cover, "Nomos," 40. As he wrote about the organization of law's violence, and, in particular, about the way "judicial authority is transmitted through the inferior layers of the administration of justice," Cover, Douglas Hay has recently claimed, "celebrated . . . the fact of the integrity of that power of command of violence" (Hay,

is cast as much by the "radical instability" of contesting, meaning-producing normative communities as by self-interested actors in an imaginary state of nature.

The language Cover used to describe a nomos that was unregulated, ungoverned, makes his fear of such a place unmistakable. "Let loose, unfettered, the worlds created would be unstable and sectarian in their social organization, dissociative and incoherent in their discourse, wary and *violent* in their interactions."[91] Note too how he described "*warring* sects" that wrap themselves in their own special law, in normative worlds where "not all interpretive trajectories are insular."[92] In the presence of such volatile dynamics, the enterprise of "maintaining the world . . . requires no less energy than creating it."[93] In this process, judges, even as they deploy violence, become, for Cover, "people of peace."[94]

Thus, the legal violence that initially seemed so inhospitable to the nomos and to the jurisgenerative work of communities and associations within that nomos is imaginatively tamed and transformed. Law's violence is neither an impediment to restraint nor a guarantee of excess. The danger is dissipated, and no price is paid for law's intimacy with violence.[95] In this imagined transformation of violence into peace, Cover moves away from critique to restate the liberal apology for the law and its reliance on force.[96]

"Time, Inequality, and Law's Violence," in this volume). Though Hay is onto something important about Cover's work, "celebrate" seems not quite right as a way of describing Cover's attitude toward the internal organization of law's violence. While continuing to press the analytic point about the relationship of violence and legal interpretation that animated his critique of others in the law and humanities movement, Cover's contemplation of the internal organization of law's violence is the contemplation of the sociologist simply investigating the facts rather than of the enthusiast celebrating what he has found. Yet it is nonetheless true that, in his sociological guise, Cover expressed much less regret about the fact of violence than he did in his reconstructive and utopian mood, and much more resigned acceptance of the need for law to do violence.

91. Cover, "Nomos," 16; italics added.
92. Cover, "Nomos," 60.
93. Cover, "Nomos," 60.
94. Cover, "Nomos," 53.
95. By appealing to judges to resist "mere administration," to avoid acceding to the violence done by others, Cover hoped that he could reconcile law's violence with a legal order hospitable to diverse normative worlds. The concern is that judges will violently and *unnecessarily* impose themselves against critique, vision, and aspiration in the normative world beyond state law and, in doing so, will destroy the nomos and narrative on which law itself deeply depends.
96. See Shklar, "Liberalism of Fear"; Roberto Unger, *Knowledge and Politics* (New York: Free Press, 1975).

The Social Organization of Law: On the
Achievements of an Orderly Violence

Having imaginatively transformed violence into peace, Cover could
further imagine that he had made peace between law's violence and
the restraint and toleration he thought was so essential to law. Thus,
it is not surprising that Cover's other two treatments of law's
violence—"Violence and the Word" and "The Bonds of Constitutional
Interpretation"—would identify the conditions that make it effective
in the world. In those articles, he paid particular attention to
the judge, now as an important role player in law's social organization, and he describes judges "from John Winthrop to Warren
Burger ... [sitting] atop a pyramid of violence."[97]

As suggested by the metaphor of the pyramid, the conception
of social organization at work in "Violence" is rigidly hierarchical
and "formalist in its apparent assumption that the hierarchy of state
violence has the same contours as the hierarchy of legal institutions."[98]
Given this picture of judges seated at the apex of such a hierarchy,
the question almost naturally becomes not so much how judges interpret legal texts and whether their interpretations circumscribe or
invite new worlds, but rather what happens to their interpretations,
what happens when the interpretive act is completed. Does anybody
listen? Does anybody care? Does anybody respond?

If the answer to those questions were to be no, then we would
face a situation in which law could not, or would not, deploy its
coercive force, a situation perhaps welcome within the nomos, but
quite unwelcome once it is acknowledged that violence and death are
already within our society and polity. As Cover himself put it, "To
stop short of suffering or imposing violence is to give law up to
those who are willing to so act."[99] Or, alternatively, if the answer is
no, then it may be that others down the chain of command deploy
coercive force as independent operators, themselves undisciplined
and lawless. It is, of course, against both of these possibilities—
uncontrollable violence at large in society or the state as renegade—
that the liberal vision of law arrays itself.[100]

If, in "Nomos and Narrative," Cover seems to ally himself with

---

97. Cover, "Violence," 1609.
98. See Hay, "Time, Inequality, and Law's Violence," in this volume.
99. Cover, "Constitutional Interpretation," 833.
100. See Sarat and Kearns, "Journey."

meaning against power, in "Violence" and "The Bonds" the alliance is, at the least, destabilized and perhaps reversed.

> So let us be explicit, if it seems a nasty thought that death and pain are at the center of legal interpretation, so be it. It would not be better were there only a community of argument, of readers and writers of texts, of interpreters. As long as death and pain are part of our political world, it is essential that they be at the center of law. The alternative is truly unacceptable— that they be within our polity but outside the discipline of *collective* decision rules and the individual efforts to achieve outcomes through those rules.[101]

In these sentences, we see no glimpse of the nomos, no bold assertion of the possibilities and virtues of a plural society where the threat of conflict is relegated to interactions at the boundaries separating normatively integrated communities. Instead, we see a Hobbesian nightmare of death and pain undisciplined, inside the body politic but outside the reach of rules, asserting itself in Cover's work.[102] Order, and some semblance of peace, can only be achieved where legal interpretation is embedded in, and is attentive to, what Cover called conditions of "effective domination."[103] Where such domination is not achieved, we face the prospect that people will find themselves in "conditions of reprisal, resistance and revenge."[104]

In Cover's praise of "collective decision rules" and persons seeking to achieve results through "rules" there is a move from Hobbes to Locke, from power against freedom to rules against disorder. Here, too, we see the imagining of a world outside of law used to conjure up and justify the "discipline" of "rules."[105] From this point, with a Hobbesian nightmare as a background condition, the next step in Cover's exploration of law's violence is to inquire about its own discipline, to ask about the adequacy of the Lockean "discipline of

---

101. Cover, "Violence," 1628.

102. For a similar analysis in a different context, see Gary Peller, "Reason and the Mob," *Tikkun* 2 (1987): 28.

103. Cover, "Violence," 1616.

104. Cover, "Violence," 1616. See also Susan Jacoby, *Wild Justice: The Evolution of Revenge* (New York: Harper and Row, 1983).

105. See Sarat and Kearns, "Journey."

collective decision rules," and, in addition, to applaud that discipline where it is found.

Such discipline, in which the deployment of force is controlled and coordinated by judges through their interpretations of legal texts, stands in stark contrast to situations of uncontrolled private violence— lynching is the example to which Cover himself referred[106]—and to lawless states in which people "disappear . . . die suddenly and without ceremony in prison, quite apart from any articulated justification and authorization of their demise."[107] Seen from the inside, against the specter of an undisciplined violence, the discipline of collective decision rules is an achievement to be respected, if not cherished and admired. In Cover's own words,". . . we have come to expect near perfect coordination of those whose role it is to inflict violence subject to the interpretive decisions of judges. . . . Such a well-coordinated form of violence is an achievement."[108]

Cover's concern was to understand that "achievement" by understanding how judicial interpretations of legal texts get translated into deeds, how judicial words become violent acts. The doing of such deeds and acts means that when judges confront an interpretive problem, they really confront two problems, not one. The first is, of course, the problem of meaning itself, namely, how to identify and justify a hermeneutically satisfactory, if not superior, rendering of a text.[109] The second is the problem of implementation, namely, how to ensure that others act on the basis of, and in the ways prescribed by, an interpretive act.

---

106. Cover, "Violence," 1624.

107. Cover, "Violence," 1624. In one place, Cover seemed to entertain a quite different proposition, namely, that "violence . . . must be viewed as problematic in much the same way whether it is being carried out by order of a federal district judge, a mafioso or a corporate vice-president." Yet even here he quickly retreated, "Please note well, here," he argued,

> that I am not saying that all violence is equally justified or unjustified. I am claiming that it is problematic in the same way. By that I mean that the form of analysis that we enter into to determine whether or not the violence is justified is the same. That same method will, of course, if it is any good at all, not yield the same answer with respect to dissimilar cases. (Cover, "Folktales," 182 and n. 15)

108. Cover, "Violence," 1624.

109. This is, of course, the stuff of much debate in legal and constitutional theory. See, for example, Sanford Levinson, "Law as Literature," *Texas Law Review* 60 (1982): 373; Ernest Weinrib, "Legal Formalism: On the Immanent Rationality of Law," *Yale Law Journal* 97 (1988): 949.

With respect to the first of these problems—the problem of
meaning—Cover again took cognizance of the social organization of
law, only this time the social organization of interpretation and justification. No judge, Cover writes, "*acts* alone. . . . The application of
legal understanding in our domain of pain and death will always
require the active or passive acquiescence of other judicial minds."[110]
Before judicial words can be translated into deeds, other judges,
whether appellate judges reviewing a trial court decision or other
members of a collegial court, must be convinced that those words
represent a reasonable interpretation of a legal text. They must be
convinced, in other words, that the action is justified, that the words
supply sufficient justification for violent acts. The community of
judges is always a community of interpretation and justification. As
Cover puts it, ". . . for those who impose the violence, the justification
is important, real and carefully cultivated."[111]

Because judges do not themselves do the deeds that their acts
authorize, they are dependent on others in preexisting institutional
roles to carry out their orders and make their decisions work in the
world. Cover illustrates this familiar fact by considering the act of
criminal sentencing, an act in which judges are "doing something
clearly within their province."[112] That act, however, depends upon a
"structure of cooperation" in which ". . . police, jailers or other
enforcers . . . restrain the prisoner . . . upon the order of the judge, and
guards who will secure the prisoner from rescue and who will protect
the judge, prosecutors, witnesses and jailers from revenge."[113] That
structure of cooperation must work to overcome substantial cultural
and moral inhibitions that curb "the infliction of pain on other

110. Cover, "Violence," 1627.
111. Cover, "Violence," 1629. The emphasis on justification is especially great
where the violence to be authorized is most severe. Thus, in the case of capital
punishment, because

> the action or *deed* is extreme and irrevocable, there is pressure placed on the
> *word*—the interpretation that establishes the legal justifications for the act. At
> the same time, the fact that capital punishment constitutes the most plain, the
> most deliberate, and the most thoughtful manifestation of legal interpretation
> as violence makes the imposition of the sentence an especially powerful test of
> the faith and commitment of the interpreters. (1622)

Faith and commitment become the ultimate test of interpretation, the ultimate standard against which the persuasive power of justifications will be measured.
112. Cover, "Violence," 1618.
113. Cover, "Violence," 1619.

people."[114] For Cover, the key fact is that those inhibitions could be overcome "upon the order of the judge."

In such a structure of cooperation, judges do the interpretive work that renders law's deeds of violence intelligible, and, in return for their "relatively automatic heed" of the orders of judges, those who carry out those orders are able ". . . to shift to the judge primary moral responsibility for the violence which they themselves carry out."[115] Cover believed that the institutional context within which legal interpretation occurs provides, and should provide, a predictable, "though not logically necessary,"[116] set of responses to judicial decisions. It is in the gap between the necessary and the merely predictable that Cover looked to see the way interpretation is itself tutored by the need both to activate and, at the same time, control those who actually do law's violence.[117]

As we move from thinking about interpretation to thinking about implementation, one might contemplate two possibilities. In the first, the problem of implementation would be resolved in the interpretive act itself and in the justifications that it provides. Readings of texts would be authoritative, even compelling, providing analyses with which no rational person could disagree. Implementation would be assured as a series of successive readers, first the judge, then the marshall, then the warden, then the executioner, all, albeit independently, read the text in the same way, all embrace the same justifications, and, as a result, all embrace the same commitments. But given Cover's own theory of interpretation, a theory in which the realm of meaning is the realm of freedom rather than authority,[118] it is not surprising that Cover looked elsewhere to understand how judicial readings are translated into deeds.

---

114. Cover, "Violence," 1613. As Cover puts it, "Were the inhibition against violence perfect, law would be unnecessary; were it not capable of being overcome through social signals, law would not be possible." For a useful discussion of the dangers of overcoming that inhibition, see Herbert Kelman and V. Lee Hamilton, *Crimes of Obedience: Toward A Social Psychology of Authority and Responsibility* (New Haven: Yale University Press, 1989).

115. Cover, "Violence," 1626–27.

116. Cover, "Violence," 1611.

117. Because responses are predictable, judges can view their own interpretive acts as having an impact in the world; because responses are not logically necessary, judges must be attentive to the conditions that maintain the predictable quality of administration and implementation.

118. See Cover, "Nomos," 18.

For him, the answer was to be found, in the first instance, in the way judges alter their readings to take into account the likely reactions of others in the chain of command, and, in the second instance, in a structure of offices and roles that assures relatively automatic compliance with any reading that emanates from someone exercising judicial power.[119] With respect to the former, if judges were poets or literary theorists, their attention to meaning might be innocent. They would be free, like Ronald Dworkin's proverbial Hercules, to act on their own sense of the best theory of meaning or political morality.[120] In so doing they might rescue meaning at the risk of relinquishing control of the apparatus of state violence.

However, judges in the usual, ordinary performance of their duty seek to ensure that that apparatus will respond, because, in Cover's view, interpretive acts mean nothing in a legal sense if they have no purchase in the world. Thus, judges ordinarily are not free;[121] they can never engage in poetic inattention to things outside the text. Judicial interpretation and the justifications judges provide are always, and must always be, attentive to the organizational context in which they will be received and translated into action. As Cover argued

> The practice of interpretation requires an understanding of what others will do with . . . a judicial utterance and, in many instances, an adjustment of that understanding, regardless of how misguided one may think the likely institutional response will be. Failing this, the interpreter sacrifices the connection between understanding what ought to be done and the deed, itself.[122]

"[R]egardless of how misguided . . . ," suggests that Cover is thinking about those who are responsible for the deed rather than the word. For that audience there is, and must be, a low threshold for influence; indeed, Cover might just as well have said that the

---

119. No wardens, guards or executioners wait for a telephone call from the latest constitutional law scholar, jurisprude or critic before executing prisoners, no matter how compelling the interpretations of those others may be. And, indeed, they await the word of judges only insofar as that word carries with it the formal indicia of having been spoken in the judicial capacity. (Cover, "Violence," 1625)

120. See Ronald Dworkin, "Hard Cases," *Harvard Law Review* 89 (1975): 1057.

121. Cover, "Violence," 1617.

122. Cover, "Violence," 1612.

rational judge, remembering that he is a judge and not a poet, will always take into account likely institutional responses to ensure that his readings will be persuasive if not pure, efficient if not excellent. Legal interpretation, in this account, is deeply and profoundly shaped by an awareness of the contingent character of implementation; meaning is altered and transformed in order to ensure that action follows utterance. An excellent reading of a legal text is one that garners not just the praise of critics, but also triggers necessary responses in those charged with carrying out the acts of violence it authorizes.

When he considers the vertical organization of law, the lower ranges of the pyramid that judges rule from the top, anarchist Cover sounds suspiciously Weberian.

When judges interpret the law in an official context, we expect a close relationship to be revealed or established between their words and the acts that they mandate. That is, we expect the judges' words to serve as virtual triggers for action. We would not, for example, expect contemplations or deliberations on the part of jailers and wardens to interfere with the actions authorized by judicial words.[123]

Judges who take into account the likely reaction of others in the chain of command, "regardless of how misguided," can, in this picture, expect the favor to be returned.

The language in which Cover describes the translation of judicial words into legal acts is particularly slippery, and notably atypical of Cover. Who is the "we" that expects a close relationship between the words judges utter and the acts others perform? Is the reference to what we "expect" empirical? Or does it instead (or in addition) have a normative dimension and refer to what we should expect? And why shouldn't "we expect" contemplation or deliberation to "interfere"? The imagined alternative that generates "our" preferences and expectations seems to be an apparatus of violence—the state— uncontrolled, undisciplined, unresponsive.

When judges interpret, they trigger agentic behavior within . . . an institution or social organization. On one level judges may

---

123. Cover, "Violence," 1613–14.

appear to be, and may in fact be, offering their understanding of the normative world to their intended audience. But on another level they are engaging a violent mechanism through which a substantial part of their audience loses its capacity to think and act autonomously.[124]

At this point, in the face of his own image of such rigid and unthinking bureaucractic behavior, one might almost expect that Cover would have rebelled against his own insights, rebelled against any use of interpretive authority to suspend the "capacity to think and act autonomously." Cover the anarchist, or Cover the normative pluralist, might have been expected to embrace and to praise a theory of social organization that allowed for and encouraged multiple sites of interpretation, sites in which alternative readings might prevail, sites of resistance. In this way, the deployment of violence would be greatly tempered by problems of coordination within law's complex chain of command. To the extent that interpretive authority is fragmented, and dispersed, that rival centers of power enter competing interpretations, the literal violence of the law might be reduced.

But there is, in fact, no rebellion, no endorsement of a loosely coupled bureaucratic structure; there is, instead, first silence and later an approving, if stark, description of wardens, guards, and doctors engaged in the process of carrying out a death sentence who "jump to the judge's tune."[125] The world of interpretation is altered by a consideration of the requisites of order; meaning (freedom) gives way to ensure that an orderly violence is done. Meaning is disciplined, in Cover's analysis, by the requisites of discipline itself. From the inside of law, and against the possibilities of undisciplined force and aggression, legal interpretation and law's social organization are looked to by Cover as the domain to achieve "whatever achievement is possible in the domesticating of violence."[126]

Violence domesticated, force turned into persuasion, war turned into peace, given this hope it is not particularly surprising that Cover accepts law's violence,[127] and writes as if that violence would have

---

124. Cover, "Violence," 1615.
125. Cover, "Violence," 1623–24.
126. Cover, "Violence," 1628.
127. Cover was not so much of an anarchist that he was indifferent to the distinction between a lynching (or run-away police machinery) and an execution

no price for law itself. Combined, the instructions regarding state law expressed in "Nomos" and "Violence" appear to be

> Wherever possible, withhold violence; let new worlds flourish. But, for the sake of life, do not forget that law's violence is sometimes necessary and that its availability is not automatic but must be provided for. And finally, effective violence that is also temperate and controlled is a considerable achievement, requiring "an organization of people" that is as complex as it is fragile.

The insistence that legal violence should be used sparingly is explained by Cover's conviction that "we inhabit a nomos—a normative universe" that is easily destroyed by such violence even though some measure of it is needed to maintain normativity. The restraint called for at the end of "Nomos" refers principally to instances or kinds of instances in which the use of force is justifiable or appropriate; to insist that such instances are relatively rare and that legal force should be used sparingly is, of course, perfectly compatible with the conviction that *some* use is actually necessary and, on those occasions, it should be applied efficiently. To do its job, then, law *must* be violent, but as little as possible. Cover's attention to law's violence (in "Violence") signals his recognition that, despite the normativity that precedes law and partly because of it, there is a need for law's violence and a need also to secure the conditions of its effective use.

But again we ask, can Cover have it both ways? Can he (and we) provide those conditions for the effective use of force that he so insightfully identified and, at the same time, develop a legal system that is restrained, tolerant, and encouraging in its attitude toward alternative normative visions? Can law be homicidal without being jurispathic?

The Difference Violence Makes

Cover believed that it is, indeed, possible to limit the jurispathic characteristic of law while making peace with a legal order that is

---

authorized after a trial and review on appeal. And this is precisely the point; Cover had neither such a romantic aversion to violence, nor such an unqualified sympathy for freedom over order, that he rejected violence entirely.

"homicidal" and that law could escape the imperatives of violence.[128] We do not.[129] Cover could imagine judges gearing up and governing an apparatus of pain-imposing, death-dealing force in one moment and then judiciously tolerating diverse and challenging normative visions. We cannot. Violence and law can never adequately and satisfactorily be reconciled. They are social facts in opposition that no amount of theoretical ingenuity can harmonize.[130]

While we grant that the central messages of "Nomos" and "Violence" are not formally or logically incompatible, they are, we believe, antagonistic to one another at the level (to borrow Cover's phrase) of practical activity. The forces at work in the arrangements described in "Violence" undercut and oppose any self-limitation on the impulse of statist judges to be jurispathic. The first of those forces is a disposition whose initial impetus is the supposed demand of rationality to universalize or objectify judgments and decisions,[131] to be governed, that is, by the maxim of "treating like cases alike and different cases differently," a purely formal requirement that is subsequently given direction—at least in Cover's account of judges' circumstances—in favor of finding similarity, not difference. Other forces derive largely from the interaction between the members of that fragile "organization of people" required, Cover contends, to make legal violence possible and, at the same time, to domesticate it.

We begin our exploration of these forces by noting, with Cover, the familiar but unfathomable distance between thought and action, especially between the judgments and decisions of some and the uncoerced but reliably certain deeds of others. In the case of law, this distance is at once a blessing and a difficulty. It is a blessing because if there were virtually no distance between a judicial decision and its actualization on another's body—if, that is, judges themselves were required to impose the pain and death that their judgments

---

128. On the possibilities of such an escape, see Tom Dumm, "Fear of Law," *Studies in Law, Politics and Society* 10 (1990): 29; Drucilla Cornell, "The Violence of the Masquerade: Law Dressed Up as Justice," *Cardozo Law Review* 11 (1990): 1047.

129. To make our case against Cover, we mean to draw on Cover himself, to use the insights of "Violence and the Word" to explain why Cover's toleration of legal violence undermines the vision and hope of "Nomos and Narrative."

130. See Taylor, "Desire of Law."

131. See Thomas Nagel, *The View from Nowhere* (New York: Oxford University Press, 1986); Richard Rorty, *Philosophy and the Mirror of Nature* (Princeton: Princeton University Press, 1979).

demand—too little violence would be done, and law would fail in its contest with the violence that is its origin. On the other hand, the distance is a difficulty, because a way must be found to traverse the gap between the judge's thought and the material act of, say, the executioner. For the reason just noted, it obviously will not do simply to force others to do law's violence; between the legal word and the deed there must be a transmission capable of linking word and action, capable of activating the deed but not causing it.

The transmission, then, does two things; first, it keeps the judge separated—distanced—from the deed itself (so that decisions that need to be made will be made) but also connected to it (so that meaning is conferred on the deed and so that, in ways yet to be described, the judge is to some extent morally implicated in that deed). Second, it connects the deed to the word by linking the agent of law's violence (for example, the executioner) to the judicial decision in some manner that overcomes cultural and moral inhibitions against inflicting pain and death. These, it appears, are the basic pathways that make possible "the organization of people" required for law to function as a practical activity, as thought in action. But matters of substance must now be added to these formal routes.

To begin from the perspective of the active agent, the actual doer of law's violence—the executioner, we can ask what is required to trigger such conduct, to make it possible for these persons to act in a manner that seems virtually "agentic" in character, that does not involve independent review or judgment on the merits of the judicial decision.[132] Here, Cover refers us to two possible accounts, one that ascribes evolutionary value to obeisance within hierarchical structures (the Milgram studies) and another (in Anna Freud) that suggests, contrary to Milgram, that a disposition to do such violence is the *natural* condition of human beings and that, except for institutionally specified occasions (as in law) where outlets for this natural aggression can be expressed, the impulse is firmly restrained.[133]

There is, of course, another story that might be told, not a causal account as the others are, but one that sounds in the language of justification, moral or otherwise. Surely it is just such a story that

---

132. See Petres Spierenburg, *The Spectacle of Suffering: Executions and the Evolution of Repression* (New York: Cambridge University Press, 1984); William Bowers, *Executions in America* (Lexington, Mass.: Lexington Books, 1974).

133. See Cover, "Violence," 1614–15.

officers and agents of the law tell themselves and one another; they believe or appear to believe that they are justified in what they do, and it is this conviction that explains their capacity to set aside the customary inhibitions against doing violence. Presumably they believe that acts of the kind that they perform are, indeed, necessary and that they, unlike others, are specifically authorized to carry them out.

But that they are disposed to act "agentically," in immediate, largely unquestioning response to the judicial decree is perhaps still both puzzling and problematic.[134] It is one thing to believe that acts of the kind being contemplated here are necessary and in some sense justified; it is, we understand, one thing to suppose that a certain *system* of rules and sanctions is justified, and another, albeit related, thing to believe that particular applications of force are justified. To bridge the latter gap, we need a reasonable assurance of the correctness of the intervening determinations, or we need the interposition of other responsible agents, or both.

Because, in Cover's view, law is not a formal system but is inescapably an interpretive enterprise,[135] it is apparent that the merit of any particular judgment is never entirely separable from the agent who makes it.[136] It does not follow that such judgments can be judged as neither correct nor incorrect; it means only that their warrantability is not fully determined by reference to the rules of the system alone.[137] Wielders of the rules always have the option to understand them anew, to see them in new light, to interpret them in new, yet fully cogent, ways.[138] Assuming this to be so, legal officials, and judges especially, are never justified in behaving agentically with respect to their texts. They must construe and measure and balance, and construe again, in ways that are never and can never be tied

---

134. But see Kelman and Hamilton, *Crimes of Obedience.*

135. See Stanley Fish, "The Law Wishes to Have A Formal Existence," in *The Fate of Law,* ed. Austin Sarat and Thomas R. Kearns (Ann Arbor: University of Michigan Press, 1991); also see Dworkin, "Law as Interpretation," 527.

136. "Interpretation," Stanley Fish argues, "is not the art of construing but the art of constructing. Interpreters do not decode poems; they make them" (Fish, *Is There A Text in This Class?* [Cambridge, Mass.: Harvard University Press, 1980], 327). See Levinson, "Law as Literature," 373.

137. For a useful discussion of this point, see H. L. A. Hart on formalism and rule skepticism in *The Concept of Law* (London: Oxford University Press, 1961), chap. 7.

138. See Fish, *Is There a Text?*

down fully. Such judgments need not be subjective (i.e., products of mere whim or bias or unsupported preference) but they *are* ineliminably personal.[139] By this we mean they bear the marks of their author, they bespeak a perspective, a set of assumptions, a point of view that is the decider's own and that cannot help but have an effect on the content of the judgments made.

That *this* defendant is to be executed for *this* crime under *this* body of law is the result of this judge's sentence, a sentence that, but for the predilections, perceptions, and turns of mind of this particular judge, could, with full warrant, have been different from what it was.[140] It does not follow, of course, that judges must bear full responsibility for the decisions they make since what they decide is powerfully shaped by considerations (pertinent statutes, previous decisions, the conduct being censured) over which they have no control.[141] But, especially in an interpretivist account of law, judges are deeply implicated in the decisions they make; moreover, it is to be expected that the capacity of these judgments to endure will depend, in large measure, on the practical activity, the argument and analyses, their authors are prepared to marshal on behalf of those decisions.

Presumably, the responsibility borne by interpretivist judges in every decision they make is part of what Cover has in mind when he imagines that law's violence might be domesticated. These judges, it seems, are "the transmission" between the standing system of rules and the inscription of pain and death on the bodies and souls of other human beings. Their responsibility is not so great that they are unable to do what needs to be done, but it is great enough to implicate them as moral agents and to give them ample reason to behave thoughtfully.[142]

---

139. On the distinction between the personal and the subjective, see Nagel, *View from Nowhere*, 152–53.

140. For a general treatment, see John Noonan, *Persons and Masks of the Law: Cardozo, Holmes, Jefferson, and Wythe as Makers of Masks* (New York: Farrar, Strauss and Giroux, 1976).

141. The question of how much constraint is imposed by such things is, of course, at the center of debates in interpretive theory. See Levinson, "Law as Literature"; Gerald Graff, "'Keep Off the Grass,' 'Drop Dead,' and Other Indeterminacies," *Texas Law Review* 60 (1982): 405.

142. On the imperative of deliberation in moral decision making, see Daniel Maguire, *The Moral Choice* (Garden City, N.Y.: Doubleday, 1978); see also Charles Larmore, *Patterns of Moral Complexity* (Cambridge: Cambridge University Press, 1987); Edmond Cahn, *The Moral Decision: Right and Wrong in the Light of American Law* (Bloomington: Indiana University Press, 1955).

It surely suffices to test "the faith and commitment" of deciding judges.[143]

Correspondingly, judges thus implicated in the "organization of people" that is required to carry out law's violence would appear to meet the conditions set out earlier for authorizing agentic behavior on the part of others, namely, reasonable assurances regarding the correctness of the decisions to be implemented or the interposition of responsible agents or both. Because judges are personally implicated in the decisions they make (so there *is* an intervening responsible agent), they have compelling reasons (at least to try) to get it right. Given the specific character of their involvement, perhaps it is not surprising that others feel at ease "jump[ing] to the judge's tune." Here, then, is another way in which judges are implicated in law's violence: they contribute to the justificatory story that induces or allows others to behave agentically.

Cover's work thus points toward a troublesome impediment to his own reconstructive project. That problem arises from the difficulty that judges and other legal officials face in marshaling the conviction necessary to use and deploy law's violence. Faced with that difficulty, they need, Cover argued, to provide compelling reasons and justifications—for themselves and within their own interpretive communities—for the violence that they authorize.[144] Without such reasons and justifications, law's violence could or would not be effectively organized and deployed.

So the presence of violence requires what might be called strong justification of legal acts.[145] The consequence of this fact is transformative; it promotes an imperialistic relationship between the legal order, in which one constant need is the generation of strong justifications, and normative communities whose ideas of the right and the good are at odds with what the law requires. In the face of such challenges, and spurred on by the strong justifications generated to sustain its own violence, the legal order becomes aggressive in its

---

143. As Cover himself put it, "a legal interpretation cannot be valid if no one is prepared to live by it" (Cover, "Nomos," 44).

144. Cover, "Violence," 1627.

145. By a strong justification we mean a justification sufficient to explain an action as having some other origin than an act of will or raw power. For an argument that all justifications, properly so called, are strong justifications, see Hadley Arkes, *First Things* (Princeton: Princeton University Press, 1986), 20.

insistence that what it proclaims as right is *the* only acceptable version of right.

When we invoke the language of morals, we praise and we blame, we commend and condemn, we applaud and deride, we approve and disapprove. It would make no sense, however, to cast these judgments on other people unless it were assumed that there are standards of judgment, accessible to others as well as ourselves, which allow these people to know what they are doing is right or wrong. . . . When we invoke the language of morals . . . we move away from statements of personal taste and private belief; we offer a judgment about the things that are universally right or wrong, just or unjust.[146]

Legal interpretation that contemplates violence must tell a story that, to borrow from Cover, tends to "objectify" the demands it would enforce.[147] That is, legal interpretation seeks to show not only that its decisions are technically sustainable, but that they *merit imposition* against those who might resist, that they are worthy of being lived in and through the pain that is done in their name.[148] This, as Cover notes, "escalates the stakes of the interpretive enterprise."[149] To meet them, judges must generate a normatively enriched story, one that suffices to overcome reticence and to persuade other officials not to intervene. Such a story will be difficult to restrain; it will tend to assert itself in new domains and to promote intolerance in the face of challenges.[150]

---

146. Arkes, *First Things*, 22, 23–24.

147. The Law of Law calls us to interpretation, and this process of interpretation appeals to the promise of a reconciled whole, or the Good, which is itself only an interpretation and not the last word on what the Good of the community actually could be. . . . Yet even so, the Law of Law is that we justify our interpretation through an appeal to the Good. . . . [W]hen one legal interpretation is vindicated as to what constitutes the Good, it is imposed upon the other as if the Good had been achieved. (Cornell, "From the Lighthouse," 1712)

148. See Martha Minow, *Making All the Difference: Inclusion, Exclusion, and American Law* (Ithaca: Cornell University Press, 1990), 60–65.

149. Cover, "Nomos," 51.

150. As Minow puts it,
Legal language seeks universal applicability, regardless of the particular traits of an individual, yet abstract universalism often "takes the part for the whole, the particular for the universal and essential, the present for the eternal." . . .

It is difficult to contemplate such stories without recalling Cover's discussion of the creation of legal meaning, a process, he says, that involves commitment, identification, and objectification. As he puts it, "Creating legal meaning ... requires ... dedication and commitment, but also the objectification of that to which one is committed."[151] Here, it seems Cover has in mind the attitudes and behavior of members of various insular and redemptive communities, but it would be strange to posit any radical disjunction between those persons and a community of statist judges. Violence cannot be done without a sense that it is justified, and, once generated, justification is unlikely to be self-limiting.

But matters are more complicated still, as Cover emphatically reminds us. The judge, as we have seen, contributes to the emergence of agents who feel themselves morally "free" to do law's violence. But these actors are not utterly without effect on the law that they enforce. Though they do not review a judge's order on its merits—if they did, they would not be behaving agentically—there are limits to what they are prepared to do and the circumstances under which they will do it. The judge who would issue orders and decisions in hopes of having them acted upon must be attentive to such limitations and fashion decrees accordingly.

Legal interpretation is never free; it is reciprocally bonded to the roles from which it issues and at which it is directed. It follows that there is always a tension between producing the most coherent legal meaning (in the manner that Dworkin might applaud) and (to quote Cover) "generating effective action in a violent context."[152] But precisely this constraint on legal interpretation, while it has the virtue of perhaps domesticating and tempering law's violence, puts in play the logical, sociopragmatic, and moral forces that dispose statist law to be jurispathic, to kill other normative orders, contrary to Cover's appeals at the end of "Nomos."

We thus return to where we began, with the suggestion that "the organization of people," described in "Violence" as being necessary if law is to deal pain and death, is a mixed blessing. Inside, it makes

Justices to this day fail to acknowledge their own perspective and its influence in the assignment of difference in relation to some unstated norm. (Minow, *All the Difference*, 64, 65)
151. Cover, "Nomos," 45.
152. Cover, "Violence," 1629.

available devices by which thought might effectively be transformed into action and law's violence might be done in a generally controlled and temperate way. But in its interactions with competing normative visions, a statist legal order that is bonded to local practices, whose judges are not free to do the work of pure, unimpeded legal interpretation but whose decisions must cater to the conditions of doing violence, will be limited by those conditions. Thus, a judge who, for example, lives in a world that includes a statute against bigamy might find cogent legal reasons for carving out an exception for a particular insular community and its embrace of plural marriages. But if the "right" or "best" decision is one that is suitably responsive to the social organization of violence, it is less likely that such an exception would be made. The lesson of "Violence" is that thought cannot issue in action without being transformed by it, that interpretation is tutored and transformed by the imperatives of its violent context.

Violence changes things; violence changes law. At issue is the capacity of people who have imposed their will on some—who have used force to assure conformity among themselves—to find reasons now, but not then, to respect multiplicity and difference in their midst. New distinctions may weaken, if they do not refute, old justifications. An excess of casuistry is surely contrary to the demands of solidarity, and, if Cover is right, solidarity, not subtlety of thought, is the sine qua non of effective legal violence.

Poets and philosophers, Cover would have us believe, unencumbered by the need to act, are free to proliferate distinctions and cultivate a taste for incompatible views. But the need to do violence, as we have said and as Cover himself recognizes, makes a difference. Where pain and death are to be done, irreversible stands must be taken. When death and pain are involved, what is done cannot be undone, and judges especially are responsible for it. In the interpretive world of law, texts and reason alone do not dictate the result; on the contrary, in a world that requires legal violence, the "right result" is shaped, in part, by the shared commitments and common meanings that make the cooperative enterprise of law possible.

These commitments and meanings, while never wholly cogent nor wholly shared and common, must be respected if law's fragile capacity to do (controlled and temperate) violence is to be sustained. The price of this capacity, we have argued, is a disposition to be hostile to the visions of other normative orders, contrary to the plea at the end of "Nomos" "to stop circumscribing the nomos" and "to invite new worlds." It appears, then, that violence ties thought to action and, as a consequence, makes law less tolerant of multiplicity and difference. Law's capacity to be homicidal tends, against Cover's fervent hope, to make it jurispathic as well.

Contributors

Elaine Scarry is professor of English and American Literature at Harvard University.

Patricia M. Wald is a judge on the United States Court of Appeals for the District of Columbia Circuit.

Carol J. Greenhouse, professor of anthropology, teaches at Indiana University.

Douglas Hay is an associate professor of history and law, York University and Osgoode Hall Law School.

Robert Weisberg is professor of law at Stanford University.

Austin Sarat is William Nelson Cromwell Professor of Jurisprudence and Political Science at Amherst College.

Thomas R. Kearns is William H. Hastie Professor of Philosophy at Amherst College.

Index

Larceny, 181, 188
Law as Fact (Olivecrona), 176–77
Law Week, 130–31
Legal cases: *DeShaney v. Winnebago County*, 95–96; *Estelle v. Gamble*, 131; *Frisbie v. Collins*, 86; *Gregg v. Georgia*, 201, 202–3; *Ker v. Illinois*, 86; Nancy Cruzan case, 88–92; *Perry v. Louisiana*, 16, 129–39; *Rhodes v. Chapman*, 85, 86; *Rochin v. California*, 86; *Sierra Club v. Morton*, 101–2; *United States v. Holmes*, 212n.6; *United States v. Toscanino*, 86–87; *Washington v. Harper*, 130; *Wilson v. Seiter*, 85–86
Legitimacy, 4–5; Hay on, 141, 169, 172; Sarat and Kearns on, 4–5, 212–14, 221–22; and self-help crime, 192; and silencing, 169
Levellers, 170
Leviathan, 216
Levinson, Sanford, 125
Liberalism, in England, 165, 177, 223n.55, 226–28, 232, 233
Locke, John, 27, 34n.21, 42n.32, 234–35
Lynchings, 144, 154–55, 235

Madison, James, 63
Maine, Henry, 105
Marriage, 29, 31; at Canaan, biblical tale of, 79; among the Ilongot, 114–16, 120; among the Kaluli, 116–17, 120
Marshall, Thurgood, 79, 89
Materiality, 44, 55–76
Mayan civilization, 179n.12
Medical care, life-sustaining, 14, 88–92
Mental illness, 129–39
Metaphor, 1, 2, 10, 219; of the pyramid, 141–43, 233, 239; of "reflective" law, 199
Metaphysics, 176, 196

Mexican War, 26, 45n.36, 46n.37, 48–49, 56, 57, 60n.62, 64
Middle class, 184–85
Milgram, Stanley, 243
Model Penal Code, 208–9
Monopoly, 176, 200–201, 202, 206, 208
Montesquieu, Charles, 106
Moore, Michael, 190
Moore, Sally Falk, 108, 110
Morality, 18–19, 74; Cover on, 22, 226, 236–37, 243, 245, 246, 247; and declaration of war, 64; and private violence, 92–93, 175–210; and sentencing, 83. *See also* Ethics
Morphine, 87
Morse, Stephen, 190
Murder. *See* Homicide

Naming, act of, 65–66, 67
Nancy Cruzan case, 88–92
Napoleonic Wars, 48
Narcissism, 185, 192
Narratives, 229, 230; and capital punishment, 131–32, 134–35; and declaration of war, 65, 70, 72, 75–76; Greenhouse on, 116, 121, 128–29, 131–32, 134–35; among the Ilongot, 116; and *nomos*, 225; Weisberg on, 128–29
National Environmental Protection Act (NEPA), 101
National Security Council, 24, 25
Natural law, 177
Nature, 3, 232
Necessity doctrine, 203–4, 207
New Guinea, 15–16, 116–23
Nietzche, Friedrich, 188, 211n.3
Nixon, Richard M., 25
Nomos, 220, 223–27, 229–34, 241, 242, 248, 249–50
Nonviolence, principle of, 184
Normative visions, 126, 215, 216; Cover on, 19–20, 223–32, 234, 240, 241, 250